INSIGHT GUIDES MUSEUMS AND GALLERIES OF LONDON

APA PUBLICATIONS

Part of the Langenscheidt Publishing Group

Editorial

Editors
Brian Bell
Clare Peel
Design
Klaus Geisler
Picture Editor
Hilary Genin
Picture Research
Britta Jaschinski

Distribution

UK & Ireland
GeoCenter International Ltd
The Viables Centre, Harrow Way
Basingstoke, Hants RG22 4BJ
Fax: (44) 1256-817988

United States
Langenscheidt Publishers, Inc.
46–35 54th Road, Maspeth, NY 11378
Fax: (718) 784-0640

Canada
Prologue Inc.
1650 Lionel Bertrand Blvd., Boisbriand
Québec, Canada J7H 1N7
Tel: (450) 434-0306. Fax: (450) 434-2627

Worldwide
Apa Publications GmbH & Co.
Verlag KG (Singapore branch)
38 Joo Koon Road, Singapore 628990
Tel: (65) 6865-1600. Fax: (65) 6861-6438

Printing

Insight Print Services (Pte) Ltd
38 Joo Koon Road, Singapore 628990
Tel: (65) 6865-1600. Fax: (65) 6861-6438

©2002 **Apa Publications GmbH & Co.**
Verlag KG (Singapore branch)
All Rights Reserved

First Edition 2002

ABOUT THIS BOOK

A public lottery funded the British Museum's foundation in 1759 and fittingly it was lottery money released in the late 1990s to celebrate the new millennium that helped finance its spectacular Great Court. The same millennial largesse aided many of London's museums and galleries and soon the government decreed that the great national collections should abolish entrance fees. Suddenly museums and galleries were sexy. Marketing initiatives abounded. The appointment of a curator for a major institution, once worthy of a note on a newspaper's arts pages, now made headlines in the news columns.

Alongside the rejuvenation of the star attractions came a rash of specialist new museums documenting topics as diverse as fashion and funerals. Not all worked: the whistle was quickly blown on a football museum and a waxworks of rock music legends melted away.

This book is designed to make sense of this dynamic sector of London's cultural life. It recognises that visitors who turn up at a major museum or gallery, pick up a leaflet at the entrance and aim to "do" it in a couple of hours will rapidly find themselves hopelessly confused. Devoting just a minute to each object in the British Museum alone would take them 12 years – more if they paused to eat or sleep. To get the most out of a visit, it's essential to prepare in advance, to ascertain what's on offer and then to put one's priorities in order. This book provides the information needed to set those priorities. It also explains, in introductory features, why these institutions developed in the way they did over the centuries.

Its reviews embrace a wide range of specialist museums and galleries likely to appeal to both Londoners and visitors. Practical information such as addresses and opening times is provided at the start of each entry. It is advisable to telephone the smaller venues before visiting to check that details are still correct – and that they have managed to survive. At the end of most entries, we suggest where to find convenient refreshments.

The writing team

The introduction to the museums section of the book was written by Brian Bell, Insight Guides' editorial director. The introductions to the Galleries and Commercial Galleries sections were written by William Feaver, a leading writer and broadcaster on the art world. Art galleries were reviewed by Judith Bumpus, an art historian, writer and critic.

Museums were visited and assessed by members of Insight Guides' London-based editorial team: Natasha Babaian, Bronwen Barber, Brian Bell, Erica Brown, Donna Dailey, Rachel Fox, Hilary Genin, Sylvia George, Zoë Goodwin, Lesley Gordon, Clare Griffiths, Freddy Hamilton, Huw Hennessy, David Isaacson, Tom le Bas, Maria Lord, Jason Mitchell, Cathy Muscat, Christina Park, Clare Peel, Jenni Rainford, Maria Randell, Dorothy Stannard, Sylvia Suddes and Martha Ellen Zenfell.

INSIDE FRONT COVER: the Great Court of the British Museum.

OPPOSITE: *The Duet* (1849) by Arthur Devis, at the Victoria and Albert Museum.

Mexican mask from the Horniman Museum.

MUSEUMS

Anglo-Saxon
helmet from
the British
Museum's
Sutton Hoo
exhibit

Henry VIII's writing
desk, from the
Victoria and Albert
Museum

German doll (1890s) from
Pollock Toy Museum

Detail from Edward Penny's
A City Shower (*c.*1764) at
the Museum of London

Greek plate,
from around
520–500BC,
in the British
Museum

FOLLOWING PAGES: touching up the *Three Graces*
at the Victoria and Albert; touching up *Bashaw
the Dog* by Matthew Coates Wyatt at the V&A;
Somerset House re-creates a Royal Academy
show as it would have looked 200 years ago

PLUNDERING THE PAST

Scrupulous archaeologists rubbed shoulders with tomb robbers to bring the world's riches to London, courtesy of the Royal Navy

In 1795 Thomas Bruce, the 7th Earl of Elgin, decided to build a mansion on his Scottish estate for himself and his vivacious bride-to-be. He favoured the style of ancient Greece and, when posted as Britain's ambassador to Turkey, he sent an aide to Athens to make sketches and plaster casts of the Parthenon's pillars and statues. Their purpose was to guide his architect. Elgin, a 29-year-old diplomat, did not plan to plunder the site, and it would have astonished him to learn that he would be viewed by future generations as the villain in a controversy that would sour political relations between Greece and Britain 200 years later.

The trouble began when his advisers informed him that, instead of making plaster casts, he would probably be allowed by the Turks, who then ruled Greece, to take home to Scotland "some" or "any" of the sculptures. This ambiguity in a translation of the official agreement was interpreted liberally by Elgin's agents, and 300 workmen spent a year packing 200 chests with the 2,300-year-old treasures. The Turks had so little respect for the architecture and graven images of the Greeks that they used the Parthenon as a gunpowder store. An explosion had already severely damaged the building and Elgin's apologists have often argued that removing the marble statues and friezes to Britain was the best guarantee of their survival.

But a Grecian variant of the mummy's curse seems to have struck Elgin. One of the ships carrying the treasures back to England sank in a gale and the heavy pieces of marble had to be expensively retrieved. While travelling home overland, Elgin was taken hostage by Napoleon's troops, then at war with England. When he finally reached London after three years, he discovered that his wife had run off with a Scottish neighbour, that he had lost his seat in the House of Lords, and that the poet Lord Byron was publicly condemning him as a thief and desecrator. To cap it all, a skin disease contracted abroad was eating away part of his nose. Running short of money, Elgin offered the priceless marbles to the nation. Grudgingly, the government paid him £35,000 – less than half what he had spent acquiring and transporting them – and in 1817 put the exquisite sculptures on display at the embryonic British Museum.

Lord Elgin: more sinned against than sinning?

The ethics of acquisition

The Elgin saga contains many of the elements that powered the remarkable growth of London's museums in the 19th century. Diplomats, who were often keen collectors, colluded with scholars, whose archaeological knowledge identified the likely sites of buried treasures, and with local middlemen, whose expertise in identifying corrupt officials eased the exporting of antiquities. The fourth vital player was the Royal Navy which, in addition to policing the British Empire, was happy to ferry the most monumental booty back to London.

LEFT: the 18th-century collector Charles Townley and friends in the Park Street Gallery.

At the same time that Britain was busily shipping Greece to London, so the French were transporting Rome to Paris. Occasionally the rivals clashed on the same territory. When the British defeated Napoleon's expeditionary force in Egypt in 1799, they relieved the French of the Rosetta Stone, the inscribed basalt block that would prove the key to deciphering

James Stuart's 1751 watercolour shows himself sketching the Erechtheum in Athens.

ancient Egyptian hieroglyphics, and routed it to the British Museum instead of the Louvre. As the Grand Tour became increasingly popular with well-to-do Britons, an appetite for antiquities was stimulated, which enterprising explorers were only too eager to satisfy by bringing back shiploads of ancient sculptures, jewellery and bronzes from Italy, Greece and Egypt. Such was the fashion for ancient artefacts that a brisk souvenir trade sprang up in England, France and Germany. A French monk, Father Géramb, remarked in 1833: "It would be hardly respectable, on one's return from Egypt, to present oneself in Europe without a mummy in one hand and a crocodile in the other."

Egypt had a long tradition of tomb robbing, going back at least to the 12th century. Locals found it a more profitable occupation than farming, and the buried riches seemed inexhaustible. Mummy cases were used as firewood and Mark Twain scarcely exaggerated when he joked that the fuel used by the country's locomotives "is composed of mummies three thousand years old, purchased by the ton or by the graveyard for that purpose". Claims were staked, as in a gold rush, with many explorers adopting the approach described by Howard Carter, the archaeologist who discovered Tutankhamun's tomb in 1922: "Anything for which a fancy was taken, from a scarab to an obelisk, was just appropriated and if there was a difference of opinion with a brother excavator one laid for him with a gun."

Eventual attempts by Egypt's Antiquities Service to regulate the trade were met with bravado. On one occasion in the 1880s when Warren Budge, an assistant keeper at the British Museum, was put under guard in Egypt with his latest hoard, accomplices posing as gardeners tunnelled their way into the basement of the house and liberated the antiquities, which were then spirited away to London as part of official military baggage.

The urge to acquire

In today's post-colonial climate, such looting seems outrageous. But prominent collectors saw themselves as the saviours of antiquities, which would otherwise be allowed to decay, while museum curators – many of whom dreamed of being private collectors but lacked the funds – argued that they were making the achievements of ancient cultures accessible to everyone, not just a well travelled elite. Warren Budge justified his beliefs thus: "Whatever blame may be attached to individual archaeologists for removing mummies from Egypt, every unprejudiced person who knows anything of the subject must admit that, when once a mummy has passed into the care of the Trustees and is lodged in the British Museum, it has a far better chance of being preserved than it could possibly have in any tomb, royal or otherwise." A great Egyptian ruler, he pointed out to doubters, would be buried with charms to guard against evils, and "in the British Museum he is placed beyond the reach of all such evils."

Whether motivated by greed, scholarship or a desire for social prestige, people have been collecting objects since prehistoric times. Traditionally, kings, emperors

An 1827 watercolour by G. Scharf shows a student artist at work in the British Museum's Townley Gallery.

and popes could best afford to own the past, but by the 18th century wealthy individuals had built up remarkable collections in their homes which they would show to friends or scholars. Sir Charles Townley, for example, assembled a superb collection of Greek and Roman marbles at his house in London's Park Street. The physician and naturalist Sir Hans Sloane (1660–1753) amassed an extraordinary array of antiquities and natural history specimens – famous enough to be visited by Voltaire, Handel and Benjamin Franklin. To some, however, the enthusiasm of such collectors seemed risible: satirising Sloane, a Chelsea coffee house set up a spoof collection of objects such as Pontius Pilate's Wife's Chambermaid's Sister's Hat.

The idea of transferring such private collections to public ownership in order to guarantee their continuity – and, with luck, perpetuate the donor's name – originated in 16th-century Italy, and it was central to the birth of the British Museum in 1759. Then, as now, British politicians were loath to spend public money on financing cultural awareness and had to be pressured by enterprising individuals. In the end, the funds to build and stock the museum were raised through a lottery. The collection was initially based in Montagu House, a handsome 17th-century mansion, since demolished, slightly south of today's museum in Bloomsbury.

Sir Hans Sloane: an avid collector.

The first acquisitions were the manuscripts of Robert Harley, 1st Earl of Oxford, the library of Sir Robert Cotton (which included two of the four extant copies of Magna Carta), and Sloane's collection of 79,575 objects and antiquities. King George II donated the 12,000 volumes of the Old Royal Library, founded by Edward IV in 1471.

Bursting at the seams

Access to the British Museum, Parliament decreed, should be limited to "studious and curious persons" – who also needed to be persistent persons since timed tickets had to be obtained in advance through a laborious process. Once admitted, they were rushed round the collections by impatient members of staff who regarded the presence of visitors as something of an intrusion, an attitude that lives on today in some of London's smaller, specialist museums.

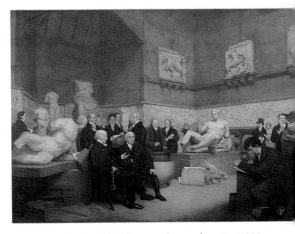

Before long, Montagu House was bursting at the seams, with larger sculptures being stored in sheds in the garden. The antiquities section was vastly expanded by Sir Charles Townley's bequest of marbles. Sir Hans Sloane's extensive collection of plant and animal specimens was later enlarged by the bequests of collectors such as Joseph Banks, the naturalist who accompanied Captain James Cook on his voyage around the world in 1768. In the 1830s, having voyaged around South America on the *Beagle*, Charles Darwin returned laden with exotic specimens that were added to the collection. A further royal donation, this time from George IV, brought in another 65,250 books.

A new building was clearly needed. Today's imposing and dignified neoclassical museum, designed by Sir Robert Smirke, was begun in 1826, with new wings being added piecemeal over the next quarter of a century, engulfing Montagu House. The circular Reading Room arose in a neglected courtyard between 1854 and 1857.

The British Museum's Temporary Elgin Room in 1819 – an oil on canvas by Archibald Archer.

But just what was the purpose of the British Museum? The eclecticism of its collections earned it the nickname of "the old curiosity shop" and led one critic to complain: "We go from the masterworks of the Parthenon straight up to the stuffed seal and buffalo; and two monster giraffes stand as sentinels before the gallery of vases." And just who would benefit from viewing such variety? Certainly not the hoi-polloi, according to the Principal Librarian, Henry Ellis, who told a parliamentary committee in 1835: "People of a higher grade would hardly wish to come to the Museum at the same time with sailors from the dock yards and girls whom they might bring with them. I do not think such people would gain any improvement from the sight of our collections."

The Great Exhibition

A turning point in determining public taste came with the 1851 Great Exhibition of the Works of Industry of All Nations, a prototype "world's fair" staged in Hyde Park in a magnificent iron and glass building dubbed the Crystal Palace. Its appeal astonished even its backers: more than 6 million people visited during its 120-day run, leaving a clear profit of £186,000. Eager to educate British manufacturers in the relationship between fine art and design, Queen Victoria's husband, Prince Albert, one of the moving spirits behind the exhibition, argued for a permanent exhibition of applied arts, and the money was used to buy a block of land in South Kensington.

The Natural History Museum.

Here, the South Kensington Museum of Science and Art opened in 1857. As with the British Museum, its collection grew rapidly and in 1899 Queen Victoria, making her last public appearance, laid the foundation stone of the present imposing building. When completed in 1909, it was renamed the Victoria & Albert Museum. Its purpose was to inspire as well as educate, a role it still fulfils for designers. The founders wanted to attract the increasingly wealthy middle classes, whose new enthusiasm for design would boost British manufacturing. It was the first museum in London to be gas-lit, which allowed working people to visit in the evening after finishing their jobs. It also symbolised a major shift in the way museums would display their wares: instead of exhibiting objects for the edification of scholars and aesthetes, they would increasingly seek to re-create the past by arranging them according to theme or period.

As well as art objects, the South Kensington Museum built up a strong collection of industrial technology. It acquired a collection of scientific instruments from a second international exhibition, in 1876, and in 1884 was given a stock of patent models including Richard Arkwright's pioneering textile machinery and George Stephenson's 1828 railway locomotive, the Rocket. It became increasingly clear that the arts and science collections had to part company and in 1928 a separate Science Museum opened in an adjacent building.

The Science Museum's model of the first hot-air balloon to carry people.

New roots for natural history

"Albertopolis", as this area of South Kensington was jokingly known, was also the site of the Natural History Museum, which opened its doors in 1881 to house the British Museum's zoological department. Managing this department within the confines of the Bloomsbury building had become a nightmare as new cases of shells, fossils, dried plants, dead insects and assorted skeletons continued to arrive. Even disposing of unwanted specimens posed a problem as nearby residents objected to "the pungent odour of burning snakes" emanating from the gardens of the British Museum. Even so, it took three decades of lobbying to persuade parsimonious parliaments to fund the new building.

The Natural History Museum (which did not achieve independence from the

British Museum until 1963) is a terracotta-faced cathedral, a Romanesque embodiment of the Victorians' reverence for science. Such inspiring architecture, while reassuring to scholars and the culturally confident, tended to intimidate the general public, but capitalism's entrepreneurs were not slow to cater for them too. In the 18th century Mrs Salmon ran a waxworks in Fleet Street and she was succeeded in the early 19th century by the more celebrated Madame Marie Tussaud, whose wax museum remains one of London's top attractions today. In 1811 the showman William Bullock opened the Egyptian Hall, an exhibition space in Piccadilly decorated with Egyptian-style mouldings, and proceeded to exhibit anything and everything, from Napoleon's coach, captured at Waterloo in 1815, to parrots brought back from the South Seas by Captain Cook.

Changing tastes

One exhibitor in the Egyptian Hall was Giovanni Battista Belzoni, a massively built barber's son from Padua who had toured Europe as a circus strongman before discovering the profitable pleasures of plundering the Middle East. His weightlifting gave him an interest in hydraulics, knowledge he put to good use in lifting such colossal pieces of marble as the head of Ramesses II. In a classic pairing of adventurer and diplomat – necessary since the Egyptian authorities had given the British and French representatives a virtual monopoly over excavations – he teamed up with Britain's consul-general, Henry Salt, to market their booty to the British Museum.

Belzoni's men removing the head of Memnon from Luxor.

Although their partnership was ultimately a successful one, they were initially dismayed to find that the museum's trustees, focused in the classical traditions of Greece and Rome, were less than rhapsodic about their Egyptian sculptures. They finally coughed up £2,000 for some very fine sculptures but couldn't agree a price for the sarcophagus of Seti I, which Belzoni then sold to the architect Sir John Soane for a further £2,000. Soane had to remove part of a wall to get it into his Bloomsbury home, where it remains today as part of the delightful Sir John Soane's Museum *(see page 61)*.

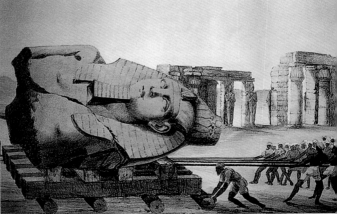

The prejudice against Egyptian antiquities did not last and by the 1880s the explorer Sir Flinders Petrie – whose work is commemorated in the Petrie Museum of Egyptian Archaeology *(see page 59)* – wrote: "A year's work in Egypt made me feel it was like a house on fire, so rapid was the destruction going on. My duty was that of a salvage man."

There had been other prejudices, too. Artefacts from less academically fashionable areas such as Africa, South Asia and Central America were regarded as primitive, less deserving of the dignity of a glass case. Curiously, much the same attitude applied to artefacts, however intricate, created by the ancient Celtic cultures of Britain and Ireland. This bias was reversed partly by the growth of municipal museums around Britain, financed by socially conscious local authorities and individuals responding to the free education movement, and by the influence of such national institutions as the Victoria and Albert Museum, which examined contemporary objects as well as historical developments. The V&A was also one of the first major museums to give prominence to the cultures of Britain's colonial territories such as India and Southeast Asia.

The spread of democracy encouraged the notion that peasants as well as potentates were worthy of study. In Egypt, Flinders Petrie recorded not only the legacy of the pharaohs but also domestic trivia such as tools and pieces of furniture that suggested how the ordinary people lived. By 1914 it was even possible for venues such as the Geffrye Museum, created from 18th-century almshouses in East London, to celebrate the virtues – and vices – of English domestic decor *(see page 76)*.

THE SHAPE OF MUSEUMS TO COME

Can traditional museums learn from Walt Disney World? Will branches of Starbucks join the artefacts? Cash-poor curators are tempted

The dispute over the true ownership of the Elgin Marbles, which had begun in the 19th century and rumbled on through the 20th, has grown even more strident in the 21st. Determined to recover the treasures in time for the staging of the 2004 Olympic Games in Athens, Greece promised to surmount environmental concerns by housing them in a new Acropolis Museum equipped with a high-tech air and chemical regulation system that would make the British Museum's look primitive. But things didn't stop there: soon every postal delivery to the British Museum seemed to bring new demands. Scotland pressed for the return of the 12th-century Lewis Chessmen. Wales wanted back the 4,000-year-old Mold Cape. Nigeria insisted that the 16th-century Benin bronzes belonged in Benin. National dignity was said to be at stake.

How different it had all been in the 19th century when a French commander, defending his right to remove an obelisk from Egypt, declared: "Antiquity is a garden that belongs by natural right to those who cultivate and harvest the fruit." Today the British Museum wheels out more tactful arguments: first, its expertise in conservation is still unsurpassed; second, far more people can enjoy such riches in London than in Athens, Lewis, Clwyd or Benin; and third, exhibiting such exquisite artefacts within the same building as other treasures enables visitors to make cross-cultural comparisons. The lobbyists remain unconvinced. Conversely, a few nations such as South Korea have begun offering their artefacts to London museums, along with funds to mount an exhibition or open a new gallery; their hope is that the publicity will promote trade and tourism.

Criticism of museums, of course, is nothing new. In 1908 Filippo Tommaso Marinetti, a founder of Italian futurism, compared a museum to a cemetery – "identical truly in the sinister promiscuity of its many objects unknown to each other." Today, as consumer goods proliferate and new media bring knowledge to a mass audience, the critical debate has intensified. What objects are really worth preserving? Does an exhibition of airline sickness bags make any sense? Why, in a market-led economy, shouldn't museums pay their own way?

Old and new intersect at an eatery in the British Museum.

Free admission

The last question was further complicated in 2001 when the government provided funds to enable the major national collections, such as the Science Museum and the Victoria and Albert, to abolish their entrance fees. This assumed that there was a pent-up demand for such a public resource, and the assumption was confirmed as attendance instantly soared. But it was clear that the government funds would not cover the museums' rising costs, never mind their accelerating ambitions, and curators began casting around for new ways to make money.

The success of Times Past, a specialist retailing chain selling historical trinkets

to tourists, pointed the way, and soon a British Museum shop powered up its electronic tills at Heathrow Airport. The Science Museum mused that outmoded galleries displaying such dull historical apparatus as weighing and measuring equipment might be put to more profitable use as corporate hospitality suites and that visitors might appreciate the provision, amid its pumping machines and flying engines, of a few branches of Burger King and Starbucks. Both museums and galleries began dreaming up increasingly spectacular temporary exhibitions – which *would* charge an admission fee.

Gadgets or gimmicks?

The challenge for the national museums was not only to continue catering for scholars and first-time visitors to London but also constantly to provide enough novelty to entice back non-specialists, whether Londoners or tourists, on a regular basis. As the Science Museum ruefully admitted, most British visitors cross its threshold just three times: once when they're eight,

Hands on at the Science Museum's Wellcome Wing.

once with their eight-year-old son or daughter, and once with their eight-year-old grandchild. If Disney can lure people to its theme parks again and again, why can't museums? A branch of the Hermitage Museum in Somerset House neatly solved this problem by changing virtually all its exhibits twice a year, drawing on the huge store available from its parent in St Petersburg.

Some curators thought the adoption of interactive technology would add allure, but others dismissed such gadgetry as a waste of money. "A lot of it is rubbish and doesn't work anyway," said the Museum of London's director, Simon Thurley. "You press the buttons too hard and you break it." But providing the right amount of information when most people won't read wall texts longer than 180 words is difficult. The smaller, more specialist museums such as the Cabinet War Rooms and the Vinopolis wine museum found it easier to avoid information overkill or underkill by providing sophisticated audioguides, allowing visitors to press various key combinations if they wanted more information about particular exhibits.

History with attitude: Madonna at Madame Tussaud's.

Keeping people in the picture helps bring the past to life, as Madame Tussaud's waxworks has proved. The practice of using "interactive people" – actors playing historical characters, for instance – attracts some curators, but it increases the payroll. The Natural History Museum found a neat solution in its new Darwin Centre: it allows the public to view its scientists through glass walls as they carry out their regular work on biodiversity, disease control and the like, and encourages the more gregarious scientists to chat to visitors about their work. This access should appeal both to the specialist and to the dilettante – the two vital constituencies which any reputable museum must seek to serve.

Changing demands

The magic of viewing such an extraordinary variety of historic artefacts for real rather than on a screen or in a book should ensure a robust future for London's museums. But, just as circuses and zoos were forced by animal rights activists to rethink their values, so traditional museums are having to respond to myriad demands from historians, politicians and an increasingly discriminating public. Their best bet might be to ponder the words of Henry Cole, who dreamed up the Great Exhibition of 1851: "I venture to think that unless museums and galleries are made subservient to education, they dwindle into very sleepy and useless institutions."

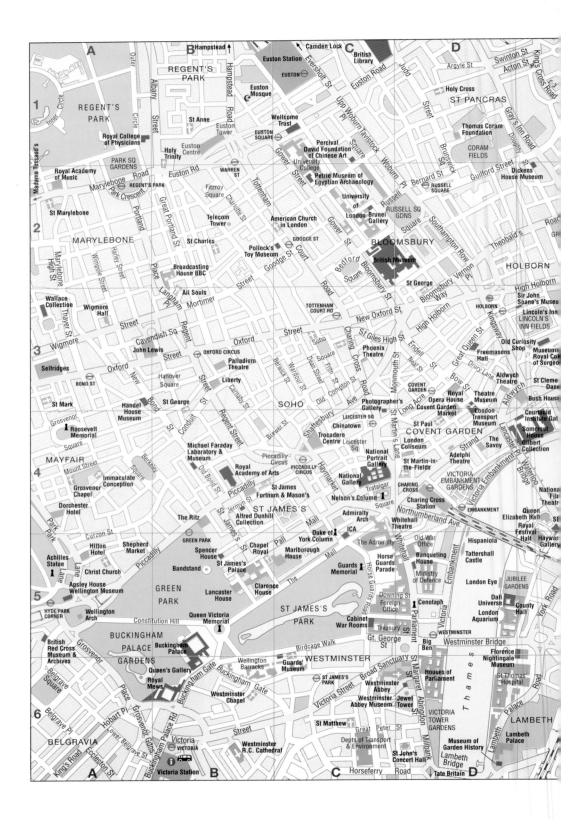

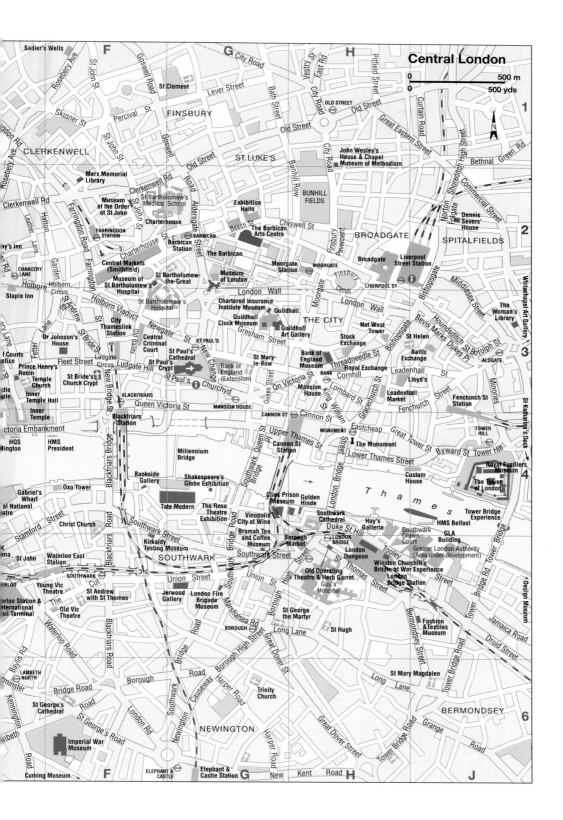

Central London

0 500 m
0 500 yds

F **G** City Road **H** Pitfield Street Curtain Road

Sadler's Wells
Roseberry Ave
St John St
Goswell Road
St Clement
Lever Street
Bath Street
Old Street
City Road
OLD STREET
Old Street
Shoreditch High Street
1

Skinner St
Percival St
Old Street
FINSBURY
ST LUKE'S
City Road
Old Street
Great Eastern Street
Commercial Street
Bethnal Green Rd

CLERKENWELL
Clerkenwell Rd
St John St
Goswell Road
Bunhill Row
John Wesley's House & Chapel Museum of Methodism
Norton Folgate
Dennis Severs' House
Whitechapel Art Gallery

Marx Memorial Library
St Bartholomew's Medical School
Exhibition Halls
BUNHILL FIELDS
BROADGATE
SPITALFIELDS

Museum of the Order of St John
Charterhouse
Aldersgate Street
Beech St
Chiswell St
The Barbican Arts Centre
Finsbury Pavement
Broadgate
Liverpool Street Station
The Woman's Library

FARRINGDON STATION
Charterhouse St
Barbican Station
The Barbican
Moorgate Station
MOORGATE
Finsbury Circus
LIVERPOOL ST
Bishopsgate
Middlesex Street

CHANCERY LANE
Central Markets (Smithfield)
St Bartholomew-the-Great
Museum of London
London Wall
Bevis Marks Dukes Pl
ALDGATE

Holborn
Holborn Circus
St Bartholomew's Hospital
St Bartholomew's Hospital
Chartered Insurance Institute Museum
Guildhall
THE CITY
London Wall
Houndsditch
St Botolph St

Staple Inn
Holborn Viaduct
Newgate
Guildhall Clock Museum
Guildhall Art Gallery
Nat West Tower
St Helen
Baltic Exchange

Dr Johnson's House
City Thameslink Station
Old Bailey
Gresham Street
Stock Exchange
Bank of England Museum
Threadneedle St
Royal Exchange
Leadenhall
Lloyd's
St

Fetter Lane
St Bride's St
Central Criminal Court
St Paul's Cathedral
St Mary-le-Bow
BANK
Cornhill
Leadenhall Market
Fenchurch St Station

Prince Henry's Room
Fleet Street
St Paul's Crypt
New Change
Bank of England (Extension)
Mansion House
Lombard St
King William
Fenchurch
Minories
St Katharine's Dock

Temple Church
Inner Temple Hall
Ludgate Circus
Ludgate Hill
St Paul's
Churchyd
Qn Victoria St
King
Eastcheap
Great Tower St
TOWER HILL

Inner Temple
New Bridge St
Queen Victoria St
MANSION HOUSE
Monument
Byward St
Tower Hill

Victoria Embankment
BLACKFRIARS
CANNON ST
Cannon St
The Monument
Lower Thames Street
Royal Fusiliers Museum

HQS Wellington
HMS President
Blackfriars Station
Blackfriars Bridge
Upper Thames St
Cannon St Station
Custom House
The Tower of London

Gabriel's Wharf
Royal National Theatre
Oxo Tower
Bankside Gallery
Millennium Bridge
Shakespeare's Globe Exhibition
Clink Prison Museum
Golden Hinde
Southwark Cathedral
Hay's Galleria
Tower Bridge Experience

Christ Church
Blackfriars Road
Southwark Street
Tate Modern
The Rose Theatre Exhibition
Vinopolis City of Wine
HMS Belfast
GLA Building

St John
Waterloo East Station
Bramah Tea and Coffee Museum
Kirkaldy Testing Museum
Borough Market
Southwark Crown Court
Greater London Authority (Area under development)

SOUTHWARK
Southwark Street
LONDON BRIDGE
London Dungeon
Tooley
Winston Churchill's Britain at War Experience
London Bridge Station

Young Vic Theatre
Union Street
Jerwood Gallery
London Fire Brigade Museum
Old Operating Theatre & Herb Garret
Guy's Hospital
Design Museum

Waterloo Station & International Rail Terminal
St Andrew with St Thomas
The Old Vic Theatre
Marshalsea Rd
St George the Martyr
St Hugh
Fashion & Textiles Museum
Jamaica Road

Waterloo Road
Blackfriars Road
BOROUGH
Long Lane
Bermondsey Street
Druid Street

LAMBETH NORTH
Borough
Southwark Bridge Road
Borough High Street
Trinity Church
St Mary Magdalen
Long Lane
Grange Road
BERMONDSEY

St George's Cathedral
St George's Road
London Rd
Newington Causeway
Harper Road
Great Dover Street
Tower Bridge Road

Imperial War Museum
NEWINGTON
Harper Road

Cuming Museum
F ELEPHANT & CASTLE Elephant & Castle Station **G** New Kent Road **H** **J**

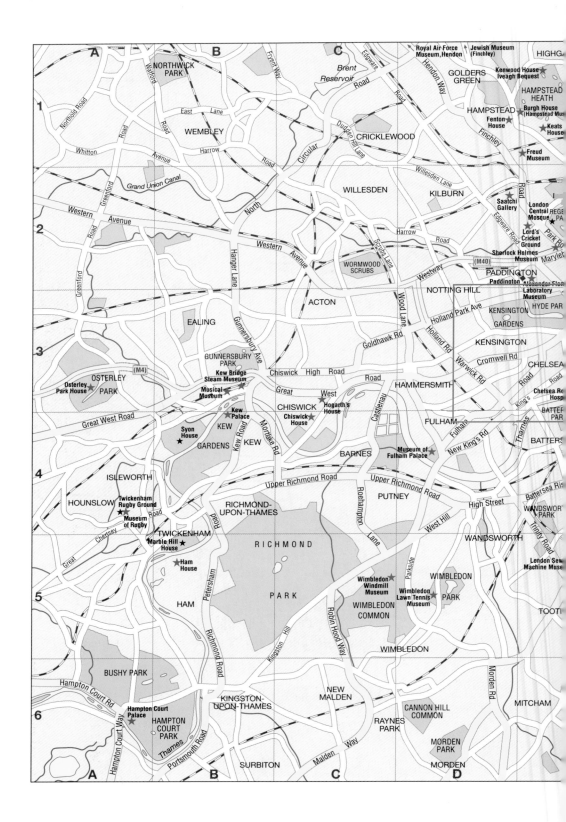

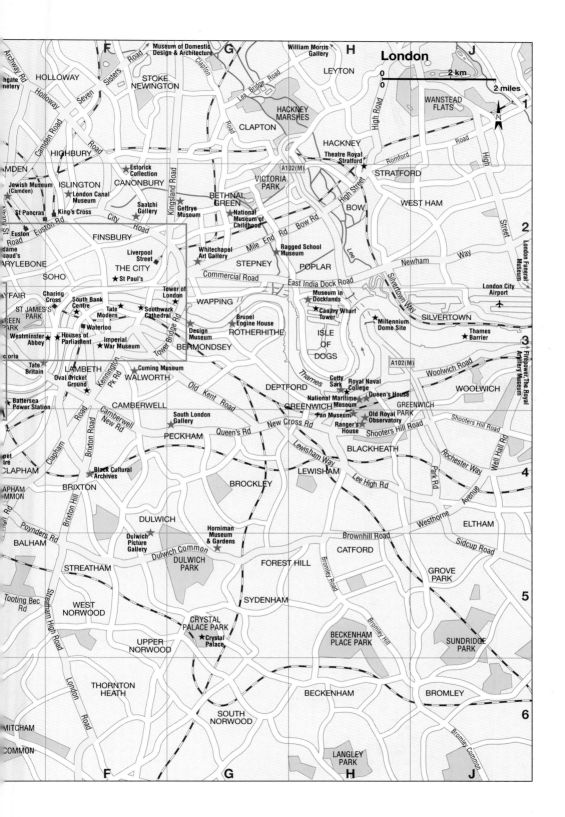

London

F

HOLLOWAY
hgate Rd
netery
Holloway Road
Seven Sisters Road
STOKE NEWINGTON
Museum of Domestic Design & Architecture

G

Clapton
William Morris Gallery

H

LEYTON
0 2 km
0 2 miles
N

J

WANSTEAD FLATS

HIGHBURY
Camden Road
HACKNEY MARSHES
CLAPTON
HACKNEY
High Road
Romford Road
Road
High Street

★Estorick Collection
ISLINGTON
CANONBURY
Kingsland Road
VICTORIA PARK
Theatre Royal Stratford
STRATFORD
A102(M)

MDEN
★Jewish Museum (Camden)
★London Canal Museum
★Saatchi Gallery
★Geffrye Museum
BETHNAL GREEN
★National Museum of Childhood
BOW
Bow Rd
WEST HAM

St Pancras
★King's Cross
City Road
Euston Rd
Euston
Road
FINSBURY
THE CITY
Liverpool Street
★Whitechapel Art Gallery
STEPNEY
Commercial Road
Mile End Rd
★Ragged School Museum
POPLAR
Lee
Newham Way
Silvertown Way
SILVERTOWN
London Funeral Museum
London City Airport

MARYLEBONE
SOHO
★St Paul's
Tower of London
WAPPING
East India Dock Road
★Museum in Docklands
★Canary Wharf Tower
★Millennium Dome Site
★Thames Barrier
Street

FAIR
Charing Cross
South Bank Centre
Tate Modern
★Southwark Cathedral
★Brunel Engine House
Design Museum
ROTHERHITHE
ISLE OF DOGS
A102(M)
Woolwich Road
Firepower The Royal Artillery Museum

ST JAMES'S PARK
REEN PARK
Waterloo
Tower Bridge Rd
BERMONDSEY
Thames

★Westminster Abbey
★Houses of Parliament
★Imperial War Museum
toria
LAMBETH
Oval Cricket Ground
WALWORTH
Kennington Pk Rd
★Cuming Museum
Old Kent Road
DEPTFORD
★Cutty Sark
★Royal Naval College
★Queen's House
GREENWICH PARK
WOOLWICH

Tate Britain
★Battersea Power Station
CAMBERWELL
Camberwell New Rd
★South London Gallery
Queen's Rd
New Cross Rd
GREENWICH
★National Maritime Museum
★Fan Museum
★Old Royal Observatory
★Ranger's House
Shooters Hill Road
Shooters Hill Road
Rochester Way
Well Hall Rd

pet tre
CLAPHAM
Brixton Road
PECKHAM
Lewisham Way
BLACKHEATH
Park Rd
Avenue

APHAM MMON
★Black Cultural Archives
BRIXTON
Brixton Hill
BROCKLEY
LEWISHAM
Lee High Rd
Westhorne
ELTHAM

BALHAM
Poynders Rd
DULWICH
★Dulwich Picture Gallery
★Horniman Museum & Gardens
Dulwich Common
Brownhill Road
CATFORD
Sidcup Road
GROVE PARK

Tooting Bec Rd
Streatham High Road
STREATHAM
WEST NORWOOD
DULWICH PARK
FOREST HILL
Bromley Road
SYDENHAM

CRYSTAL PALACE PARK
★Crystal Palace
UPPER NORWOOD
BECKENHAM PLACE PARK
Bromley Hill
SUNDRIDGE PARK

THORNTON HEATH
London Road
SOUTH NORWOOD
BECKENHAM
BROMLEY
Bromley Common

MITCHAM COMMON
LANGLEY PARK

F **G** **H** **J**

1
2
3
4
5
6

The Major Collections

Viking longships and Venetian glass, Egyptian mummies and Wellington's boots, iron lungs and lunar modules... the astonishing range of exhibits to be found in these impressive museums is unmatched anywhere in the world

British Library

The national library of the United Kingdom

Map reference: page 20, C1
96 Euston Road, NW1. Tel: 020-7412 7332.
www.bl.uk
Tube: King's Cross St Pancras, Euston, Euston
Square, bus: 10, 18, 30, 59, 68, 73, 91, 253.
Mon, Wed–Fri 9.30am–6pm, Tues 9.30am–8pm,
Sat 9.30am–5pm, Sun/public holidays 11am–5pm.
Applications for admission to the reading
rooms should be made through the Reader
Admissions Office, tel: 020 7412 7677. Full
wheelchair access to all public areas. Tours on
Mon, Wed, Fri 3pm, Sat 10.30am and 3 pm.
Tours including a reading room Tues 6.30pm,
Sun and public holidays 11.30am and 3pm.
Free admission, charges for tours.

With more than 16 million books and periodicals, and vast holdings of sound recordings, newspapers, maps and stamps, the British Library (part of the British Museum until 1973) is one of the world's greatest library collections. Early aquisitions and donations included Sir Hans Sloane's library (1753), the old Royal Library (1757) and the library of George III (1823).

As the museum became a copyright library (entitled to a free copy of every book printed in the UK), space began to run out. In the 1990s a new library was built on Euston Road with 267 miles (430 km) of shelving, mostly underground. On the west side of the building are four public exhibition galleries: the John Ritblat Gallery: Treasures of the British Library, the Pearson Gallery, the Workshop of Words, Sounds and Images, and the Philatelic Display.

The John Ritblat Gallery houses a display of some of the library's most valuable books and manuscripts. Its "Maps and Views" display includes the 13th-century map of Great Britain drawn by the monk Matthew Paris. Another area houses sacred texts from around the world with a separate display of Bibles and Christian manuscripts. Among these are a 3rd-century Egyptian codex of the Gospel of St John, possibly the library's oldest manuscript.

Alongside these are the illuminated manuscripts. Particularly fine works include the histories of the Mughal emperors Babur and Akbar, the *Baburnama* and *Akbarnama*, and the 8th-century Japanese Buddhist *dharani* (religious texts), whose printing was ordered by the Empress Shotoku. In the same case is a copy of the *Gutenberg Bible* (1454), the earliest European work printed using movable type.

A case dedicated to science has a wide spread of documents, from Leonardo da Vinci's notebook to letters from Newton and Darwin. In the sections on literature, historical documents and musical manuscripts, Shakespeare figures prominently, with a copy of the first folio (collected edition) of his plays, printed in London in 1623. Also worth noting are copies of the 1215 Magna Carta, Nelson's last letter, Scott's Antarctic journal and the draft of Britain's 1939 ultimatum to Germany.

Cases of musical manuscripts include the autograph of Handel's oratorio *Messiah* (1741), Beethoven's sketches for his 6th Symphony (1808) and Mahler's manuscript for *Des Knaben Wunderhorn* (1893). There is a special display of loaned pieces relating to The Beatles, including the original copies of their song lyrics, with a listening post supplied.

Food and drink*: The library has two cafés and a restaurant. Terra Brasil (36–38 Chalton Street, 020-7388 6554) offers a cheap and tasty Brazilian buffet.*

OPPOSITE: the hall and staircase of the British Museum from Ackermann's *Microcosm of London.*

BELOW: The building of the Tower of Babel, a French parchment (*c.* 1423) in the British Library.

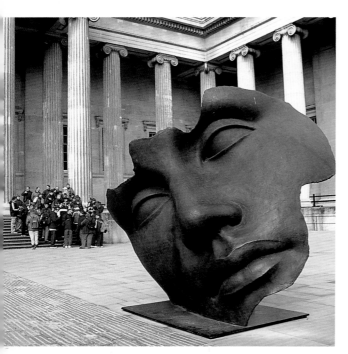

Tsuki-no-Hikari, a 1991 bronze by Igor Mitoraj, sits outside the museum's main entrance.

British Museum

Two million years of human history

Map reference: page 20, C2
Great Russell Street, WC1. Tel: 020-7323 8299.
www.thebritishmuseum.ac.uk
Tube: Holborn, Russell Square, Tottenham Court Road.
Sat–Wed 10am–5.30pm; on Thurs–Fri some galleries stay open until 8.30pm. Free admission.

The British Museum contains 6½ million objects, ranging from prehistoric pots to a Cona coffee machine. Devote just 60 seconds to each one and you'd be there, without sleep or meal breaks, for more than 12 years. Even though only 50,000 objects are on display at any given time, this is clearly not a place to "do" in a couple of hours. It is a treasure house that caters for scholars as well as tourists and, as the scholars do, it is best to concentrate initially on what interests you most. A tour of the highlights *(see page 28)* is a good start. As you seek out any particular objects in the 100 or so galleries, you will be diverted by enough intriguing displays to justify future visits.

This is one of the oldest museums in the world, founded by an Act of Parliament in 1753 and opened in 1759 *(for its full history, see page 15)*. It is also the most traditional of museums, with most objects in glass cases and few buttons and levers for children to manipulate, but it is rarely boring. The best time to visit is soon after opening, before the crowds begin aiming their flashguns unwisely at the reflective glass cases and panning their video cameras.

The Great Court

In 1857, the celebrated Reading Room – where Karl Marx researched *Das Kapital* – was added in the central courtyard to house most of the museum's immense library. In 1997, the British Library was relocated to new premises on the Euston Road *(see page 25)*, allowing the British Museum to make radical changes to its overcrowded building. The most radical change was the glassing over of the Great Court, the area around the Reading Room in the centre of the building, to create the largest covered public square in Europe – as well as one of the most striking museum experiences in the world. The curators see the Great Court not just as an essential improvement to the museum's existing facilities but as a free public space in its own right. As a result, it opens every day at 9am, staying open until 9pm Sunday to Wednesday and until 11pm on Thursday to Saturday (subject to funding). Even as a superior place to shelter from the rain, it's hard to beat.

It is also indisputably a remarkable architectural achievement. In part, this is the result of the mix of styles – the hi-tech panelling of the new roof, with its 3,312 unique glass triangles, set against the sturdy, measured classicism of the original 19th-century buildings. In part, it's the result of the spectacular new space that has been created, with an elegant, curving walkway on two levels around the old Reading Room, from where there is easy access to all parts of the museum. Shops, cafés and a new restaurant have been added, together with a few striking artefacts such as the majestic Lion of Cnidos and an Easter Island statue.

But, above all, the museum has taken full advantage of the project to create vastly improved facilities and relieve the overcrowding as the number of visitors each year approached 6 million.

Important new galleries have been built under the Great Court: the Clore Exhibition Centre, which contains two

The 1st-century Portland Vase.

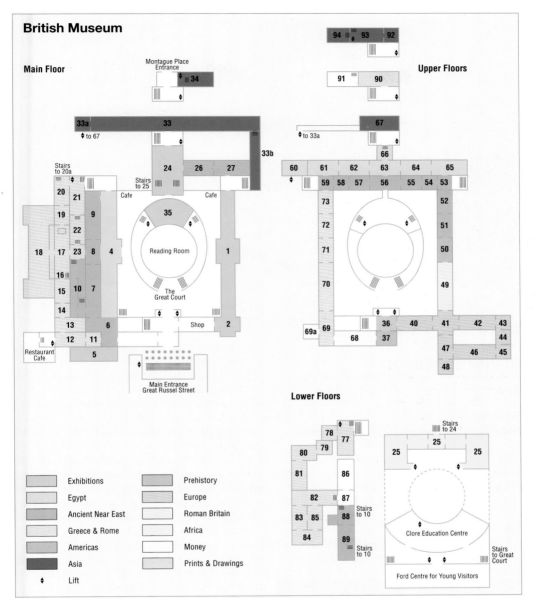

British Museum

Main Floor

Montague Place Entrance

Upper Floors

Lower Floors

Exhibitions

Egypt

Ancient Near East

Greece & Rome

Americas

Asia

Lift

Prehistory

Europe

Roman Britain

Africa

Money

Prints & Drawings

theatres and a space for temporary exhibitions; and the Sainsbury African Galleries. The latter is a particular step forward for the British Museum. In 1970, pressure on space forced it to rehouse the ethnography collections in the Museum of Mankind in Mayfair, near Piccadilly. Bringing them all back to the main building in Bloomsbury has not only allowed the museum to display these exceptional objects in new, purpose-built galleries but also to show many more of them at any one time.

The Reading Room

Readers here included Marx, Lenin, George Bernard Shaw, Thomas Hardy, Rudyard Kipling and Oscar Wilde. To gain access to its majestic interior, they needed readers' tickets, but today, following the relocation of the British Library, it is open to all. The Collections Multimedia Public Access System (Compass) is located here, its touchscreens enabling visitors to plan a tour of the galleries, browse objects on-line and order prints of selected images (services

A section of
the frieze
from the
Sculptures of
the Parthenon.

also available on the museum's website). A new reference library, sponsored by the late publisher Paul Hamlyn, has assembled more than 12,000 books to complement the museum's collections.

But the main attraction is the room itself, described by the *Publishers' Circular* when it opened in 1857 as "a circular temple of marvellous dimensions, rich in blue, and white, and gold." The soaring dome, with a diameter larger than that of St Paul's Cathedral, is supported on cast-iron ribs.

The highlights

Although the British Museum's collections span 2 million years, it is best known for its antiquities from Greece and Egypt and these dominate the highlights which should be seen on any first visit.

The Egyptian mummies

The hallowed Reading Room.

Rooms 62–63, on the upper floors, are the rooms to see first, simply because they can get wildly overcrowded as the day goes on – 98 percent of visitors want to see the mummies. They're worth seeing, too: thanks to the enthusiastic plundering of 19th-century explorers, this is the richest collection of Egyptian funerary art outside Egypt itself.

The size and ornamentation of the coffins and sarcophagi are immediately striking. The richly gilded inner coffin of the priestess Henutmehyt, for example, which dates from 1290 BC, is a work of considerable art. Scans displayed beside the coffin of Cleopatra (not *the* Cleopatra) show how well the body inside is preserved, and the process of embalming is explained in detail – one tool on display was used for hooking the brain and extracting it through the nose, and an accompanying skull shows the damage this caused to the nasal bone.

Apart from the princely humans who were destined to spend their afterlife in London's Bloomsbury, there are mummified cats, dogs, fish and crocodiles, as well as a variety of amulets and jewellery buried with them and various Canopic jars holding the mummies' preserved organs. One great strength of the British Museum is that one can compare how disparate ancient cultures in Europe, Africa and Asia handled their illustrious corpses – there are some startling similarities.

If you wish to meditate further on mortality, a glass case in Room 64 contains the body of a truly ancient Egyptian, his flesh preserved in the sands for 5,400 years. He is familiarly known as Ginger.

The Sculptures of the Parthenon

Commonly known as the Elgin Marbles *(see page 13),*

these have been given their own spacious quarters on the main floor (Room 18). Carved in the 5th century BC for the Temple of Athena Parthenos, patron goddess of Athens, these are, even in their damaged state, some of the greatest sculptures ever created, their muscular detail and fluidity of movement airily transcending their origins as blocks of marble. A model shows the harmony and proportion of the Parthenon before gunpowder stored there by the occupying Turks exploded in 1687, destroying most of the building and causing much of the damage seen on the statues and friezes today.

The Rosetta Stone

From the west side of the Great Court, enter Room 4 and turn left to find the granite tablet from the 2nd century BC which provided the key in the 19th century to deciphering ancient Egypt's hieroglyphic script. In the same room is the colossal sandstone head of the pharaoh Ramesses II, said to be the inspiration for *Ozymandias*, Shelley's poetic meditation on the transience of power.

The Nereid Monument

Room 17 contains the imposing facade of this 4th-century monument from Xanthos in Turkey, destroyed by an earthquake and reconstructed by the British Museum.

The Mausoleum of Halikarnassos

This giant tomb (Room 21), finished around 351 BC in southwest Turkey, was one of the seven wonders of the ancient world. The 10-ft (3-metre) statues of a man and woman hint at the tomb's enormity.

The Sutton Hoo Ship Burial

Room 42, on the first floor, contains the richest treasure ever dug from British soil, an early 7th-century longboat likely to have been the burial chamber of Raedwald, an East Anglian king. The acidic sand had destroyed all organic material well before the excavation in 1939, but a rich hoard of weapons, armour, coins, bowls and jewellery has survived. There's a superb iron helmet which manages to look curiously modern and deeply threatening at the same time.

The Lewis Chessmen

Also in Room 42 are these 82 elaborately carved 12th-century chess pieces, probably made in Norway and found on the Isle of Lewis in Scotland's Outer Hebrides. (Scotland would like to have them back to join the 11 pieces held in its National Museum in Edinburgh.) The lumpy, helmeted figures, their faces set in curious scowls, are strangely beautiful.

Lindow Man

A quiet corner of Room 50 is the final resting place of one of Britain's most senior citizens, found in a

The gilded inner coffin of the priestess Henutmehyt, from around 1290 BC.

The Lewis Chessmen.

to the Assyrian royal palace at Nimrud, and a giant pair of human-headed winged bulls from the palace of Assyria's Sargon III (721–705 BC) at Khorsabad.

Exhibits in the upstairs rooms depict everyday life in the ancient world, in peace and war. Jugs, spoons, saucepans and a cheese grater show how little basic kitchen utensils have altered in 20 centuries. A gladiator's helmet and weapons of battle show that some activities have changed. The arts are well represented, from the intricate motif of a mosaic pavement to the whimsy of a glass bottle in the shape of a fish. Room 70 contains the Portland Vase, a superbly crafted cameo-glass vessel from the early 1st century.

Ancient Egypt

In scale and quality, the museum's collections of Egyptian artefacts rival those even of its Greek and Roman collections, eloquent proof of the energies and interests of the 19th- and early 20th-century archaeologists who so painstakingly assembled them. There are two principal collections: sculptures, on the ground floor; and, among much else, mummies on the first floor.

The ancient Egyptians stocked tombs with everything the departed might need for the next (and apparently strikingly similar) life – from cosmetics to clothing, from writing materials to furniture – and the country's dry climate preserved many of these objects, to the delight of 19th-century tomb robbers.

Ancient Near East

As befits the area of the world which saw the first human civilisations, the museum's collections from the Ancient Near East are exceptionally rich. Among the highlights are a number of clay tablets with cuneiform inscriptions, one of the oldest forms of

peat bog, Lindow Moss, in Cheshire in 1984. Instantly dubbed Pete Marsh, he was identifed as the 25-year-old victim of a Druidic sacrifice (clubbed, garotted and throat cut) who had eaten some cake shortly before his death and was blood group O. So well was the body preserved that scientists were able to construct a likeness, which hangs on a wall alongside the somewhat gruesome corpse.

The Benin bronzes

In Room 25, in the basement, are around five dozen of the 900 brass plaques found in Benin City, Nigeria, in 1897. Probably cast in the 16th century to clad the wooden pillars of the palace, they depict court life and ritual in fascinating detail.

The Cassiobury Park Turret Clock

The intricate workings of this 1610 weight-driven clock, originally installed in a country house in Hertfordshire, are fascinating to behold. This is a good starting point for viewing the museum's remarkable collection of clocks and watches in Room 44.

The main collections

Greece and Rome

The museum's vast holdings from the Classical world are divided between Rooms 11–23 on the ground floor (the larger exhibits) and Rooms 69–73 on the first floor.

Lindow Man, also known as Pete Marsh.

Apart from highlights such as the Parthenon Sculptures, described above, treasures worth seeking out on the ground floor include the pair of colossal 9th-century BC lions which guarded the entrance

writing. One, nearly 5,000 years old, records the delivery of barley to a temple. Among somewhat younger objects, the highlight is probably the series of carved Assyrian reliefs, originally part of the monumental gateways from a variety of royal palaces: at Nimrud, at Khorsabad and at Nineveh. The majority of these superb slabs are a mere 3,000 years old.

Those with an interest in genuinely ancient objects, however, should seek out the plastered skull from Jericho, the oldest continuously inhabited city in the world. It is around 9,000 years old.

Early Europe

Apart from Lindow Man *(see highlights, above)*, a perennial attraction here is a Neolithic trackway, a simple raised path of leather and wood made by herders almost 6,000 years ago to help them cross the marshy ground of the Somerset Levels. But for many visitors the elaborate Celtic artefacts – highly refined and often of extraordinary craftsmanship – are even more remarkable. Shields, coins, a wide variety of jewellery and drinking vessels testify to the vigour and achievements of Celtic culture. Room 49 has a wide range of Roman treasures unearthed in Britain over the years.

Medieval and Modern Europe

Though not as rich in medieval artefacts as the Victoria and Albert Museum, the British Museum has some exceptional medieval pieces. Chief among them is the Sutton Hoo treasure *(see highlights, above)*. Other medieval objects include a series of richly decorated ecclesiastical artefacts. A highlight is an intricately patterned and decorated 12th-century gilt cross from Germany, a striking example of the high levels of craftmanship in the so-called Dark Ages.

More recent artefacts are eclecticism gone insane. A random selection would include a 15th-century bronze medal of Cosimo de' Medici the Elder, painted earthenware jugs from 17th-century Frankfurt, Russian revolutionary ceramics, and a 1919 Charles Rennie Mackintosh clock.

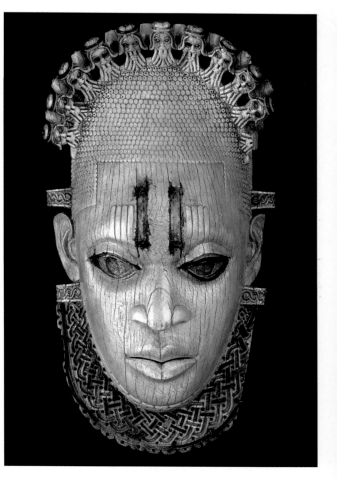

Africa

The Sainsbury African Galleries in the basement combine ancient and modern, showing how cultural traditions are still alive today. Thus one can view traditional textiles, masquerade masks and woodcarving, and then see how they have inspired the work of some of Africa's leading contemporary artists. This is one of the most colourful collections in the museum. Some of the shields used by Masai, Zulu and Matabele warriors are remarkably elaborate, and quilted horse armour from 19th-century Sudan is so vivid that a surprise attack would have been out of the question. Cast bronzes and ivory carvings are well represented.

Asia

The museum's collections of Chinese, Japanese and Korean artefacts are astonishingly large and varied, with a series of vast galleries given over to them (33–34 on the ground floor; 67 and 91–94 on the

An ivory mask made by the Edo peoples of Benin, Nigeria.

Young Nobleman on Horseback, a handscroll painting by Qian Xuan (AD 1290).

first floor). Not surprisingly, they attract large numbers of Asian visitors. There are examples from all periods and all styles, many of them highlighting just how far in advance of the West China in particular was for much of its history.

Those with a taste for Ming vases will find it more than satisfied. The Japanese collections, though not as old, contain objects every bit as sophisticated: wall hangings, furniture, masks, ceramics of all kinds, lacquer work and jade.

Spotting an incomparable opportunity to promote its culture to an international audience, Korea has cooperated closely with the British Museum, which now has the most important collection of Korean artefacts outside Korea. Room 67 includes a scholar's house constructed by Korean master craftsmen.

Exhibits from India include some exquisite bronzes, including a large dancing figure of the Hindu god Shiva. There's a seated Buddha from Burma and rare examples of early central Asian art.

The Americas

Although relatively less strong in collections from South America, the museum has superb collections from Central and North America in Rooms 26–27 on the ground floor. There are a number of hugely impressive Olmec statues and other works from around 1000 BC, as well as magnificent carved Mayan slabs from the 8th century AD. The rather later Aztec artefacts are equally striking. An early 16th-century mosaic mask, for example, made from jade and turquoise, is all the more memorable for having been set on a real skull. The relatively little known peoples of North America before the European invasion, from the Innuit in the far north to the peoples of the Mississippi in the south, are equally well represented.

A stoneware figure from the Ming dynasty (16th century).

Money and Medals

A collection of 750,000 coins dates from the 7th century BC to the present day, and there are notes dating back to 14th-century China (Room 68). The museum regards its collection of commemorative and art medals as providing an unparalleled insight into historical events and schools of art since the Italian Renaissance.

Prints and Drawings

For conservation and space reasons, only a fraction of the museum's 3 million works on paper are displayed at any one time. Highlights include Old Master prints and drawings, and satires of the 18th and 19th centuries.

In Sickness and In Health

A new Wellcome Trust Gallery, due to open in 2003, will be built around ethnological exhibits, particularly those relating to illness and health. The brief will be broad enough to encompass images of gods and ancestors, masks and costumes, and even consciousness-raising substances. Until it opens, an exhibition by Foster and Partners, architects of the Great Court, explores their ideas about urban regeneration and the use of public space, using models of some of their actual and imagined buildings.

Food and drink: The Court restaurant (020-7323 899) on the upper floor of the great Court has waiter-service morning coffee, lunch, afternoon tea and, on Thurs–Sat, dinner until 9pm. The Court café serves snacks and the Gallery café next to Room 12 has self-service meals.

A few minutes away, Poons (50 Woburn Place, 020-7580 1188) is an old-style Chinese restaurant, and serves dim sum noon–4pm. Wagamama (4A Streatham Street, 020-7736 2333) offers quicker and cheaper oriental food.

Museum of London

The world's largest museum of urban history

Map reference: page 20, G2
London Wall, EC2Y. Tel: 020-7600 3699.
www.museum-london.org.uk
Tube: Barbican, St Paul's, Moorgate, Bank.
Railway: Moorgate, Liverpool Street,
City Thameslink. Bus: 4, 56, 141, 172.
Mon–Sat 10am–5.50pm, Sun noon–5.50pm.
Café, shop, education services, research facilities/
picture library, wheelchair access and disabled
parking, suitable for children. Free admission.

The museum stands in the southwest corner of the Barbican complex (Gate 7), overlooking fragments of the old London wall, the busy city streets and layers of history buried underneath. It holds more than a million objects in its stores, making it the world's largest urban history museum. Aside from important prehistoric and Roman collections, it has a vast archaeological archive, a costume and decorative arts collection, and a photographic archive of 280,000 images. Only a small proportion of its collections are on permanent display.

London's history is traced chronologically across two floors, from prehistory to the Tudors and Stuarts at the entrance level and from the late Stuarts to the modern day at the lower level. The same thematic threads run through each period – architecture, trade and industry, transport, health, multiculturalism, religion, fashions, leisure pursuits. There are a lot of detailed information panels; you may find that, an hour into your visit, you're still with the Romans.

Londinium Life

Prehistory from 400,000BC to AD50 is covered by a new "London before London" gallery. The star exhibits of the next gallery, devoted to Roman London, are the hoard of gold coins (1st–2nd century AD) found buried in a safety deposit box near Fenchurch Street and the gilded arms of what must have been a life-size statue of a god or emperor. Other artefacts include Samian pottery from France, Mithraic sculptures made from Italian marble, a necklace made with Egyptian emeralds, and an amphora with the inscription "Lucius Tettius Africanus supplies the finest fish sauce from Antibes". A street exhibition displays craftsmen's tools alongside their finished product: studded shoes, phials and jeweller, knives of all shapes and sizes.

Saxon London is more scantily documented. Shining out from among the coins, cooking pots and weaponry is the Floral Street brooch found in one of the graves uncovered in Covent Garden in 2000. This elegant 7th-century brooch made of garnets and gold, may have belonged to an Anglo-Saxon noblewoman.

The Middle Ages section emphasises foreign trade, with exhibits of Spanish, Dutch and Flemish pottery, Venetian and Syrian glass and German arms. A "capital at play" display includes a pair of ice-skates (the Thames often froze over), arrowheads and hawkbells used for hunting and a swindler's set of loaded dice.

Tudors to the early Stuarts

The two engraved copperplate maps (c.1559) in the Tudor gallery are the earliest known maps of London and detail the area north of the river from London Bridge to Shoreditch. A model of London Bridge in around 1600, lined with timber-framed buildings before it all went up in smoke, leads to the popular Great Fire Experience, where you stand in a dark room and watch a rather basic mock-up of London licked by flames while listening to Samuel Pepys's account of its devastating progress.

The museum's Civil War collection includes Cromwell's death mask and bible, but more captivating is the cabinet filled with the glittering Cheapside Hoard. In 1912, a workman digging in

A re-creation of an 18th-century room in Poyle Park.

George William Joy's 1895 oil painting, *The Bayswater Omnibus.*

Cheapside hit on a box containing 230 pieces of finely crafted jewellery set with precious stones. The treasure is thought to have belonged to a goldsmith forced to hide his precious stock during the civil war.

Before heading down the ramp into Georgian London, take a breath of air in the well-planted Nursery Gardens (open in summer), an organic history of London's nursery trade.

Restoration London

The chronological tour continues on the lower level with the late Stuart period, a time of intense cultural, architectural and scientific activity. When Charles II returned to the throne in 1660, he concentrated his efforts on expanding his colonies abroad and the pursuit of pleasure at home. The objects in the Foreign Trade section provide a quick visual summary of the source of London's burgeoning wealth. A reproduction of Hogarth's portrait of tea magnate Thomas Twining hangs behind early 18th-century tea and coffee pots, a ginger jar and a pile of guineas minted from African gold.

The Royal Society was also established during Charles II's reign. Timepieces, mathematical and medical instruments show scientific and technological progress, though the instruments used for dental extraction look horrifyingly primitive.

Changes in society are examined with exhibits on music and theatre, taverns and early tourism, fashion and the calico craze, interior décor and tableware. Look out for the series of four amusing prints satirising the excesses of the period. One depicts a fashionable lady sporting a ridiculous wig; another is of a stay maker gleefully measuring a woman's waist. The star attraction on the lower level is the Lord Mayor's gilded coach (1757), an elaborate if gaudy display of the exquisite craftsmanship that characterised the age. It is taken out of the museum once a year for the Lord Mayor's Show.

World City Gallery

This new gallery presents a dynamic illustration of "the long 19th century" from the French Revolution through the Victorian age and Industrial Revolution to World War I. Exhibits include Wellington's boots, hat and duelling pistols, a jewelled sword presented to Nelson by the Corporation of London, Queen Victoria's parliamentary robes and one of the first motorised taxis.

The post-1914 collections are in storage.

Food and drink: On level 0 of the Barbican, the pleasant Waterside Cafe (inexpensive), is a self-service spot with open-air lakeside seating. On level 1 is the Balcony Café (tel: 020-7628 3331; moderate), a minimal restaurant with snacks or full meal. On level 2 is the acclaimed Searcy's Restaurant (tel: 020-7588 3008; expensive), where Modern British food with a French twist is served with style.

National Maritime Museum and Queen's House

Unrivalled collection of maritime art and artefacts displayed in a classical palace

Map reference: page 22, H3
Romney Road, Greenwich.
Tel: 020-8312 6608. www.nmm.ac.uk
By rail: Docklands Light Railway: Cutty Sark.
Mainline: Greenwich, Maze Hill. By river:
pleasure boats leave from Westminster,
Tower and Embankment piers.
By bus: 177, 180, 188, 199, 286, 386.
10am–5pm daily (summer 6pm).
Café and restaurant, shop, research facilities,
wheelchair access/disabled parking, suitable for
children, guided tours. Free admission.

The National Maritime Museum, the largest of its kind in the world, explores the sea and sea-faring from every aspect. The cream of its vast collection, comprising more than 2 million objects, is spread across 16 themed galleries.

Ground level: Columbus to Cunard

The six main galleries on the ground floor are arranged in and around the glass-roofed Neptune's Courtyard. Two are dedicated to the great explorers, from the Vikings who powered their longboats as far south as North Africa, to the European explorers of the 16th and 17th centuries and the great polar expeditions of the 19th century. Mementoes of these heroic seafarers include a silver-gilt cup given to Sir Frances Drake by Elizabeth I after he circumnavigated the world, a Chinese geomancer's compass and the "last message" written by Sir John Franklin before his mysterious disappearance in the Arctic.

The adjacent Passengers gallery focuses on the mass migrations from Europe to America during the 19th and early 20th centuries. It also celebrates the romance of sea travel with early tourism posters and models of the great luxury liners.

The Cargoes gallery covers post-war maritime trade and the evolution of the cargo ship, from the first roll-on roll-off ferry to the world's biggest container vessel. A large map shows the main shipping routes, ports and trading countries.

In the middle of the central courtyard, the Maritime London gallery explores the city's maritime heritage and its role today. The dual panorama of the north and south banks of the Thames shows how radically the face of London has changed.

Next door, the Rank and Style gallery displays practical and ceremonial clothing worn at sea. Prince Albert (later Edward VII) set a nautical trend for children with his sailor suit. But the garment with the most compelling tale to tell is Tony Bullimore's survival suit. Made from the latest synthetic materials, it kept the round-the-world yachtsman from freezing to death when his boat capsized in 1997.

Neptune Courtyard

This courtyard has been renovated and glazed over to provide an airy, light-filled space for larger exhibits. These are lined up along three "streets". South Street is dominated by Prince Frederick's golden barge (1732), a symbol of royal power. East Street is taken up by a new interactive display called "Making Waves" where you can learn all about tides, waves and the weather. Other exhibits include a lighthouse lamp, the hulking "grasshopper" engine of the 1950s paddle tug *Reliant* and the 1930s speedboat, *Miss Britain III*, which held the open water speed record for several years.

First floor: Ruling and polluting the waves

The presentation of the second-level galleries is more traditional, but no less interesting. The Trade and Empire section covers the growth of maritime trade and the expansion of the British Empire, focusing on slavery, the tea trade and opium wars, and Cook's Pacific voyages. The seeds of the empire were sown in 1600 when a royal charter granted the East India Company the monopoly of trade in the East. In 1601, John Lancaster, whose portrait hangs here, commandeered the first East India Company voyage to the "spice islands". He was dismayed to discover that his cargo of tweed had no commercial value in the hot tropics, so he plundered a Portuguese ship whose cargo of light Indian cotton was much more useful. He was

Figurehead from the 174-gun *Implacable*, originally French but captured by the Royal Navy in the early 1800s.

Captain Graham in his Cabin by William Hogarth (1697–1764).

able to trade it for spices and proved on his return that the company could turn a good profit. Another historically significant painting depicts the signing of the Treaty of Nanking that ended the first Opium War (1839–42). The treaty was signed between Britain and China on board the HMS *Cornwallis* (a model of this 74-gun ship, displayed in All Hands gallery, is the pride of the museum's model collection). A minor clause of this treaty leased Hong Kong to Britain, which China had no qualms handing over as they considered the island a barren backwater.

Only a small proportion of the museum's collection of artworks is on view (though the recent transformation of the Queen's House into an art gallery should ease the pressure). The Art and the Sea gallery is crammed with works of European marine art from the 17th to the 20th centuries which are not given the space or lighting they deserve. There are a couple of impressive ink and oil drawings by William Van der Velde the Elder (1611–93), an early war correspondent who included himself in all the battle scenes he painted. The series of etchings of the Thames by Whistler (1834–1903) add a human element to a space dominated by ships, seascapes and battle scenes. Two videos at either end of the gallery running extracts from Noël Coward and David Lean's 1942 stiff-upper-lip navy film *In Which We Serve*

and Peter Greenaway's *Beside the Sea* anti-documentary add an interesting perspective.

The third main gallery on this floor is the Sea Power gallery, tucked away in the southwest wing (with the Regatta café). It covers the history of the Navy and the maritime rivalries of the 20th century. One side of the gallery is dominated by brooding images of war. Other highlights include the life-size replica of a torpedo compartment accompanied by video extracts from *Das Boot* – the acclaimed 1981 film about life on a German U boat – and the frigate operations room simulator where you can plan and launch an attack on an enemy vessel.

The courtyard area at this level examines the state of the marine environment today and the Future of the Sea. Step into the giant silvery sphere and be hypnotised by 32 screens with a cleverly choreographed film showing both the beauty of the oceans and our destruction of them.

Third Floor: All Hands on Deck

A whole gallery is dedicated to Horatio Nelson (1758–1805), Britain's most popular hero in the 19th century, who has gone down in history as much for his passionate affair with Lady Hamilton (one of her many portraits painted by George Romney hangs in the gallery) as for his naval victories. The museum's most prized possession is the uniform coat Nelson was wearing when he was killed in the Battle of Trafalgar on board the *Victory*. The bullet hole at the shoulder and the bloodstains on his stockings are clearly visible. Nearby hangs Turner's controversial interpretation of the historic battle. Around the corner in the Ship of War room is a selection of warships from the museum's model collection.

This is the floor that will amuse restless children. A large area is given over to two interactive galleries: the All Hands gallery, where you can send a morse code message, have a go at gunnery target practice or try out a diver's suit; and the Bridge, where you can take the helm of a Viking longship or try to steer a virtual paddle steamer through the Thames.

New Visions of the Sea is a collection of specially commissioned art works by contemporary artists dotted around the museum. At the entrance you are greeted by an evocative short film by Lucy Blakstad based on Radio 4's Shipping Forecast. On the mezzanine level is Rosie Leverton's glass and stainless steel sculpture inspired by the salvaged stern of *HMS Implacable* suspended on the wall behind. The most recent addition to the Art and the Sea section is Humphrey Ocean's painting of a cross channel ferry drifting in to Dover.

THE QUEEN'S HOUSE

With its high windows and Ionic columns, this was England's first classical Renaissance building. It was designed as a summer palace for Queen Anne of Denmark, the wife of James I (reigned 1603–25). The story goes that the king proposed the building of a palace as a peace offering for swearing at her in public after she accidentally shot one of his

favourite hunting dogs. The Queen commissioned Inigo Jones (1573–1652) to design her new retreat in 1616. Inspired by the Renaissance villas he had seen in Italy, the royal architect came up with a clean, symmetrical design, in marked contrast to the

The South Sea Company's coat of arms, from around 1712.

WHERE EAST MEETS WEST

It's a short, but steep walk from the National Maritime Museum to the Royal Observatory *(see page 144)*, but worth the effort to stand on one of London's most historic spots and enjoy one of its finest views. The statue of General Wolfe, a gift from the Canadian government, has been king of the hill since 1930. James Wolfe was Commander of the British Army when Quebec was captured in 1759, but was killed in battle in the same year, just before Canada became a British territory. His body was returned to his family home in Greenwich and is buried in St Alfege's Church. Sit on the steps or benches at the foot of the statue and take in the view. A concise history of maritime London can be mapped out in the skyline. Dominating the scene are Inigo Jones's resplendent white palace and the colonnades of the Maritime Museum. Rising behind each side of the Queen's House, in perfect symmetry, are the twin domes of the Royal Naval College, designed as a seaman's hospital by Christopher Wren, with the assistance of Nicholas Hawksmoor. It was here that Nelson lay in state after his death at the Battle of Trafalgar. To the left you can see the tall masts of the racing tea clipper, *Cutty Sark (see page 133)*. Further west along the Thames is Deptford, where Henry VIII founded the Royal Naval Dockyard and from where Sir Walter Raleigh set sail for North America. On the north side of the river, the London Docklands are dominated by Canary Wharf and its sister towers, the latest additions to the city skyline. The dome of St Paul's is visible on the far horizon. Among the financial institutions clustered around the cathedral and the Bank of England is the Lloyd's building, which remains the centre of the marine insurance market. (For more information about historic Greenwich, visit the Tourist Information Centre next to the *Cutty Sark*).

Sir Christopher Wren's Royal Naval Hospital.

red-brick confusion that characterised many Tudor palaces. The Greenwich Palace, which stood on the site now occupied by the Royal Naval College, was a favourite with Henry VIII, who was born here, and with Elizabeth I, who spent her summers here.

Work on the Queen's House stopped when Queen Anne died in 1619 and wasn't resumed until 1629 when her son, Charles I, passed Greenwich to his French queen, Henrietta Maria. Under her supervision, the palace was finally completed in 1638. Following the example of the great European courts, the royal couple employed leading artists of the day to create works of art for their palaces, but, after Charles's execution in 1649, the works of art were removed. All that remains of the original grandeur is the wrought-iron balustrade of the tulip spiral staircase, the black-and-white marble floor in the Great Hall, and Matthew Gooderick's "grotesque work" painted on the ceiling of the Queen's Bedchamber.

When the monarchy was restored in 1660, the palace was extended and Charles II commissioned top French landscape architect, Le Nôtre, to create a formal landscape to the south. In the late 17th century, the house was used to accommodate royal servants. The astronomer royal, John Flamsteed, lived here while the observatory was being built *(see page 144)*, and the Dutch

Hogarth's portrait of Inigo Jones (1573–1652).

marine artists, the Van de Veldes, used one of its rooms as their studio. In the 18th century it was occupied by the Governor of the Royal Hospital and later by the Ranger of Greenwich Park until 1805 when the building was given to the Royal Naval Asylum, an orphanage school.

The wings, joined by two long, airy colonnades, were added in 1807, to commemorate the Battle of Trafalgar. The Queen's House finally became home to the Maritime Museum in 1937.

Despite renovations in the 1980s, when the stately home was reconstructed to evoke the extravagant lifestyle of the Stuart monarchs, it was decided that the building would be put to better use as an art gallery. It is now being used to showcase the National Maritime Museum's art collections through rotating exhibitions, each mounted for about a year.

Food and drink: In the museum, the Upper Court Coffee Bar (level 2) serves drinks and snacks while the Regatta Café has a more substantial menu and a terrace overlooking the park. There are countless pubs, tea rooms, cafés and restaurants in Greenwich. Among the old favourites are the Trafalgar Tavern (Park Row; 020-8858 2437, moderate, a historic pub overlooking the river with a good fish menu, and the Bar du Musée (17 Nelson Rd; 020-8858 4710, inexpensive), a cosy wine bar with a cold platter menu and wine list with a Spanish bias. For a real treat try the Spread Eagle (Nevada Street; 020-8305 1666, expensive), which offers traditional, fine French cooking.

Natural History Museum

Life forms, from termites to dinosaurs

Map reference: page 40, B3
Cromwell Road, SW7. Tel: 020-7942 5000.
www.nhm.ac.uk
Tube: South Kensington; buses: C1, 14 and 74.
10am–5.50pm, Sun 11am–5.50pm.
Excellent for children of all ages (children
under 12 must be accompanied by an adult).
Activity sheets available at information desks.
Free admission. Free guided tours throughout
the day (register at the information desk).
Wheelchair access.

If any of London's museums encapsulates the Victorians' quest for knowledge and passion for sifting and cataloguing data, it's this one, with its colossal collection of 75 million plants, animals, fossils, rocks and minerals. But the museum is no relic of a bygone age: its collection is expanding at a rate of 50,000 new specimens a year, many of them "type" specimens (the first of their type to be discovered), and forms the basis of research for around 350 leading scientists working on solutions to global problems. It also offers some of the country's most impressive high-tech exhibits (such as animatronic dinosaurs and a simulated earthquake).

The collection was originally a department of the British Museum, but by the mid-19th century it had outgrown the available space and in 1881 the present museum opened on Cromwell Road *(full history on page 16)*. In spite of its vast size, the layout is easy to master. It divides between the "Life" galleries, starting from Cromwell Road, and the "Earth" galleries, beginning from Exhibition Road. Waterhouse Way connects the two.

One of the museum's greatest delights is the way it presents superb high-tech exhibits alongside beautifully kept Victorian-style galleries filled with meticulously labelled cabinets. Many of the latter are found in quiet by-ways, but one vintage member of the collection appreciated both by excited children and reflective adults is the magnificent wood and plaster model of a blue whale (Life Gallery 24), which has been the centrepiece of the Mammals section since it was built in 1938.

This tour of the museum's highlights sets off from the main Cromwell Road entrance, which leads into the Central Hall. Numbers in brackets in the text refer to the number of the gallery being discussed.

The Central Hall

The hub of the museum, this contains the ticket office, the meeting point for guided tours and a shop. It is also dotted with a selection of exhibits that serve as tasters for the main galleries. Explore the alcoves to discover such things as a spider trapped in amber or a coelacanth, a type of fish which, until its discovery in 1938, was thought to have been extinct for more than 70 million years.

In the centre of the hall is the much-photographed cast of a diplodocus dinosaur unearthed in Wyoming in 1899. At 85 ft (26 metres), it is the longest complete skeleton of a dinosaur ever discovered (though incomplete skeletons of dinosaurs twice this size have been found).

The Central Hall is the best place to appreciate

the architectural details of the building *(see panel "A Gothic Extravaganza", page 42)*. On the landing overlooking the hall is a statue of Richard Owen, the museum's first director and the first person to recognise the existence of giant prehistoric land reptiles and to call them dinosaurs ("terrible lizards").

Dinosaurs remain a big attraction.

At the top of the stairs above the entrance is a cross-section of a giant sequoia from the Sierra Nevada; aged 1,335 years when felled, it was relatively youthful for a tree of this type, which can live for as long as 3,000 years.

The Life Galleries

Dinosaurs (21)
One of the busiest sections of the museum, this gallery can easily absorb an hour or more. But many

visitors make a bee-line for the robotic dinosaurs at the end of the room. Two menacing Deinonychus serve as warm-ups to the full-scale animatronic T-Rex on long-term loan from Japan. Responsive to human movement, the roaring, life-like model twists and turns convincingly, delighting most children.

Human Biology (22)

Examining the workings behind every part of the human body, from hormones to genes, this section is packed with interactive exhibits: you can test your memory and senses or be tricked by optical illusions. It is a credit to the museum that its presentation of the oft-told story of puberty and reproduction enthralls both jaded parents as well as the children encouraged to view it.

More on genetics and the possibilities of genetic engineering can be found in the exhibition on Darwin and the Origin of Species (105) on the first floor. To learn about man's relationship with other primates, visit Primates (07), also on the first floor.

Mammals (23 and 24)

As well as displaying an astonishing array of taxidermy and correcting some erroneous ideas that visitors might have been picked up in school biology (not all mammals give birth to live young: witness the duck-billed platypus and echidna), these galleries contain sobering statistics on the rate at which species are becoming extinct. Upstairs on the balcony, a section is devoted to cetaceans (sea-living mammals), and you can listen to whale songs and dolphin clicks.

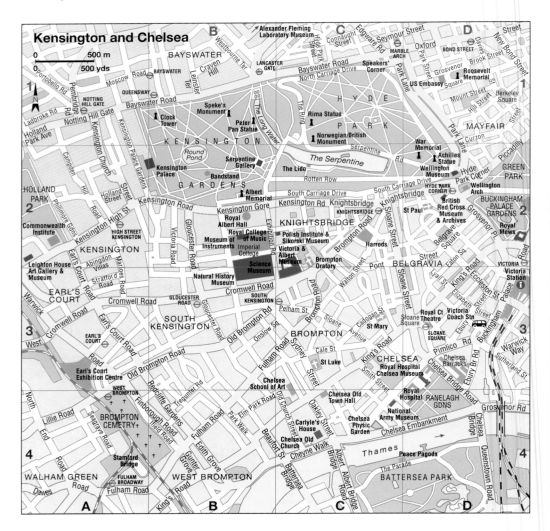

Skeleton and full-size model of a blue whale.

Fish and Amphibians (12)

This gallery highlights many fascinating species, including fish that live between the sea's twilight zone at 1,300 ft (400 metres) and total darkness at 3,300 ft (1,000 metres); some generate their own light. Next door is the wonderfully serene Marine Invertebrates (13), where cabinets of exquisite corals, shells and sea fans are enhanced by the sound of waves breaking on a shore.

Waterhouse Way

The walls of this central corridor are lined with impressive marine fossils, many discovered by the Victorian fossil-hunter Mary Anning (1799–1847). At the age of 11, she discovered a complete icthyosaur in the undercliff near her home in Lyme Regis in Dorset, a find that triggered a life-long interest in collecting fossils and selling them on to scientists (inspiring the old English tongue-twister "She sells sea-shells on the sea shore").

Among the other marine fossils here, look out for an ichthyosaur with the broken skeletons of three unborn young, found in Germany. On the opposite wall is the hip section of a stegosaur, a plated dinosaur, from Wiltshire; it is from one of only two stegosaurs discovered in Britain.

Creepy Crawlies (33)

Another big hit with children, this section, off Waterhouse Way, has many interactive exhibits and is a mine of astonishing and sometimes flesh-crawling facts. You can wander through a house and learn about the many uninvited housemates in an average home; sit in a life-size model of a termite mound; and watch a colony of leaf-cutter ants, whose activities can also be followed on the web (www.nhm.ac.uk/antcast).

The Earth Galleries

This section, based on the once separate Geological Museum, is brought to life by exciting special effects and atmospheric sound and lighting. A central

---

THE DARWIN CENTRE

Accommodating, let alone exhibiting, the NHM's collection is a perennial challenge. Until recently only 1 percent of the collection could be displayed; the rest, including some historic collections, such as that acquired by Captain Cook on his voyage through the South Seas in 1768, and the specimens brought back from the Galápagos by Charles Darwin, were stacked in research departments or stored in the suburbs.

The new Darwin Centre should help alleviate the problem. Situated next to the main museum, on Queen's Gate, the seven-storey building is designed to be both a top-class centre for scientific study and a public resource; guided tours of the centre and "meet-the-scientists" sessions are planned.

In Phase One of its development (2002), some 22 million specimens were moved here from the Spirit Building (named after the methylated spirit in which the specimens are preserved). In Phase Two, a phenomenal 28 million insects and 6 million plants (there are 25,000 jars of plankton alone) will follow, as will stuffed mammals and birds at a later date.

The new building is undeniably modernist, but, like Alfred Waterhouse's original, the design includes witty allusions to nature. Stainless steel spiders, for example, are bolted on to the solar wall; and the inflatable roof is likened to a caterpillar.

From the Beginning (63) relates the mind-bending story of the universe from the time of the big bang 15,000 million years ago to the end of the solar system, predicted 5,000 million years from now.

For sheer pleasure in the planet's beauty, visit Earth's Treasury (64), displaying rocks, gems and minerals glittering in the gallery's semi-darkness.

The Jerwood Gallery (26)

Often overlooked by visitors is the museum's superb collection of watercolours, oils, prints and drawings, some of which are the original illustrations to books by 19th-century explorers such as Richard Burton and David Livingstone. The gallery also stages temporary exhibitions, including the annual Wildlife Photographer of the Year competition.

The Wildlife Garden

The wildlife garden around the west lawn is a microcosm of the main wildlife habitats of Britain. Although hardly a haven of tranquillity (traffic thunders along nearby Cromwell Road to and from the M4), it is a lush spot in which frogs plop and dragonflies hover. There's a tour of the garden twice daily in spring and summer (enquire at the information desk in the Central Hall), which is a refreshing way to end a visit to the museum.

The Earth Galleries. escalator transports visitors into a gigantic rotating globe. At the top (second floor), Restless Surface (62) includes imaginative coverage of earthquakes and volcanoes: the tremors of an earthquake are simulated in a mock-up of a Japanese mini-market; a bank of TV sets next to a car covered in volcanic ash replays news reports of the 1991 eruption of Mount Pinitubo in the Philippines.

It is in this area, too, that you learn how a lightning bolt hit desert sand and changed it into a hollow tube of glass.

Food and drink: In the Life galleries there are the Waterhouse Café (pleasant and airy; self-service; coffee, tea, sandwiches and cakes), the Life Galleries Restaurant (self-service; hot meals and snacks) and a basement snack bar. In the Earth Galleries there is the Globe Fast Food Café (self-service; burgers, chips, baked potatoes). During school holidays and at weekends an area for eating packed lunches is made available next to the basement snack bar in the Life galleries. Alternatively, you can walk to the many cafés and restaurants in nearby Knightsbridge.

A GOTHIC EXTRAVAGANZA

Almost as famous as the NHM's colossal collection is the extravagant building itself. Designed by Alfred Waterhouse, who reworked earlier designs by an architect called Captain Fowke, it is in the Gothic Romanesque style. It was the first building in Britain to be faced entirely in terracotta, a cheap but versatile material that could be easily cleaned and came in lovely shades of buff and pale-blue.

With its Romanesque arches, Gothic pinnacles, stained-glass windows and nave-like Central Hall, it's more like a cathedral than a museum, a similarity intended by Professor Richard Owen, its first director. As well as being a brilliant scientist, Owen was a deeply religious man who rejected Darwin's theory of natural selection. He felt the building should celebrate God's creation and wanted the ornamental elements to symbolise this in the same way that stonework does in medieval cathedrals. The result is a joy. Terracotta monkeys scramble up pillars; cranes, hares and lizards peep through foliage; songbirds are everywhere. Follow the lines of the soaring architecture upwards to see the beautifully painted ceiling panels depicting medicinal plants.

Science Museum

Great inventions, inventively presented

Map reference: page 40, B2
Exhibition Road, SW7. Tel: 0870-870 4771.
www.sciencemuseum.org.uk
Tube: South Kensington (a tunnel leads from the station to the museum).
Daily 10am–6pm. Free admission.

When we visited, the artefact greeting us just inside the main entrance was the massive landing gear of an Airbus. It was both unexpected and entirely appropriate, representing what the museum does superbly well: encouraging visitors to contemplate the marriage of form (separated from the rest of the aircraft, the landing gear looked like a masterful sculpture) and function (a consideration of vital importance to Airbus passengers dropping towards a runway).

With more than 10,000 exhibits, plus additional attractions such as an IMAX theatre, this museum could occupy a full day, and visitors pressed for time should assign priorities. An important point to note is the distinction between the main wing, dating back to 1928, and the Wellcome Wing, opened in 2000 with sponsorship mainly from the Wellcome Trust. You can walk between the two wings at five of the museum's seven levels, but the ambience of the wings is quite different and it is more satisfying to explore one wing at a time.

One thing's for sure: anyone downcast after a visit to the Imperial War Museum should head straight for the Science Museum. If the first chronicles the evil that mankind has perpetrated, the second, while not ignoring the disreputable uses to which many inventions have been put, is a resounding tribute to the astonishing ingenuity that has been devoted over the centuries to improving humanity's lot.

Main Wing: Ground Floor

This is the Science Museum at its spectacular best, featuring three main areas: Power, Space and Making the Modern World.

The Power hall is dominated by a massive 1903 mill engine which worked 1,700 looms in Burnley until 1970 and still rotates with great elegance. An impressive variety of engines, some models but many full-size, trace the development of steam power from the early 18th century. James Watt, whose private workshop has been reconstructed at mezzanine level, said of his 1777 pumping engine: "The velocity, violence, magnitude and horrible noise of the engine give universal satisfaction to all beholders, believers or not." What gives satisfaction today is the beauty and precision of these machines as well as the ability to observe exactly how they work – a gratification seldom provided by modern high-tech contraptions. Coming up to date, a cutaway model show what's inside the cooling tower of a modern thermal power station.

The Exploration of Space gallery's big attraction is a replica of the Apollo 11 lunar excursion module, but its scope encompasses videos of early rocket experiments in the 1920s (most ended humiliatingly) and a dissection of a V2 rocket, showing why it struck fear into Londoners during World War II. There's the spacesuit Helen Sharman wore when she took the Union Jack to the Mir space station in 1991, plus a video of her describing the experience.

Making the Modern World is an excuse to bring together many of the museum's most important exhibits. "Modern" is defined as post-1750 and the stars include the world's oldest surviving steam locomotive, the coal-hauling Puffing Billy (*circa* 1815), Stephenson's pioneering *Rocket* passenger

Reconstruction of the 1969 lunar landing module that put Neil Armstrong and Buzz Aldrin on the moon.

Transports of delight in the Making the Modern World gallery.

locomotive (1829), a Ford Model T (1916), a Lockheed Electra airliner hanging in silvery splendour from the ceiling (1935), a copy of Crick and Watson's DNA spiral model (1953) and the battered Apollo 10 command module (1969). Specialists might wish to study Troughton's Dividing Engine (1778) and Ramsden's Three-Foot Theodolite (1791), while the rest of us marvel at their ingenuity and refinement. A host of less spectacular exhibits include the world's first sewing machine.

First Floor

Galleries include materials, telecommunications, gas, agriculture, surveying, time measurement, food and weather.

These are more education-oriented galleries, though some of the 750 classic timepieces are just beautiful to behold. The Challenge of Materials gallery is wide-ranging enough to include a prototype pod from the London Eye observation wheel and an Axminster carpet dress designed by Vivienne Westwood. The telecommunications exhibit allows visitors to call from one telephone to another via one of Britain's last mechanical exchanges, watching the switches operate as they do so. The agriculture gallery is big enough to accommodate a combine harvester, and the weather gallery has one of the world's best collections of scientific barom-

eters. Most of the galleries have hands-on exhibits to appeal particularly to children, as well as intriguing displays such as "What is a motorcycle helmet made of?"

Second Floor

Galleries here cover everyday chemistry, printing and papermaking, weighing and measuring, lighting, nuclear physics and power, computing and mathematics, ships, marine engineering and diving.

Highlights include some of Thomas Edison's early lamps, the Difference Engine No. 2 with which in the 1830s Charles Babbage anticipated modern computing, a working Monotype machine from the days of hot-metal printing, and a full-size reconstruction of a ship's bridge.

Third floor

Galleries are devoted to heat and temperature, geophysics and oceanography, optics, photography and cinematography, health, flight and broadcasting.

Dominating this floor is the magnificent Flight Gallery, with exhibits ranging from a seaplane to a Spitfire, from hot-air balloons to helicopters. The 1919 Vickers Vimy in which Alcock & Brown made the first non-stop transatlantic flight is here, as is Amy Johnson's Gipsy Moth Jason. There's a replica of the Wright Flyer in which Wilbur and

Orville Wright pioneered powered flight at Kitty Hawk, North Carolina, in 1903 (Orville donated the original to the museum in 1928 after a row with the Smithsonian Institute, but it was returned to the US in 1948 after this exact copy had been made). Other eye-catching exhibits in this hangar-style space include a Messerschmitt rocket-propelled fighter and the first British jet aircraft, the Gloster Whittle E28/39. Visitors can peer into the cockpit of a Douglas DC3 and participate in interactive exhibits illustrating the principles of flight. A flight simulator offers a rodeo-style ride, for which a fee is charged.

Also on the third floor is a radio studio, where a computer simulation allows you to compile a sound mix and hear how it plays. A serendipity selection of other exhibits might include a colourful mechanical model of the solar system from 1712, early cameras from the 19th century, an 1870s tide-predicting machine, and an early iron lung.

Fourth and Fifth Floors

These cover medicine and veterinary history. With exhibits ranging from early surgical instruments to a 1905 pharmacy, and from an 1890s dental extraction to 1980s open-heart surgery, these displays are a hypochondriac's nightmare. Among the 5,000 objects on display in the Science and Art of Medicine section are many appealingly decorative items, including a Tibetan doctor's medicine bag and an English 19th-century leech jar.

Basement

We've left this to last because it is a more recreational area and is a good place to bring younger children if they tire of the more serious exhibits. It contains The Garden, a play area for children aged 3–6, and Things, a hands-on "how do things work?" gallery suitable for 7–11-year-olds.

Also in the basement is The Secret Life of the Home, a collection of domestic appliances and gadgets that provoke nostalgia in adults and disbelief in children. A range of models charts the development of the electric toaster since 1923. Hundreds of other items include a 1925 Sol hairdryer and a 1945 Goblin Teasmade. The thought occurs, as it so often does throughout the Science Museum, that older artefacts often seem more visually appealing than their modern equivalents. After viewing a selection of gloriously ornate 19th-century stoves, for example, the cutaway of a modern gas central heating boiler seems much less interesting.

The Wellcome Wing

Providing further interest for children, Launch Pad, in the Wellcome Wing section of the basement, is a spacious interactive gallery with an emphasis on learning about science and technology. A highlight is provided by two enormous sound receivers. A message spoken quietly into one is easily picked up by the other one on the far side of the room.

The remaining floors of the new wing, opened in 2000, are quite different in look and feel to the museum's older wing. Aiming at a younger audience, they look to the future rather than the past, concentrating on digital technology, biomedical science and information technology. The new wing is windowless, apart from one wall whose translucent blue glass bathes the display areas in what is meant to be a modernistic, if not futuristic, glow.

One problem is that the workings of digital technology are not as transparent as those of a steam engine. Another is that, to hold the attention, didactic displays on computer screens must match the graphic agitation of computer games. The result often reminds one of a popular science programme on television, packed with dazzling graphics but not

An installation in the Digitopolis section of the Wellcome Wing.

really leaving one much the wiser about its subject.

On the ground floor, Antenna is a series of changing exhibits based around current science news, its topicality enchanced by a live feed from the BBC's online science pages. These have an edifying feel, which is balanced by the all-out entertainment of Virtual Voyages, a simulator creating the effect of a comet impact or a trip to Mars, and an IMAX film theatre conjuring up dinosaurs or outer space on a screen 65 ft (20 metres) wide.

The theme of the first floor is "Who am I?" This explores such questions as "How does the immune system work?" and "Why are men and women different?" Addressing the latter theme, one screen photographs your face and morphs it into a similar face of the opposite sex.

Digitopolis, on the second floor, shows how digital technology may change our lives. The more interesting displays demonstrate how special effects are created in movies and how developments in digital speech may allow us to discuss our health problems over the telephone with computers.

In Future, the display on the third floor, is essentially a series of large digital board games on which contestants are invited to vote on health, communications and lifestyle topics – for example, "Should men be allowed to give birth?"

Food and drink: The Deep Blue Café (ground floor, Wellcome Wing) has waiter service. There are three other self-service cafés, plus picnic areas. A few minutes' walk away, Bombay Brasserie (Courtfield Street, 020-7370 4040) is one of London's top Indian restaurants. Pricey.

Victoria and Albert Museum

The world's largest collection of decorative and applied arts

Map reference: page 40, C2
Cromwell Road, SW7. Tel: 020 7942 2000.
Recorded info: 0870-442 0808. www.vam.ac.uk
Tube: South Kensington; buses: C1, 14, 74.
Daily 10am–5.45pm, until 10pm Wed and the last Fri in the month.
Free admission. Free guided tours.
Wheelchair access. Many children's activities.

With 5 million objects and almost 8 miles (13 km) of galleries, the Victoria and Albert Museum (founded in 1852) is colossal. Its exhibits range from exquisite Persian miniatures to a whole room designed by Frank Lloyd Wright. One minute one can be admiring Raphael's cartoons for the tapestries in the Sistine Chapel, and the next examining E.H. Shepard's illustrations for Winnie-the-Pooh or gaping at a towering plaster cast of Trajan's Column in Rome.

The sheer breadth of the V&A's collection was often cited as the main reason for a decline in the museum's popularity. Conveying the appeal of its rambling collection to an ever more selective public has defeated even the brightest copy-writers. One slogan – "an ace café with a rather nice museum attached" – seemed an open admission of defeat. But the abolition of admission charges in 2001, coincid-

17th-century displays from the V&A's British Galleries.

ing with a redesign of the British Galleries, led to a huge increase in visitor numbers and optimism for the future. Startling plans for a modernist spiral extension by the US architect Daniel Libeskind may now go ahead as part of a £150 million overhaul.

Much has already been achieved. The ground floor is clearly laid out, with major sections on the decorative arts of the world's great civilisations; exhibits are well-labelled and beautifully displayed. But large parts of the upper levels remain a labyrinth of rooms and corridors, packed with overstuffed and poorly labelled cabinets. It is here that you stumble upon many of the minor members of the decorative arts, such as knitting, lace and church plate.

The Highlights

You can't cover all the galleries in one visit, so study the map and pinpoint the areas you particularly want to see. You can also take one of the free guided tours (times are posted on a board near the ticket desk) or buy the V&A's booklet *A Hundred Highlights*. The order of the galleries listed below starts from the Cromwell Road entrance.

Glass sculpture

(hanging in foyer, Cromwell Road entrance)
This immense work is by the American glass artist Dale Chihuly. The amazing accretion of blue and green glass was erected in 1999 as a spectacular talking-point for the otherwise staid Victorian foyer. An exhibition of Chihuly's work at the V&A in 2001 saw the sculpture double in size, reaching a height of 33 ft (10 metres). The sculpture was assembled *in situ* by a team of technicians, each piece of glass slotted over an angled rod. Inspired by the Venetian glass-making tradition, Chihuly's work combines brilliant colours and extravagant shapes.

Europe and America 1800–1900

(downstairs, right from the entrance hall)
This includes pieces shown at the Great Exhibition of 1851, the inspiration for the V&A. The massive bookcases and armoires in extravagant Gothic Revival style were made for exhibition purposes only, as showcases for fine craftsmanship, but the wealthy middle classes soon ordered them for their homes.

The Sculpture Courts

(ground floor, right past the entrance)
These contain British and European neoclassical works from the late 18th and early 19th centuries. Just inside the entrance are several works by Canova

(1757–1822), including a striking early piece, *Theseus and the Minotaur*, and *The Sleeping Nymph*, a lovely reclining nude of 1822. His *Three Graces* is now in the British Galleries *(see page 50)*.

The Rotunda Chandelier by Dale Chihuly.

Among the many other works on display, including large fireplaces and doorways, look out for the collection of terracotta statuettes that served as preliminary models for monumental works. At the far end of the second sculpture gallery are several glazed terracottas by the della Robbia family, including Giovanni della Robbia's *The Last Supper*, based on Leonardo da Vinci's painting.

Raphael Cartoons

(ground floor, left from the entrance, past the shop)
The vast Raphael Cartoons (1515–16), on loan from the Queen, are among the museum's most valuable items. These highly finished preparatory drawings were commissioned by Pope Leo X (Giovanni de' Medici) as templates for a series of tapestries in the Sistine Chapel.

Depicting scenes from the lives of St Peter and St Paul, the cartoons were painted in distemper (a mix of pigment, water and animal glue), then cut into strips, which the master weavers of Brussels would use as guides. The strips were reassembled and

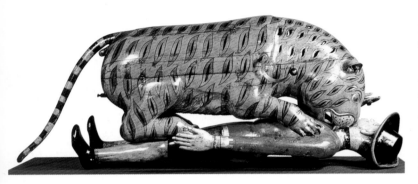

The Asian and Islamic Collections
(ground floor)

Next to Dress is a series of large rooms focusing on the superb Asian and Islamic collections: Indian Art (1550–1900), Arts of the Islamic World and, beyond the Medieval Treasury, the China, Japan, Southeast Asia and Korea galleries.

Probably the most rewarding for the non-specialist is the outstanding Nehru Gallery of Indian Art. Many items are from the Mogul period (1526–1707), when imperialist expansion led to immense wealth and a unique artistic flowering that culminated under Shah Jahan, the builder of the Taj Mahal. Small, portable items were particularly in demand, as the court was constantly on the move. Fine examples include the Shah Jahan wine cup, carved from jade in the shape of a half gourd with a handle shaped like a goat's head.

Next door, Arts of the Islamic World covers the range of Islamic decorative arts from Persia, Turkey, Iraq, Syria and Egypt. In line with Islamic prohibitions, most items here do not include figurative representations, but a beautiful exception is a 10th-century ewer carved from a single block of rock crystal and decorated with sensuous birds and beasts.

Tipu's Tiger, made around 1790 for the amusement of Sultan Tipu. A miniature organ mimics the sounds of the dying British officer.

mounted on canvas in the late 17th century, after which copies of Raphael's cartoons inspired tapestries in many of Europe's great houses.

Dress
(ground floor)

Directly opposite the Raphael Cartoons is the entrance to Dress (1600 to present day), a section well known for its interesting temporary exhibitions. Its permanent collection chronicles the history of male and female costume, relating each new trend to developments in society in general, such as the great watershed of World War I (leading to the uncorseted figure of the 1920s flapper), retrenchment in World War II (slim-line utility clothing), post-war regeneration (Dior's New Look of 1947) and the advent of the Pill in the 1960s (Mary Quant's mini-skirt).

A staircase in the centre of Dress leads up to Musical Instruments, though this can also be accessed from the first floor.

Plaster Casts and Fakes & Forgeries
(ground floor, past the Korea section)

These two great cast courts are all the more intriguing for the fact that everything is fake. Here you will find copies of vast monuments, tombs, pillars,

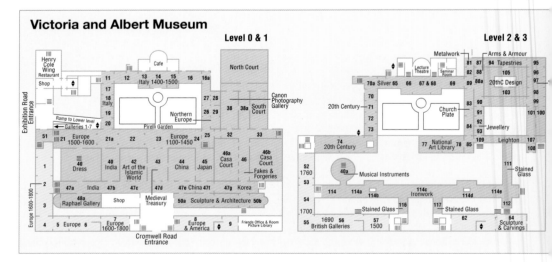

Victoria and Albert Museum

friezes and effigies. Probably the most outstanding is a cast (in two pieces) of Trajan's column in Rome, though the casts of the Portico de la Gloria with Christ in Majesty from the Cathedral de Santiago de Compostella and Michelangelo's *David* are also compelling. Until 1953 the cast of *David* wore a fig leaf, a measure demanded by Queen Victoria: it can still be seen if you look behind the statue.

Plaster cast collections became popular in the 19th century both as a means of recording some of the world's greatest monuments and as a way of showing the classical sites to a non-travelling public. Prince Albert helped set up cast museums all over Europe, believing they would be a valuable resource for scholars. The V&A's collection is one of the few to have survived. In some cases the casts are the only copies of monuments destroyed during World War II.

The Italian Collection

This section, flanking the great courtyard known as the Pirelli Gardens, contains many outstanding Renaissance pieces, concentrated in Rooms 12–20.

The highlight of Room 12 is Andrea Briosco's (1470–1532) *Shouting Horseman*, which captures the pent-up energy of the horse and the alarm of the rider. Also in the room are a Lucca della Robbia terracotta *(see below)* above the fireplace and three highly decorated "birth trays", traditionally used to present food and drink to a woman in labour.

Room 14 contains terracottas by the Florentine sculptor Andrea della Robbia (1435–1525) and his sons, including the lovely *Adoration of the Maji*. Glazed terracotta was often used to adorn the facades of palazzi. The magnificent stemma (coat

of arms) of King René of Anjou is a typical example; the heavy wreath of fruit and foliage is a trademark of the della Robbia workshop.

Room 16 contains the finest collection of work by Donatello (1386–1466) outside Italy. On the wall, notice the three relief carvings. In the middle one, depicting the *Ascension with Christ giving the keys to St Peter*, Donatello used a new technique known as "squashed relief" that he developed for gaining perspective. The other highlight of the room is a lovely bronze roundel portraying the *Virgin and Child with Four Angels* that Donatello presented to his doctor, Giovanni Chellini, in 1456.

Apart from the main Italian collection, Room 21 has a powerful statue of *Samson Slaying a Philistine* by Giambologna (1529–1608).

Costumes Parisiens, a 1913 drawing by Pichebot in the V&A.

Refreshment Rooms and the Ceramic Staircase

At the end of the Italian collection, near the Ceramic Staircase *(see below)*, are the three original refreshment rooms, which served first, second and third-class menus before World War II, with main courses costing upward of one shilling (5p). Allusions to food and drink are worked into the decoration.

The first, the Poynter Room, known as the Dutch

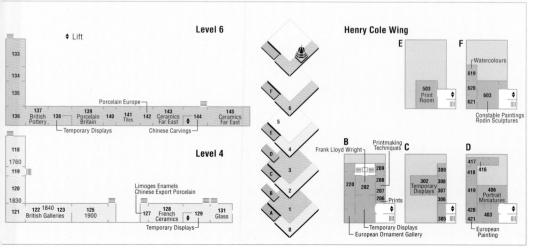

The Hereford Screen,
designed by Sir George
Gilbert Scott.

kitchen, was designed by Sir Edward Poynter in 1866–74. Next to it is the fabulously ornate Gamble Room (1868), one of London's finest Victorian interiors. The third room is the Morris Room (Green Dining Room), 1866–69, designed by William Morris, Philip Webb and Edward Burne-Jones.

Next to the Morris room is the magnificent Ceramic Staircase, completed in 1869 and symbolising the symbiotic relationship between art and science. The twin circular ceilings illustrate the theme: Ceres, Mercury and Vulcan stand for agriculture, commerce and industry; Apollo and Minerva represent the arts. On the landing of the Ceramic Staircase, the memorial to Henry Cole, the museum's first director, is by his niece, a pupil of the museum's mosaic class; the floor was laid by female members of Woking Gaol.

The Upper Levels

Many of the upper galleries focus on materials or techniques, such as silver, ironwork, stained glass, ceramics (the whole of the top floor), textiles and jewellery. The British Galleries are also here *(see below)*, along with 20th-century Design, exploring themes ranging from the influence of functionalism as exemplified by Bauhaus to the virtuoso contributions of people such as the British potter Richard Slee.

Unless you want to make a bee-line for a particular section, it can be enjoyable to explore the warren of rooms at random. At some point you are bound to pass the classically inspired Leighton Frescoes by the popular Victorian painter Frederic

Leighton *(see page 207)*. Entitled *The Arts of Industry as Applied to War* and *The Arts of Industry as Applied to Peace*, they were designed to underline the link between art and manufacturing, a favourite theme in the museum's early days. Until a remodelling of this part of the museum boxed them into a gloomy corridor, the frescoes overlooked the south court, from where they could be fully appreciated.

The British Galleries

One might expect these simply to display the work of British designers, but they follow the much more interesting course of documenting British taste, exploring "what was hot and what was new from the time of Henry VIII and the Tudors to William Morris". This has allowed many non-British items to enter the galleries, which are as much about the movement of ideas as the ideas themselves.

Ranged over two floors of the southwest wing, the galleries cover the period 1500–1900. Though assembled chronologically, the exhibits relate to four key themes – Style, Who Led Taste?, Fashionable Living, and What Was New? They develop a strong narrative, picking up many interesting threads along the way, such as how fashions for pets or tea were expressed in portraits and sculptures.

Among the many highlights is the fabulous late 16th-century Great Bed of Ware, a four-poster of such enormous proportions that it was already a tourist attraction in 1596 and mentioned by Sir Toby Belch in Shakespeare's *Twelfth Night*.

Several highlights from other galleries have been moved to the British Galleries, including Antonio Canova's *The Three Graces*, the world's most expensive statue. The V&A and the National Galleries of Scotland (with whom the statue is shared) kept it in the UK by topping a £7.6 million bid from the John Paul Getty Museum in California. It was commissioned in 1814 by the 6th Duke of Bedford, an admirer of a similar statue (now in the Hermitage in St Petersburg) that Canova had carved for the Empress Josephine.

The galleries offer opportunities for hands-on fun, from trying on a gauntlet, a hooped petticoat or a ruff to writing a mini-saga, weaving a tapestry or designing a coat of arms. Touch screens supply background information and, in some areas, headphones provide music to help set the scene (gaze at a massive wall-to-wall silk and wool embroidery of Stoke Edith in Herefordshire, for example, while listening to late Stuart music). Each floor has a well-equipped study area and a room showing short films on key influences on British art and design.

The Hereford Screen

Surprisingly, one of the star exhibits on the upper floors is found in the Ironwork Gallery, overlooking the museum's foyer. The stunning Hereford Screen, an intricate choir screen of cast iron and burnished brass, studded with semi-precious stones and mosaics reaches 36ft (10.5 metres) high and 34 ft (11 metres) wide. Designed by Sir George Gilbert Scott in 1862, it shows Christ in the centre with angels on either side welcoming his ascension. Hailed as a masterpiece, it was installed in Hereford Cathedral in 1863 as the finishing touch in Scott's renovation of the cathedral.

By 1964 Victorian Gothic had gone out of fashion, even in cathedrals, and the screen was criticised for blocking the view of the chancel. In spite of protests by art historians, it was dismantled and packed into 46 crates. In 1990 funds were found to repair and reassemble the 14,000 pieces – the museum's largest and most expensive (£800,000) conservation project.

Glass, Jewellery, Silver and Ceramics

All these galleries are well worth dipping into. As with Ceramics and Glass *(see below)*, the size of the Jewellery collection is overwhelming, but background information on each of the tightly packed exhibits can be found on touch-screen computers.

Silver is surprisingly child-friendly, with interactive displays and games; the Glass Gallery, comprising the National Collection of some 8,000 pieces, is enchanting. Among the many kinds on display are brilliant Venetian glass, high Victorian glass, Arts and Craft glass, French Art Nouveau glass and stunning modern sculptures, including a rippling glass staircase (1992) by the American glass artist Danny Lane which leads up to a mezzanine gallery.

Ceramics (comprising European and British porcelain, pottery, tiles, and Far Eastern ceramics), on the top floor of the museum, is a staircase too far for many visitors, but the section attracts connoisseurs. The collection is said to be the largest in the world. To get the most out of the Ceramics galleries, it is worth joining one of the specialist guided tours.

The Henry Cole Wing

This wing is devoted mainly to prints, drawings, paintings and photographs. Spread over six floors, the changing displays range from large oil paintings by John Constable to a superb collection of British miniatures, works by Raoul Dufy, E.H. Shepard's illustrations for Winnie-the-Pooh, Beatrix Potter watercolours, and contemporary photographs.

Also in the Henry Cole Wing is the Frank Lloyd Wright Room, transplanted here from Pittsburgh. Commissioned in 1935 as the office of Edgar J. Kaufmann, the proprietor of a department store, it is a stylish but rather oppressive interior lined top to bottom in wood (hollow-core plywood veneered with swamp cypress). It is the only work of Frank Lloyd Wright in Europe.

Food and drink: The self-service New Restaurant (ground floor, Henry Cole Wing) serves hot dishes, salads, snacks, beer and wine; live music on Sunday lunchtime. In summer, light food and drink are served from a marquee in the Pirelli Garden, a magnificent central courtyard with shady trees and a fountain. Alternatively, at 215 Brompton Road, Patisserie Valerie has cakes and pastries, as well as hot dishes and snacks such as croque monsieur and eggs benedict.

Platform shoes created in 1993 by Vivienne Westwood.

Ancient and Modern History

Coptic pots and ancient armour, musical instruments from India and plank masks from Burkino Faso – the plunder and souvenirs collected by early explorers and builders of the British Empire help bring the past vividly alive

Bank of England Museum

The history of the nation's Central Bank

Map reference: page 21, H3
Address: Threadneedle Street (entrance,
Bartholomew Lane), EC2. Tel: 020-7601 5545 or
020-7601 5491 to arrange wheelchair access.
Web: www.bankofengland.co.uk/mus_arch.htm
Tube: Bank. Rail: Liverpool Street, Fenchurch
Street, Cannon Street (weekdays only).
10am–5pm Mon–Fri, closed weekends and
public holidays, Free admission.
Pre-booked tours for children take place on the
hour 10am–4pm, with film presentation.

The stern but grand exterior of the Bank clothes this small, salubrious museum tracing the institution's flamboyant history from its foundation in 1694 by Royal Charter through the creation of the banknote (which evolved from the hand-written receipt given for substantial loans by the money-lending goldsmiths) and the controversial nationalising of the Bank in 1946. The Bank moved from nearby rented premises to this site in 1734, acquiring the enduring nickname the Old Lady of Threadneedle Street.

Presentations narrate how the Bank helped to finance Britain's war effort against France in 1688, how it became one of the first institutions in the City to employ women, and how it controlled government borrowing during World War II.

The museum's grand architecture is a fittingly splendid setting in which to illustrate 17th-century banking practice. Waxwork mannequins of clerks and customers carry on their business at the dealing desk at the far end of the Bank Stock Office, designed by Sir John Soane, a leading architect of the late 18th century (this is widely considered to be Europe's finest neo-classical interior).

Moving past the Roman mosaic, discovered when the building was rebuilt between the wars, you enter Sir Herbert Baker's marvellous and airy Rotunda containing a display of Roman gold bars as well as modern 28-lb (13-kg) ones, traded on the London bullion market. The banknote gallery, which exhibits a complete collection of Bank of England notes, has special features on how the watermark is used in an attempt to prevent forgery plus an explanation of the different print processes and machinery. Interactive terminals are noisy but go a long way in answering points such as why the Chief Cashier's

signature appears on all notes, and how the Promise on the bank note has been shortened but retains its important meaning.

Food and drink: There's no shortage of bars, pubs and cafés, often tucked away in side streets. Pavarotti's (directly opposite the Bank) offers a fine selection of cakes, pastries, rolls and pasta to take out – it's good for hot-filled potatoes. If you turn left out of the museum exit and then right into Throgmorton Street, you reach the Throgmorton pub, offering traditional pub grub and good beer.

ABOVE:
The Bank of England Museum.

OPPOSITE:
The Tower of London, with Traitor's Gate in the foreground.

Horniman Museum and Gardens

Rich collections of ethnography, natural history and musical instruments

Map reference: page 23, G5
100 London Road, Forest Hill, SE23.
Tel: 020 8699 1872.
www.horniman.ac.uk
Mainline station: Forest Hill (direct service from London Bridge). Buses: 176, 185, 312, 352, P4.
10.30am–5.30pm Mon–Fri, 2–5.30pm Sun;
garden 7.30am–dusk.
Café, shop, library, wheelchair access.
Free admission (fee for temporary exhibitions).

The Horniman Museum is one of South London's unsung treasures. It was founded in 1901 by a wealthy tea merchant and collector, Frederick Horniman, who followed in the footsteps of

Midnight Robbers, in the African Worlds gallery.

African Worlds

The exhibits in this gallery come from Africa and other countries influenced by the diaspora of African people caused by the slave trade and colonialism. One wall is strikingly dedicated to a psychedelic Haitian Voudou altar, an equally colourful Benin Voudou altar and a Brazilian Candomblé altar. Each has been created with the guidance of priests from the respective communities, in an attempt to demystify African cults – particularly voodoo, which is largely misunderstood by Western society. The bizarre mixture of objects, ranging from clay pots, old bones and bowls of grain to sequin-covered bottles, fat cigars and plastic crocodiles, arranged around religious icons, are typical of the type of offerings brought to honour ancestors or bargain with the deities.

A large part of the gallery is dedicated to the museum's mask collection. The most impressive are the towering Dogon masks and plank masks from Burkino Faso, a sinister skull-laden mask from Trinidad and the spectacular Igbo Ijele, Africa's largest mask and one of just three existing outside the continent. Look out for the two beautifully carved Eloi maternity figures from Nigeria; motherhood is a popular subject for African sculpture.

Among the most valuable (and controversial) exhibits in the Africa collection are the 16th-century bronze plaques from the royal palace of Benin, once a powerful kingdom of West Africa and now a province of Nigeria. When Benin was ransacked by a British military expedition in 1897, the palace was stripped of its exquisitely crafted plaques and ivories which were taken to London and auctioned off (many of the bronzes ended up in the British Museum). The entire Benin palace was decorated with these finely detailed bronze casts, each a portrait of a different ruler or priest, warrior or high-ranking official. A video explains the royal art form of bronze casting, still practised today.

Living Waters

The first section of the aquarium follows the journey of a river from the source at the top of the stairs to the estuary at the bottom, encountering different environments and fish along the way. Various other aquatic environments, particularly endangered ones, have been re-created, and there are some fascinating fish species. You can see no-eyed fish in the cave environment, four-eyed fish in the mangrove swamp, and dainty tropical fish in the coral sections. The museum takes its conservationist role seriously,

his father, "Honest" John Horniman, a respected businessman, philanthropist and collector from a Quaker family. First he relied on offerings from soldiers, merchants and missionaries to expand his father's collections, then he began to travel himself, visiting India and taking a world tour encompassing America, Japan, China, Burma and Egypt. In Egypt he met Howard Carter (who later discovered Tutankhamun's tomb) and developed an enthusiasm for mummies, one of the museum's big attractions.

To house his collections, Horniman commissioned the Arts and Crafts designer Charles Harrison Townsend to build a museum on his estate. The clock tower, made of Bath stone, is decorated with eyelid motifs, an Indian symbol for tea plants. The large mosaic at the entrance is made with 117,000 pieces laid by a team of women. In 1901, Horniman presented the museum to the People of London for their "instruction, enjoyment and recreation".

The main ethos of the Horniman Museum today is to encourage a wider appreciation of world cultures and environments. Its collection covers three main areas: natural history, human culture and beliefs and musical instruments.

backing conservation projects and breeding endangered species such as seahorses.

The Vivarium, next door in the natural history gallery, keeps a small number of reptiles and amphibians from around the world. The orange and black king snake is spectacular, if you catch him out of hiding.

Victorian Gallery

Frederick Horniman was fascinated by natural history and amassed a large proportion of the 200,000-strong collection. The content and layout of this gallery has changed little over time and it retains a Victorian atmosphere. The stuffed mammals, birds, fish and insects have been left in their original wood-framed cabinets, and the iconic giant walrus still takes centre stage. The taxidermist working on it in 1870 had no clue what a walrus looked like and over-stuffed the beast by 30 percent. The end section of the gallery is dedicated to extinct and endangered bird species with a particular focus on British birds that are diminishing through pesticides.

It's worth a quick detour to the upper balcony to see the 150-year old Apostle clock. At 4pm all the apostles file out to pay tribute to Jesus – except Judas, who turns away.

World Cultures and World Music

The Horniman's new extension has four new galleries and a new main entrance linking the museum and the gardens, which was Horniman's original plan. The World Cultures Gallery complements the African Gallery with over 1,000 objects representing all other corners of the globe, and the musical instrument collection has been given a new home. A wide selection of instruments – from ancient Egyptian clappers to Western classical instruments to more recent aquisitions from Uzbekistan and India – are displayed around activator tables where you can hear samples of them being played. The gallery has a space for performances and a hands-on area where you can try a range of instruments.

The handling collection is a parallel collection of objects, such as fossils, masks, puppets and stuffed animals, which visitors can pick up and examine.

Bwa plank mask from Burkino Faso.

The Gardens

The 16 acres (6.5 hectares) of parkland attached to the museum are a mixture of formal and natural landscapes, with great views across London. There's a small animal enclosure, a bandstand for summer concerts and a Dutch Barn used for educational activities. The Conservatory, built in 1894, is used for concerts and private functions.

The park is bordered along the bottom by the Horniman Railway Nature Trail, a shady semi-wild stretch with a wildlife pond that children can have a fine time exploring.

***Food and drink**: The museum has its own reasonably priced café overlooking the gardens, which are perfect for picnics in fine weather.*

A 20th-century Ethiopian painting by Jemlieri Hailu Kegneketa of Gondar showing the 16th-century burning of churches by Muslims.

London Jewish Bakers' Union banner, *circa* 1926.

Jewish Museum

Two locations cover British Jewry's history

Camden Town location:
Map reference: page 23, E2
Raymond Burton House, 129–131 Albert Street, NW1. Tel: 020-7284 1997.
www.jewmusm.ort.org
Tube: Camden Town.
Mon–Thur 10am–4pm (Sun 5pm); closed Jewish & public holidays.
Admission fee; disabled facilities; tours of the historical Jewish East End neighbourhood.
Finchley location:
Map reference: page 22, D1
The Sternberg Centre, 80 East End Road, N3. Tel: 020-8349 1143.
www.jewmusm.ort.org
82 bus from Baker St, then 5-minute walk.
Mon–Thur 10.30am–5pm (Sun 4.30pm); closed Jewish & public holidays, 24 Dec–4 Jan, Sun in Aug, bank holiday weekends.
Admission fee. Disabled facilities.

Fayeme Passover dish, *circa* 1613–14.

Founded in 1932, the Jewish Museum has branched out into two locations. The branch in Camden Town chronicles the history of British Jewry, and has a gallery devoted to Judaica (ceremonial art). The Finchley site (which is nowhere near the East End, despite the street name) depicts the two mass migrations of Jews to London in modern times, and has a Holocaust Education Gallery. Both museums feature temporary exhibitions.

The Camden museum is set in an elegant 1840 listed building with original walls. The interior is a modern, sophisticated affair with audio-visual programmes and hands-on exhibits, such as an interactive map showing centres of Jewish population in different periods. Concise, well-written narrative panels present the key events in Anglo-Jewish history, from the Norman Conquest in 1066 to the 20th century. Artefacts include an 8th-century gold medallion with Jewish symbols and Greek inscription; silver dishes and porcelain figures; and a gigantic London Jewish Bakers banner (1926) emblazoned with the Marxist slogan "Workers of the World Unite".

The Judaica Gallery, designed to resemble a Star of David, is more ethnographic – it illustrates religious rituals as passed down through the centuries. The exhibits range from the arcane – a 1690 marriage belt from Breslau, Germany – to the magnificence of a massive, walnut ark decorated with gilded and marbled paintwork. In the 16th century, the ark, complete with five Torah scrolls, would have been the focal point of a Venetian synagogue. By 1932, it had become an English servant's wardrobe.

The museum in Finchley, situated in a bright, modern airy building within the Jewish community's Sternberg Centre, frequently hosts school groups, and its exhibitions are less dry than their Camden Town counterparts. The social history section covers the 1881–1914 influx of Jews from Eastern Europe, and the wave of 60,000 refugees of the Nazis who fled from Germany, Austria and Czechoslovakia before war broke out. The everyday life of immigrants starting anew in London is vividly evoked through personal effects. Diverse domestic items – the tools of a 19th-century surgeon/barber, a poster advertising Russian vapour baths in the East End's Brick Lane, a Yiddish-language gramophone record from 1950 – show how the newcomers brought their old-world customs with them.

The relics of the Kindertransporte children – 10,000 Jewish youngsters sent to Britain from Germany and Austria by parents fated never to join them – are the most poignant: a child's printing set, a songbook, the notorious yellow star that Jews were forced to wear by the Nazis. One 15-year-old boy's suitcase retains his belongings: a set of phylacteries, prayer book, photographs.

Upstairs, a gallery tells the story of the Holocaust through the experience of Leon Greenman, an Auschwitz survivor. Mr Greenman is often present to speak to visitors on Sundays. This exhibition upstairs is specifically designed for secondary-school pupils but is none the less moving for that. The photographs of Leon's two-year-old son, later killed in Auschwitz, may bring tears to your eyes.

Food and drink: There is no on-site restaurant but the (signposted) walk from Camden Town Tube passes Italian, Vietnamese and Lebanese eateries, and a Starbucks. The Sternberg Centre canteen does cheap, vegetarian meals, 12–2pm; or you can bring a (vegetarian) picnic to eat in pleasant grounds that include a biblical garden.

Museum in Docklands

The story of London's river, port and people

Map reference: page 23, H3
No. 1 Warehouse, West India Quay, Hertsmere Road, E14. Tel: 020-7001 9800.
www.museumindocklands.org.uk
Tube: Canary Wharf. Docklands Light Railway: West India Quay.
Open daily; phone for hours. Entrance fee.

Of all London's "local" museums, this has the richest story to tell: the development of the riverside from the trading activities of the Romans 2,000 years ago to the regeneration of the semi-derelict Docklands over recent decades. In between, the medieval port developed into the mighty home port of the British Empire and suffered some of the worst bombing of World War II.

The museum opened in 2002 on five floors of a warehouse built in the early 19th century to store rum, sugar and molasses. It has a strong educational slant, aimed at a generation which has never known London as a major port, but its artefacts, models, film projections and taped oral history keep adults interested. There's a 20-ft (6-metre) model of Old London Bridge, complete with housing and shops, and a re-creation of the huge *Rhinebeck Panorama*, which shows the upper Pool of London teeming with activity around 1810. A ride to the museum by Docklands Light Railway gives a good overview of the area's patchwork development, including the massive bulk of the adjacent Canary Wharf office complex.

Petrie Museum of Egyptian Archaeology

21st Dynasty fragment from the Petrie.

A major collection of Egyptian antiquities

Map reference: page 20, C2
University College London, Malet Place, WC1. Tel: 020-7679 2884.
www.ucl.ac.uk/collections/petrie/museum/
Tube: Euston, Euston Square, Goodge Street, Russell Square, Warren Street, bus: 18, 24, 29, 30, 73, 134, 176, 253.
Tues–Fri 1–5pm, Sat 10am–1pm, closed one week at Christmas and Easter.
Wheelchair access via lift but two steps at the museum entrance. Free admission.

The Petrie Museum is based around the collection of the archaeologist William Flinders Petrie (1853–1942), professor of Egyptology at University College. The university acquired the collection in 1913 and important additions have been made since. Entry is via the UCL Science Library; go in the main door and up the stairs on the right, turn right at the top and go through the double doors at the end. The two-room museum is primarily a research collection for students and academics, and the more casual visitor may initially be baffled by the closely packed cases and the small typed slips describing each exhibit. However, a little perserverance uncovers many rare treasures.

The first, smaller, room is given over largely to chronologically displayed pottery, from Neolithic (*c*. 5000 BCE) shards to Coptic (3rd- to 7th-century CE) pots. Some items are finely decorated with some startling cobalt-blue fragments dating from the XVIII Dynasty (*c*.1500 BCE). The room's real treasures, however, are the textiles. On the left as you enter the room are the "Gurob sleeves", detachable linen sleeves from a child's dress dating from *c*. 1320 BCE, excavated from a tomb in 1889, and on the opposite wall is the "Tarkhan dress", the world's oldest known garment (*c*. 2800 BCE). This linen dress, made for a teenager, has been meticulously conserved, preserving the fine pleating across the shoulders and sleeves.

The main room also has a broadly chronological layout (cases A–H cover the Paleolithic to Middle Kingdom periods, and WEC1–11 New Kingdom to Roman times, and the inscription cases 1–12), and within the cases the finds are grouped according to the site at which they were discovered. Outstanding among the many everyday, ritual and funerary objects collected here are the finds from Akhetaten (WEC4–5 and 11), which include some wonderful fragments of faïence. Also of interest are the tools and toys found at Kahun, dating from around 2140 BCE. Case N is particularly noteworthy, containing fine examples from the museum's collection of facial portraits from Graeco-Roman mummies. A prize exhibit, limestone lions from Koptos in Upper Egypt, is displayed in the college's main cloister.

Food and drink: Pizza Paradiso (35 Store Street, 020-7255 2554) is an above-average pizza place. Poons (50 Woburn Place, 020-7580 1188) is an old-style Chinese restaurant, and serves dim sum from noon–4pm.

St Bride's Church Crypt

Roman artefacts in "the journalists' church"

Map reference: page 21, F3
Fleet Street, EC4. Tel: 020-7427 0133.
Tube and rail: Blackfriars.
Open daily but Eucharist (Holy Communion) is celebrated in the crypt chapel each morning at 8.30am, choral evensong 6.30pm each Sunday and in the evenings. No entrance fee, but donations welcome. No wheelchair access to crypt.

Named after St Bridget (Bride) of Kildare, this church brims with history – Romans, Saxons, Celts, Normans and Angles have all

congregated on this site. When Sir Christopher Wren (architect of St Paul's Cathedral) created this church, he built it on the site of six previous churches, thus forming extensive crypts.

Like most City of London churches, St Bride's has had its fair share of torment; it was razed during the 1666 Great Fire and suffered extensive bomb damage in World War II. It was this bombing that unearthed the Crypt, adding 1,000 years to the church's known history.

In the small and slightly airless Crypt exists a veritable timeline depicting the site's development – a Roman pavement, as well as clay pots and oyster shells from this period. Saxon finds include clay tobacco pipes, a lead plate and wine bottles plus cast iron and porcelain. Piecing together the archaeological evidence, historians believe the site has been used as a church since at least Saxon times.

The church is also notable for its spire, which was not only the highest Wren ever built but was also the inspiration for the first tiered wedding cake, made by William Rich.

Because of its location just behind Fleet Street, St Bride's Church has well-established links with press, publishing and literary society. Wynkyn de Worde, Chaucer, Thomas Becket and Shakespeare were all familiar with St Bride's. Pepys was christened here, Milton lived in the churchyard and Dr Johnson lived across the road, as did Charles Dickens. The location was, for centuries, the heart of London's printing trade and, in 1500, William Caxton's original printing press was taken by Wynkyn de Worde from Westminster Abbey to the more fitting home of St Bride's. New technology enabled national newspapers to abandon Fleet Street for cheaper locations, but St Bride's is still used for journalists' memorial services.

Food and drink: Fleet Street is buzzing with coffee shops and cafés. For something more substantial, try the trendy Jamie's, a little further east, towards St Paul's Cathedral, just past Ludgate Circus.

St Paul's Crypt

Treasury of the Diocese of London

Map reference: page 21, G3
Ludgate Hill, EC4. Tel: 020 7246 8348.
www.stpauls.co.uk
Tube: St Paul's.
Mon–Sat 8.30am–4pm (last admission). The Cathedral is sometimes closed for special services and events. Its Crypt shop and café are open 9am–5pm Mon–Sat and 10.30am–5pm Sun. There is wheelchair access to the ground floor of St Paul's via the south side entrance; the Crypt may then be reached by lift.
Entrance fee. Tours available.

Beneath Sir Christopher Wren's ecclesiastical masterpiece, built between 1675 and 1710, is the Cathedral's Crypt, home to St Paul's Treasury, its burial chamber and a chapel dedicated to members of the Order of the British Empire (OBE), who may be married or have members of their families baptised here. The Crypt runs the full 515-ft (157-metre) length of the Cathedral, making it the largest vault of its kind in Europe.

Originally the area below St Paul's was nothing more than a cellar with an earth-covered floor, under which coffins were buried. The Victorian fascination with all things morbid changed this, and a more substantial floor was laid down in the 19th century, enabling visitors to include the Crypt in their tours of the Cathedral. The mosaic floor that was put down at minimal expense by female

prisoners from Woking Gaol is still visible today.

The highlights of this cavernous undercroft include the tombs of the Duke of Wellington (whose casket was so huge that it had to be lowered into its resting place via a hole in the Cathedral floor) and of Admiral Lord Nelson, who was foresighted enough to take a coffin with him to the Battle of Trafalgar. (His body was pickled first in French brandy, then distilled wine to preserve it on the journey home.) There are memorials and tombs of scientists including Alexander Fleming, Henry Wellcome and Florence Nightingale, leading lights from the art world such as Joshua Reynolds, William Blake, J. W. M. Turner, John Constable and Henry Moore and, perhaps most fittingly, Wren himself. The plaque above his gravestone translates: "Reader, if you seek his monument, look around you."

One wing of the Crypt has a display of the Cathedral's Treasury. Most of the gold and silver ceremonial vessels, including chalices, patens, ciboria, almsdishes, cruets and straining spoons, are on loan from other churches in London, as the majority of St Paul's own treasures have been lost over the centuries through theft or fire. Of note in the collection is the Cathedral's own "Jubilee" Cope, a cape made to commemorate the Silver Jubilee of Queen Elizabeth II in 1977 and finely decorated with the

Lord Nelson's grand tomb.

embroidered spires of 73 London churches, St Paul's itself and three Royal Peculiars. Also worth seeing are two effigies that pre-date the Great Fire of London (seemingly made of wood but actually from stone), a section on the Fire of London and the damage it caused, plus architectural models of St Paul's across the centuries.

A ticket into the Crypt enables visitors to go into the main body of the Cathedral, including access to the "Whispering Gallery" and, if you have a head for heights, two higher outer galleries from where there are good views across London.

Food and drink: The Cathedral has its own café and restaurant, both of which are located next to the Crypt. The cafe does a range of inexpensive salads, savoury pastries, soups and cakes, plus coffees and soft drinks. The restaurant, which is stylishly set out, serves set menus, at moderate prices. Oppostite St Paul's, on Ludgate Hill, is a branch of the brasserie-style Dôme, which has excellent views over the Cathedral and gorgeous old-fashioned chandeliers.

Sir John Soane's Museum

A British Museum in miniature

Map reference: page 20, E3
13 Lincoln's Inn Fields, WC2. Tel: 020-7405 2107.
www.soane.com
Tube: Chancery Lane, Holborn.
Tues–Sat 10am–5pm, 6–9pm on first Tues of the month, closed public holidays, Christmas

Eve. Lecture tour Sat 2.30pm, tickets on sale from 2pm, 22 people only.
No wheelchair access.
Free admission, charges for tours.

This is a wonderfully eclectic collection, acquired by Sir John Soane (1753–1837) over his lifetime and as eccentric in its content as its display. One of England's greatest architects, Soane trained at the Royal Academy before spending two formative years in Italy on a scholarship. Among his works are the Bank of England building (1788), Dulwich Art Gallery (1811) and the remodelling of the buildings at Lincoln's Inn Fields (1792–1823). These latter buildings were his home and, from 1813, also formed a museum. He moved into number 12 in 1792, number 13 in 1813 and acquired number 14 in 1823, each time rebuilding and extending the existing buildings. It is numbers 12 and 13 that house the museum (although the yard of number 14 was used to build an extension to the museum). Number 13 is particularly striking architecturally, with the existing balcony forming the basis of a neoclassical extension to the facade.

The museum was conceived as an aid to Soane's architectural students at the Royal Academy, to which he was appointed as professor in 1806. Its interior is preserved as Soane left it, and he recommended a route around the houses, described here, starting in the Library and Dining Room (on your

LEFT: the Breakfast Parlour in Sir John Soane's Museum

RIGHT: the Dome mixes sculptures, mouldings and casts.

An Election Entertainment, part of William Hogarth's Election sequence painted in 1754–55.

right as you enter the building). Note the use of mirrors to spread natural light around the room and to increase the sense of space.

On the right-hand side at the rear of the room a door leads through Soane's study to the Picture Room, on the right at the back of the house. This was constructed on the yard of number 14. The ingenious use of a number of hinged screens means that many pictures can be displayed here, hidden behind each other, and the screens open out over the Crypt *(see below)* both to let in more light and to reveal a cast of a statue of a nymph by Sir Richard Westmacott (the original is at Castle Howard in Yorkshire). This is where the two series of Hogarth paintings, *The Rake's Progress* and *An Election*, can be seen, as well as a Turner of Kirkstall Abbey in Leeds and a number of Piranesi drawings.

Directly below the Picture Room is the Monk's Parlour and Cell, an expression of the taste for the Gothic during the early 19th century. This is slightly tongue-in-cheek, however, as the Monk's Grave, that of "Padre Giovanni", actually marks the grave of Fanny, a dog belonging to Soane's wife. The Parlour has several pieces rescued from the old Palace of Westminster. The rest of the basement is given over to the Crypt, an evocation of a Roman catacomb. The most noteworthy exhibit here is the limestone Egyptian sarcophagus of Seti I (*circa* 1370BCE) that was acquired by Soane in 1825 from the famous Italian adventurer Giovanni Battista Belzoni, who

plundered it from the Valley of the Kings in 1817. Soane marked its arrival with a three-day reception to which he invited 1,000 people. The modest mandapa that is marked as the grave of John Soane does not, in fact, contain his body. He is buried in London's St Pancras graveyard, alongside his wife.

Ascending the stairs by the Monk's Parlour brings you to the Colonnade and Dome, a delightful confusion of fragments of sculptures, mouldings and casts of Antiquity (evidence of Soane's belief in the supremacy of Classical architectural and artistic principles), lit by long light-wells that bring daylight to the lowest level of the building. Many of the pieces are not labelled. There is also a bust of Soane by Francis Chantrey. At the end of the Colonnade is the New Picture Room, added in 1890 to display the three very fine paintings by Canaletto (views of the Rialto, San Marco and Salute, all in Venice) owned by Soane.

The route then passes into house number 12, and the Breakfast Parlour. This light and airy room has a lovely decorated ceiling, restored in 1995, and is lined with bookcases and pictures. The Dining Room, towards the front of the house, has been converted into a gallery showing temporary exhibitions drawn from the the museum's considerable collections of prints, architectural drawings, and paintings.

Passing back through the linking passage, you arrive in the Breakfast Parlour of number 13. Another light and airy room, even though it lies at the centre of the building, it is cleverly lit by a combination of a shallow dome, concealed skylights and, as in the Dining Room and Library, by the use of mirrors.

From the entrance hallway, take the curving stairs up to the Drawing Rooms. Halfway up on the left is a niche containing a bust of Shakespeare, cast from the original in Stratford-upon-Avon. The two rooms, painted a distinctive shade of yellow, contain a number of treasures. Along with some of his architectural drawings, there are portraits of Soane, architectural models and his certificate of admittance to the Royal Academy (1795). Two prize exhibits are a collection of medals (1796–1815) celebrating the life of Napoleon, said to have been assembled for the Empress Josephine, and Turner's painting *Admiral van Tromp's Barge Entering the Texel* (1831). The first floor of number 12 contains a display of architectural models made by Soane; for admission, ask the warder at the front door.

Food and drink: Na Zdrowie, a Polish bar, is just around the corner at 11 Little Turnstile. Apart from possessing a fine selection of vodka, it also serves substantial Polish dishes and good coffee at reasonable prices.

Tower Bridge Experience

The story of a London landmark

Map reference: page 21, J4
Tower Bridge, London SE1. Tel: 020-7940 3985.
www.towerbridge.org.uk
Tube: Tower Hill.

10am–6.30pm Apr–Oct, 9.30am–6pm Nov–Mar; admission charge; last entry 1¼ hours before closing. Wheelchair access.

In the 19th century, a time of great industrial expansion, there was a pressing need to improve circulation along the River Thames without hindering the access of ships into London's docks. The result was Tower Bridge, a triumph of Victorian engineering, built between 1886 and 1894, its steel frame held together with 3 million rivets and clad with decorative stonework in High Gothic style.

The entrance to the Tower Bridge Experience is near the northern bank of the Thames. The tour opens with a short film. A large clock at the centre of the screen spins backwards while images pertinent to past decades are projected onto the screen, until reaching the 1890s.

Visitors ascend the staircase of the North Tower where they meet "Harry Stoner", one of two mechanised mannequins. Stoner represents the raft of painters who worked on Tower Bridge. He argues in favour of a river crossing for East End workers, who at the time had to walk to London Bridge if they needed to work in south London. The bridge could and did become clogged with pedestrians and traffic who faced queuing for several hours; curiously, there were no crossings east of London Bridge. His opponent is the former lord mayor, who had, of course, his own financial interests at heart, owning shipping rights to wharves further upstream.

At the next level, a film is shown describing the

Tower Bridge can open to let through tall ships.

design of the hydraulically operated bascule bridge. The counterweighted bascules (from the French for seesaw) are the lifting flaps, enabling tall ships to pass through.

Visitors continue up the North Tower to the high-level walkway, 139 ft (42 metres) above Mean High Water and 110 ft (34 metres) above the roadway. On a clear day in particular, views of the capital are stunning. A great photographic exhibition along the east walkway shows the construction of the bridge in progress, along with typical life from the 1880s onwards. This is the highlight of Tower Bridge.

Descending the South Tower, the final part of the tour is in the Hands-On Gallery and Engine Rooms. For those interested in engineering, there is plenty of detail on how the bascules work (they have been electrically operated since 1977), and the original hydraulic equipment is preserved immaculately. A pleasant little theatre shows a loop of film of Tower Bridge through the ages. For details of when the bridge is scheduled to be raised, tel: 020-7940 3984.

Food and drink: On the south side of the bridge are two pricey Terence Conran restaurants, Butler's Wharf Chop House (36E Shad Thames, 020-7403 3403) and La Pont de la Tour (36D Shad Thames, 020-7403 8403). Both have great views; the second has better food than the first.

Tower of London

Where traitors lost their heads

Map reference: page 21, J4
Tower Hill, EC3. Tel: 020-7709 0765.
www.hrp.org.uk
Tube: Tower Hill.
Mon–Sat 9am–5pm, Sun 10am–5pm Mar–Oct;
Tues–Sat 9am–4pm, Sun–Mon 10am–4pm
Nov–Feb.
Entrance fee. Tickets may be bought in advance at most Tube stations.
Four shops sell a wide range of souvenirs, from jewellery to Tower of London baseball caps.

Directly across the river from the idiosyncratically shaped glass offices of the Greater London Authority, centre of the capital's administration in the 21st century, stands the bulk of the Tower of London, a stolid reminder of how power was exercised in less democratic times. Two of Henry VIII's wives, Anne Boleyn and Catherine Howard, were beheaded here in 1536 and 1542. So were Sir Thomas More,

"Beefeaters", whose nickname may derive from the French *buffetier,* a servant.

Henry's principled Lord Chancellor (1535), and Sir Walter Raleigh, the last of the great Elizabethan adventurers (1618). The uncrowned Edward V, aged 12, and his 10-year-old brother Richard were murdered here in 1483, allegedly on the orders of Richard III. William Penn, the future founder of Pennsylvania, was imprisoned here in 1669, and the diarist Samuel Pepys in 1679. As recently as 1941, Rudolph Hess, Germany's Deputy Führer, was locked in the Tower.

Encircled by a moat (now dry), with 22 towers, the Tower of London, begun by William the Conqueror in 1078, is Britain's most celebrated military monument. Yet, given that so much of the country's turbulent history was played out within these walls, it conspicuously lacks the romantic aura that many visitors expect. The reason is that, until comparatively recently, its buildings were functional – as well as serving as a fort, arsenal, palace and prison, it also contained at various times a treasury, public record office, observatory, royal mint and zoo. As a result, it was frequently remodelled and renovated, especially in the 19th century, so that many floors and staircases, for example, look more modern than medieval. But then, how could the

How it looked in 1805: Thomas and William Daniell's *Tower of London from the East* is held by the Guildhall Library.

boards that Henry VIII trod hope to survive the footfalls of 2½ million tourists a year?

Any sense of awe is also undermined by the brightly uniformed "Beefeaters", the 40 yeoman warders who live with their families in houses within the grounds and who act as tour guides (their nickname may derive from the French *buffetier*, a servant). Although all have previously served in the armed forces for at least 22 years, some have enthusiastically embraced showbiz, apparently auditioning for the role of pantomime villain by alternating jocular banter with visitors and melodramatically delivered descriptions of torture and beheadings. In contrast, pike and musket drills by the English Civil War Society are conducted with the masterful lethargy of confirmed pacifists.

Given that the Tower's 18 acres (7.3 hectares) contain enough important buildings and collections to occupy three hours, you may prefer to skip the one-hour Beefeater-led tour and strike out on your own, relying on your imagination and the comprehensive official guidebook or free map. An audio guide can be hired, though

THE RAVENS

The ravens are a symbol of the Tower. Nine live here, looked after by a yeoman warder. Legend has it that, the day the ravens leave the Tower, England will fall. As a precaution, their wings have been clipped.

what the Tower desperately needs is some well-designed computer technology, with touch screens providing a real educational resource for those who would appreciate it. In summer, it's best to arrive early, giving priority to the Crown Jewels and the Bloody Tower, which can attract long queues later in the day. Note that the spiral staircases in some of the towers require a degree of agility. Below are the main sights to see.

Traitor's Gate

After entering through Middle Tower, you pass through Byward Tower; both date from the 13th century but have been much rebuilt. Mint Street, in whose 18th-century houses some of the Beefeaters live, is on the left. Ahead, past the Bell Tower (1190s) is Water Lane. Along this lane, on the right, is Traitor's Gate, the water entrance created by Edward I in 1275–79; barges would carry suspected traitors down the Thames and through this gate.

The Medieval Palace

Just before Traitor's Gate is the entrance to the residential part of the Tower, used by monarchs when they lived here. St Thomas's Tower, built in 1275–79 but much altered, displays archaeological evidence of its many uses. Parts of the Wakefield Tower (1220–40) have been furnished in 13th-century style, complete with a throne copied from the Coronation Chair in

Westminster Abbey. A spiral staircase leads to a walkway on top of the south wall, which provides a good view of the riverside defences. The wall runs to the Lanthorn Tower, an 1883 replacement for an earlier building; it contains various 13th-century artefacts.

The Wall Walk

The walk along this defensive outer wall takes in the eastern towers. Access is through the Salt Tower, often used as a prison. Next are the Broad Arrow Tower, also once a lock-up, the Constable Tower, which contains a model depicting the Tower in the 14th century, and the Martin Tower, which houses an exhibition on the Crown Jewels.

The Crown Jewels

These are displayed in the neo-Gothic Waterloo Barracks, built in 1845 to house nearly 1,000 soldiers. The queues here can be long and, while snaking slowly through airport-style barriers, visitors are treated to large-screen footage of the Queen's coronation in 1953. At the centre of the display are a dozen crowns and a glittering array of swords, sceptres and orbs used on royal occasions. The Imperial State Crown, made in 1937, contains 2,868 diamonds and is topped with a sapphire dating from the reign of Edward the Confessor, whose death in 1066 led to the Norman Conquest.

A moving walkway ensures that visitors cannot linger over the principal exhibits, but many other glass cases contain gold dishes, chalices and altar dishes that can be viewed at leisure. The eye is caught by a massive wine cistern weighing a quarter of a ton (250 kg).

The Imperial State Crown has 2,868 diamonds.

Costume drama for the tourists on Tower Green.

The White Tower

The oldest part of the fortress, the White Tower was probably designed in 1078 by a Norman monk, Gandulf, a prolific builder of castles and churches. It has walls 15 ft (5 metres) thick and was intended by William the Conqueror to intimidate. Its original form remains, but virtually every part has been refurbished or rebuilt over the centuries: the door surrounds and most of the windows were replaced in the 17th and 18th centuries, and much of the external Normandy stone was replaced with more durable Portland stone from Dorset.

Its basement contains an 11th-century well, still providing fresh water, and the first floor gives access to the austere Chapel of St John the Evangelist, a fine example of early Norman architecture. Much of the remaining space is devoted to extensive displays from the Royal Armouries: shields, suits of armour, cutlasses, broadswords, pistols, matchlock muskets, mortars and cannon. The Line of Kings, first recorded at the Tower in 1660, is a row of 10 full-size sculpted horses with royal armour from the 11th to the 17th centuries.

Traitor's Gate, the water entrance through which many prisoners passed on their last journey.

Tower Green

This grassy area, west of the White Tower, gives access (but only as part of tours) to the much rebuilt Chapel Royal of St Peter ad Vincula. It contains memorials and ornate monuments, plus the headless remains of many famous prisoners executed in the Tower. During a restoration in 1876, bones found under the nave were reinterred in the crypt. In front of the chapel is the Scaffold Site where nobles were beheaded (the less illus-trious, denied this privacy, were executed in public on Tower Hill, outside the castle walls).

Close by, the Beauchamp Tower (1281) housed high-ranking prisoners, some for many years. In the upper chamber, you can see inscriptions they carved on the walls. The timber-framed building to the south, the Queen's House (1530), is the residence of the Tower's governor, and the adjacent 19th-century houses are occupied by yeoman warders.

Sir Walter Raleigh's room, re-created in the Bloody Tower.

The Bloody Tower

Built in the 1220s and once known as the Garden Tower, this popular attraction was renamed in Tudor times because the young sons of Edward IV had been cynically murdered there during the brief reign of their uncle, Richard III. It later housed the most eminent prisoners, including Archbishop Thomas Cranmer (in 1553–54), Archbishop William Laud (1640–45) and Sir Walter Raleigh (1603–16). The rooms are now furnished as they might have been during Raleigh's internment and contain his books.

The Royal Fusiliers Museum

This is covered in a separate entry on page 130.

Food and drink: The New Armouries Café, housed in a 1663 storehouse, serves hot and cold dishes. There are also several Prêt à Manger sandwich shops. Chez Gerard (14 Trinity Square, 020-7480 5500) has good steak and chips.

Westminster Abbey Museum

The abbey's collection of royal and other funeral effigies

Map reference: page 20, D6
Westminster Abbey, SW1. Tel: 020-7654 4831.
www.westminster-abbey.org
Tube: Westminster or St James's Park. Buses:
11, 24, 88, 211.
Open daily, 10.30am–4pm.
Admission charge. Wheelchair access.

The museum at Westminster Abbey is a bizarre, macabre and rather fascinating adjunct to London's famous Gothic sanctuary. Housed in the oldest part of the abbey, the 11th-century undercroft below the former monk's dormitory, it consists primarily of a collection of wooden and wax effigies of monarchs and other notables. The effigies were used over the years at the many funerals that have taken place in the abbey, the traditional burial place of English sovereigns and their families.

Between 1307 and 1660, a wooden likeness of the deceased monarch was dressed in full coronation regalia and placed on top of the coffin for the funeral procession. The earliest effigy in the collection is that of Edward III (1312–77), of which the head and most of the body remain. Edward's face was cast from a death mask made shortly after his passing. In other words, this is a very good representation of what he looked like as he breathed his last. Look closely and you'll see a drooping mouth and flattened cheek, caused by the stroke he suffered just before he died.

Other wooden effigies include Henry VII (1457–1509), a realistic likeness also taken from a death mask; Anne of Bohemia (1366–94), wife of Richard II, whose freakishly elongated face wouldn't have won many medieval beauty contests; and Anne of Denmark (1574–1619), James I's queen, whose portrait features a pimple on the left cheek.

After 1660, the effigies' heads and hands were made of wax. Charles II (1630–85) is dressed in his own garter robes and (apparently) monogrammed underwear. The Duchess of Richmond and Lennox (1647–1702) is accompanied by her pet West African parrot, possibly the oldest stuffed bird in England. Also here is the effigy of naval hero Horatio Nelson (1758–1805), said at the time to be an amazingly accurate portrait. These later figures are all dressed in original, contemporary costume.

Display cases around the walls exhibit other artefacts associated with the abbey. A coronation chair first employed in the double ceremony of William and Mary in 1689 sits alongside a dull-looking replica set of crown jewels used in coronation rehearsals. Elsewhere are panels of 13th-century stained glass, alabaster reliefs from the 17th century, fragments of medieval masonry work and a Roman sarcophagus re-used in Saxon times.

The ticket price includes entry to the nearby Pyx Chamber and Chapter House. The former, part of the same ancient structure as the museum, was once used as the Royal Treasury and was the scene of a notorious crown-jewel robbery in 1303. Now it houses a collection of church plate from the abbey and next-door St Margaret's Church. The Chapter House, built for Henry III around 1250, features medieval frescoes and restored 13th-century floor tiles.

Food and drink: *A stall in the North Cloister sells hot and cold drinks and sandwiches. Shepherd's (Marsham Court, Marsham Street, 020-7834 9552), a politicians' haunt, serves traditional British food. Moderate.*

The wax effigy of Lord Nelson.

Museums of
Social History

People rather than objects are the focus here: the lives they led, the oppressions they suffered, the clothes they wore, the furniture they bought, the flowers they planted, the beliefs they held and the causes they championed

Black Cultural Archives

One of the largest collections of historical artefacts and memorabilia documenting the black presence in Britain

Map reference: page 23. F4
378 Coldharbour Lane, Brixton, London SW9.
Tel: 020-7738 4591; fax: 020-7738 7168.
Tube: Brixton. Buses 2, 3, 35, 45, 133, 159, 109, 196, 37.
Open: Mon–Fri by appointment only. Free.

The Archives were set up during the 1980s as the black presence grew in Britain. Reference material stored here plots the history of black people in Europe from AD 208 to the 1890s, and in Britain from 1900 to the present day.

Housed in a cramped building in the heart of Brixton, the archive is a mine of fascinating information. One of the country's largest collections of historical artefacts, it includes letters, photographs, interviews, magazines, newspapers and documents, many donated. One treasured document is an original bill of sale detailing the age, sex and price of slaves sold on the auction block in England.

There are also video footage and newspaper articles that reveal social and political changes throughout the country in the 20th century. These range from the arrival of Somali seamen in Cardiff, which has the oldest black community in Britain, to the Caribbean migrants who arrived on the *Empire Windrush* in 1948. The consequences of opposition from anti-immigration politicians is recorded.

Communities have developed as far afield as Devon, Bristol, Liverpool, Edinburgh, Glasgow and London and so the BCA catalogues and preserves material about the diverse experience of people, such as those who served in the allied armed forces in the two world wars.

A free resource, which charges a small fee for photocopying, the BCA is primarily used for research by students, but is open to everyone. Though exhibitions in the BCA building are rare, parts of the collection can be seen in visiting displays throughout the year in institutions such as the Victoria and Albert Museum. The BCA also organises talks and events, especially in October during Black History Month.

In partnership with Middlesex University, the BCA has secured lottery funding to create a national Museum of Black Heritage, which will incorporate the archive. The hope is to house it eventually in a dedicated museum and library building with exhibition space.

Food and drink: Asmara, 386 Coldharbour Lane (020-7737 4144) offers inexpensive and authentic Eritrean food served in a relaxed atmosphere; cheap–moderate. Bamboula (12 Acre Lane, 020-7737 6633) serves good hearty portions of tasty Caribbean cuisine; cheap–moderate.

ABOVE: Tea etiquette illustrated at the Bramah Tea & Coffee Museum.

OPPOSITE: *Gone* by Frank Holl (1845–88) at the Geffrye Museum.

Bramah Tea & Coffee Museum

How the beverages became big business

Map reference: page page 21, G5
40 Southwark Street, SE1. Tel: 020-7403 5650.
www.bramahmuseum.co.uk
Tube: London Bridge (Borough High St exit).
Daily 10am–6pm. Admission fee to museum; free entry to tea and coffee room.

This is a place for serious lovers of the world's favourite hot beverages. Divided into two separate galleries, Mr Bramah's charming little museum tells the history of the tea and coffee trades, with an array of antique tea and coffee pots, old posters, enormous copper urns and blending machines. The centrepiece of the tea museum is a giant teapot, with a capacity of 800 cups, using 3–4 lbs (1.5–3kg) of tea leaves. "Bedouins say that a camel, a gun and tea are the three essentials of life," it's claimed on *Tea Revives the World*, an illustrated wall map.

A fine selection of teas and coffees (with cakes) are served in the museum's café, and your pot of tea is accompanied by a timer, allowing you to wait for the recommended five minutes before pouring your cup of steaming golden nectar (remembering to put the milk in the cup first – a proviso which, if you didn't know already, you will soon find out here).

Chelsea Physic Garden

Delightful walled garden dedicated to rare and medicinal plants

Map reference: page 40, C4
66 Royal Hospital Road, SW3. Tel: 020-7352.
5646. www.cpgarden.demon.co.uk
Tube: Sloane Square (then 5-minute walk).
Open: Wed noon–5pm, Sun 2–6pm Apr–Oct
only. Admission fee. Wheelchair access.

London's "Secret Garden" is now a 3½-acre (2-hectare) haven of tranquillity full of birdsong and the scent of flowering plants, but it was established in 1673 by the Society of Apothecaries for a serious purpose. Plants were the major source of medicine, and this ancient garden was founded to teach physicians and apothecaries how to recognise and use them. At that time, the belief still prevailed that all plants had been put on earth by God for man's benefit and it was felt that they must be useful even if that use was not immediately apparent.

Early access to the garden was by boat and the steps leading directly to the riverbank disappeared only when the Embankment was created in the 19th century. As the area became built-up, the garden seemed like a green island in a sea of brick, yet the microclimate that was created enables rare and tender plants to thrive in these urban surroundings.

After an auspicious start followed by a decline, the garden was virtually reinvented by Sir Hans Sloane (1660–1753), a leading physician and one of the Society of Apothecaries' former students. He bought the Manor of Chelsea from Lord Cheyne and granted the Apothecaries a conditional lease in virtual perpetuity and a nominal rent. A herb garden, he said, is "a place you can learn to distinguish good and usefull plants from those that bear resemblance to them yet are hurtfull."

Today's garden is thriving and well cared-for. It is divided into contrasting sections, including a Garden of Medicine, History of Medicine, Herbs, Culinary Plants and the National Cistus collection. Another section has a rare plants, endangered peo-

LEFT: Gallica rose, from *A Curious Herbal* by Elizabeth Blackwell, 1837.

RIGHT: The Artists of Leonard Fuchs, from *De Historia Stirpium*, 1542.

ples and lost knowledge trail, explaining why plants are endangered – for example, by the destruction of habitat, overgrazing, or uprooting by collectors. A woodland area has birds' nesting boxes, gardens of American and South American plants and systematic order beds, a native plants section and rock gardens. The Garden of Medicine has beds dealing with such medical disciplines as oncology, ENT (ears, nose, throat) and lung diseases and ophthalmology.

Food and drink: There is a small shop, and refreshments are available in the nearby Ranelegh Gardens. The Gordon Ramsay restaurant, first-class but expensive, is close by (68–69 Royal Hospital Road, 020-7352 4441). Foxtrot-Oscar (79 Royal Hospital Road, 020-7352 7179) is more relaxed but the bistro-style food is fairly routine.

Clink Prison Museum

An attraction evoking the horror of prison life from the 12th to the 18th centuries

Map reference: page 21, H4
1 Clink Street, London SE1. Tel: 020-7378 1558.
www.clink.co.uk
Tube: London Bridge (Borough High St exit).
Open: daily 10am–6pm. Entrance fee.

Founded as early as the 12th century to deal with overenthusiastic revellers, the Clink functioned until 1780, latterly as a debtors' prison, and the word "clink" became a synonym for jail. The museum, whose future has recently seemed uncertain, can be identified by the emaciated figure suspended within a cage from the gable end.

Dimly lit steps lead down into the entrance of the museum, where tacky trinkets and souvenirs, and an interesting short history of the prison, are on sale. You then enter a dismal series of rooms that represent cell interiors, while a disembodied voice drones in the background, sentencing miscreants to a range of ever-worsening punishments. Effigies of scrawny inmates are shown in varying degrees of discomfort.

Beside each exhibit, plaques give information on various aspects of prison life and history; for example, that the Clink was allegedly the first English prison to admit women inmates, mainly prostitutes, for crimes as benign as "chiding" their clients. One frightening punishment was to "gently" pull apart the erring whore by attaching ropes to her limbs, the other ends being fastened to a couple of horses. The cells have replicas of many of the horrific instruments of torture used by the prison wardens;

some are truly ingenious. In 1530, Henry VIII ordered a new and particularly gruesome punishment: slow-boiling in oil.

With the Clink being outside the jurisdiction of London in those days, the area swarmed with brothels, bear- and bull-baiting rings, and theatres and taverns – all considered forms of "suspect" entertainment by the authorities. The area was under the control of the bishops of Winchester, who ruled by their own laws and founded the Clink Prison. The jail was never short of inmates, including, among others, monks and priests with views differing from those of the sovereign. On at least one occasion, the entire cast of one of the South Bank theatres was thrown into the Clink for lewd behaviour.

Food and drink: The museum has a small café. A few yards to the west, Cantina Vinopolis (tel: 020-7940 8333), built under railway arches to give a cathedral effect, serves moderately priced "modern British" food and has more than 200 wines by the glass. Opposite it, at 34 Park Street, the venerable Anchor Inn (020-7407 1577) is a maze of quirky rooms with a reasonably priced restaurant upstairs giving a great view of St Paul's.

Cuming Museum

Charts the history of Southwark, with a strong orientation towards schoolchildren

Map reference: page 23, F3
155–157 Walworth Road, London SE17.
Tel: 020-7701 1342.
cuming.museum@southwark.gov.uk
Tube: Elephant and Castle.
Open: Tues–Sat 10am–5pm. Admission free.

This modest museum, on the first floor of a public library, makes a big effort to give local children a taste for the past. The gift of some fossils and an old coin on his fifth birthday in 1782 inspired Richard Cuming to become a collector, and the undisciplined result was fancifully called "the British Museum in miniature" after its

Gilt head from an Egyptian coffin, *circa* 1200BC.

Dennis Severs' House

An 18th-century candlelit timewarp

Map reference: page 21, J2
18 Folgate Street, Spitalfields, E1 6BX. Tel/fax:
020-7247 4013. www.dennissevershouse.co.uk.
Tube/train: Liverpool Street.
Open first Sunday of the month 2–5pm, first
Monday of the month 12–2pm, no booking.
Also every Monday "Silent Night" by candlelight,
times vary, booking necessary. Entrance fee.
Not suitable for young children.

1906 opening. A World War II bomb curbed such ambitions. A ragbag of relics dates back to pilgrim badges from Chaucer's time and includes relics associated with Charles Dickens's childhood, a water pump from Marshalsea Debtors' Prison and an electrical generator once owned by the locally born scientist Michael Faraday *(see page 143)*. A speciality is London superstitions; exhibits range from charms to ward off rheumatism and diarrhoea to tusks offering protection against the evil eye.

Although off the beaten track, it's only a 10-minute walk from the Imperial War Museum.

This is a museum quite unlike any other. Indeed, its creator, Dennis Severs, might not have been happy with it being called a museum at all. A life-long collector and anglophile, Severs moved from his native California in 1967. He bought 18 Folgate Street, a former silk weaver's house, in 1979, and got to know it by living in each room in turn, much as its original occupants might have done, without benefit of electricity or modern appliances. Gradually he re-created its early 18th-century state, restoring its Georgian harmony.

To give the 10-room house coherence, he invented the Jervis family, and provided evidence of their occupation in the form of a half-eaten scone or half-drunk cup of tea, a smouldering fire, and a unique smell and atmosphere. Severs wanted his visitors to

The drawing room of Dennis Severs' House.

participate in this domestic history by using their imaginations, by losing themselves in another time. "You either see it or you don't," he would say.

The aim is wonderfully achieved; as you walk round the house in silence it is easy to believe that the family will come back into the room at any moment. Severs was renowned for ejecting those visitors he felt did not properly appreciate his "still-life drama" and, since his death in 1999, the staff have kept up the tradition by being equally cantankerous. Highly recommended.

Food and drink: The Arkansas Café (Unit 12, 107b Commercial Street, 020-7377 6999) serves hearty North American-style meat dishes at nearby Spitalfields Market. Vegetarians will be happier at the reasonably priced Futures ((2 Exchange Square, 020-7638 6341).

Fashion & Textile Museum

Zandra Rhodes sets the style

*Map reference: page 21, J5
83 Bermondsey Street, SE1. Tel: 020-7403-0222.
www.ftmlondon.org. Call for opening hours.
Tube: London Bridge, then 15-minute walk.
Bus: 47 from Liverpool Street. Rail: London
Bridge. Giftshop with designer goodies.
Entrance fee.*

What they're wearing at the Fashion & Textile Museum.

The brainchild of Zandra Rhodes, the "high priestess of pink" whose distinctive, textile-led clothes have been an exuberant fixture on the fashion scene since the 1970s, this museum is dedicated to exhibiting and recording the works of fashion and textiles designers, with an emphasis on British design from the 1950s to the 21st century.

Rhodes is at pains to explain that it is not a museum for her work alone (although there will be a permanent collection of Rhodes originals upstairs). Instead, changing exhibitions will feature style-setting names such as Vivienne Westwood, John Galliano (Dior), Alexander McQueen (Givenchy), Paul Smith, Jean Muir and Mary Quant, who created the mini-skirt. Textile designers – seldom given credit for their contribution – will also be represented. The museum will have a library and textile archives, and will be an educational centre for students, with possible classes in textile printing.

The flamboyant Rhodes teamed up with Mexican architect Ricardo Legorreta for the look of the building itself, a spectacular pink-and-orange creation in trendy Bermondsey. This former warehouse is the first building in Europe by Legorreta, winner of the Gold Metal Award given by the American Institute of Architects. (Previous winners include Sir Aston Webb, who designed the V&A, and Charles Barrie, who did the same for the Houses of Parliament.) The landmark façade gives way inside to a pink high-arched entranceway, followed by a corridor painted deep lapis-lazuli blue. A bold slash of yellow rivets the eye to the staircase which gleams with built-in lights, Hollywood-style. All in all, a fitting showcase for fashionable folk.

Food and drink: There will be a café in the museum, so think pink. Close by, at 50 Bermondsey Street, is Delfina (020-7357 0244), a spacious, stylish restaurant-cum-gallery where the food is as good-looking as the premises. Less self-conscious is the Honest Cabbage, at 99 Bermondsey Street, (020-7234 0080); daily dishes at reasonable prices.

An 1897 lithograph shows the Grand Lodge marking Queen Victoria's Golden Jubilee.

Freemasons' Hall

A mysterious society opens its doors

Map reference: page 20, D3
Great Queen Street, WC2. Tel: 020-7395 9258.
www.grandlodge-england.org
Tube: Holborn.
Mon–Fri 10am–5pm (library and museum also open Sat 10am–1pm), can be closed at short notice. Hourly tours 11am–4pm.
Gift shop sells books and Masonic items.
Free. Wheelchair access.

Freemasonry, one of the world's oldest fraternal societies, has long been shrouded in secrecy, and this museum lifts few veils. While tours allow the public to see around the working rooms and halls of the United Grand Lodge of England, and a museum and research library are open to all, there's little indication for the non-initiated of what Freemasonry is really about – in fact, their website gives more helpful information.

The Freemasons' Hall is worth seeing, though: this Grade II listed building, opened in 1933 and dedicated to peace, contains perhaps the most spectacularly colourful and elaborate internal decoration of the Art-Deco era to be found in London.

Freemasonry is steeped in symbolism, and the museum displays an immense collection of Masonic regalia and memorabilia: painted porcelain, engraved glassware, ceremonial swords, banners, jewels (medals) and the ritual tools of the organisation: squares, compasses and so on. Among the more interesting pieces on show are sets of tools made from scraps by World War II Freemason prisoners-of-war and minutes of their meetings, along with examples of anti-Masonic literature from the Nazi era.

A guided tour, obligatory if you want to see beyond the museum and library, takes visitors through the Grand Officers' Robing Room, hung with portraits of past Grand Masters, and down the mahogany-panelled Processional Corridor to the stunning First Vestibule. The colours of the glass windows are gloriously intense. The focal point is the Memorial Window, below which an ornate casket contains a roll of honour of Freemasons who died during World War I. Finance for the construction of this building was raised by many lodges and individuals; their names are inscribed on the walls.

Behind two massive bronze doors, weighing well over a ton each and embellished with scenes of the construction of Solomon's Temple, is the inner sanctum of the complex. The Grand Temple, a 2,000-seater auditorium for ceremonies, is splendidly ornamented, most notably by a 15-ft (4.6-metre) deep coving in which allegorical illustrations and dictums are depicted entirely in Italian mosaic.

Food and drink: In an alley off Long Acre, Café des Amis du Vin (11–14 Hanover Square, 020-7379 3444) is a good-value brasserie. The atmospheric Sarastro (126 Drury lane, 020-7836 0101) has Turkish-influenced food, and opera singers perform on Sunday and Monday evenings.

Geffrye Museum

Exposing English domestic exteriors

Map reference: page 23, G2
Kingsland Road, Shoreditch, London E2. Tel: 020 7739 9893. www.geffrye-museum.org.uk
Tube: Liverpool Street, rail: Liverpool Street or Dalston Kingsland, bus: 67, 149, 242, 243.
Tues–Sat 10am–5pm, Sun and public holidays 12–5pm, closed Good Friday, 24–26 Dec, 1 Jan.

Free admission. Full wheelchair access, wheelchairs available from front desk.

The only British museum to deal with domestic interiors of the urban middle class, the Geffrye chronicles the development of English home decoration from 1600 to the present day. It is housed in a square of former almshouses of the Ironmonger's Company on Kingsland Road, built in 1714 from the proceeds of the will of Sir Robert Geffrye. These were sold off in 1911, when the almshouses relocated to the suburbs, and re-opened as the London County Council museum of furniture and woodwork in 1914.

The aim of the collection was to provide a resource and inspiration for workers in the East End furniture trade. By 1935, much of this industry had moved elsewhere and the museum was reorganised into a series of period rooms which show the furniture in context. The gardens have been redesigned to include a herb garden and "period garden rooms".

The rooms – all of which are "sitting" or "living" rooms – are arranged chronologically and each century is preceded by a room giving background information on characteristic house layouts and furniture designs of the century. The very first room gives an overview of furniture styles from 1620 to 1990, roughly the span of the museum's exhibits. The next section is devoted to the interiors of the 17th century with three rooms: an Elizabethan and Jacobean interior (1580–1640), a Stuart room (1660–85) and a Queen Anne room (1685–1714). There is a noticable change in taste from the heavy, dark panelling and furniture of the earlier rooms, to the much lighter Queen Anne designs. The middle room begins to show the influence of the voyages of discovery and of overseas colonies with its "exotic" curios, such as the stuffed armadillo and a charming print of an elephant.

The 18th century carries on the lighter, less oppressive trend of the Queen Anne display, and is represented by two rooms, Early (1720–60) and Late (1760–1800) Georgian. By the end of the 18th century, the dark wooden panelling had, by and large, disappeared in favour of walls decorated with paint, fabric or wallpaper, lightening the overall look. Also interesting is the emergence of technology in the home, with a clock now usually present.

The 19th-century rooms begin with a Regency (1800–30) drawing room. By this time, the previously ornate plaster and wooden decoration on walls, ceilings and surrounds had become much plainer, and the use of carpeting had become well established. The room has Wedgwood blue walls that match the upholstery and pick out the blue in the carpet. The cast-iron fireplace also establishes a 19th-century norm, a product of the burgeoning industrial revolution. The mid-century is represented by a Victorian room (1840–70), with lush fabrics

LEFT: Thomas Cantrell Dugdale's *The Arrival of the Jarrow Marchers* (1936) at the Geffrye Museum.

RIGHT: Regency period room, 1800–30, at the Geffrye.

Harry Brooker's
Oranges and Lemons
(1890) at the
Geffrye Museum.

and furnishings, and a large number of ornaments (note also the sentimentally moral painting). Gas lighting had been introduced in London in around 1840, supplanting candlelight, and the room boasts a large metal chandelier with four gas lamps.

A reaction against such a "cluttered" environment wasn't long in coming and the final 19th-century room is dedicated to the Aesthetic style (1875–90). Much of the inspiration for the style came from East Asia, particularly Japan, with simple, angular lines and abstract patterns dominating the decoration.

At this point you enter a new extension, with the café on your left and the museum shop on your right. Through the doors in front of you are the 20th-century displays. From this point on the interiors become much more familiar, starting on the left with the Edwardian (1900–14) room. Many suburban houses were built during this period and the display re-creates a living room from one of these. The decor is quite plain and the influence of the Arts and Crafts movement can be seen in the textiles and furniture.

The next room shows a flat dating from the 1930s. By this time Modernism had made its mark on the taste of the middle class, and electric heating was starting to take over from coal.

By the mid-century (1955–65), Modernist design and architecture had become the norm for new houses and the next display features an open-plan living/dining room showing the influence of Scandinavian design. This is also the period when the television set begins to dominate the living area. Bringing the museum almost up to date, the last room is devoted to a 1990s loft-style apartment, many of which now exist in Shoreditch and Clerkenwell, close by the museum. Opposite the room displays are cabinets showing classics of 20th-century design, from a wonderful 1930s "vogue" teaset by Eric Slater, to a Phillipe Stark lemon squeezer.

Downstairs from the main displays is the Geffrye Design Centre (a study centre for contemporary crafts and design), a gallery for temporary exhibitions and rooms for educational activities. Outside, behind the buildings, are the museum's gardens (open Apr–Oct during museum opening hours).

Laid out from 1990 onwards, these include the walled herb garden with a wide range of plants traditionally grown for cosmetic, culinary and medicinal use, and the "garden rooms". These are a series of period gardens that complement the displays inside, from a 16th/17th-century knot garden, through late Elizabethan (1550–1620), mid to late Georgian (1760–1800) and mid to late Victorian (1860–90) gardens, to an Edwardian (1900–14) garden at the southern end.

Food and drink: The museum has a lovely café and restaurant, the At Home Restaurant, in the new wing, overlooking the gardens (Tues–Sat 10am–5pm, Sun and Bank Holidays 12–5pm, last orders 4.45pm). It serves good-value traditional and modern English food plus snacks (afternoon tea with English dessert wine is especially good).

London Dungeon

**Gruesome reminders of historical horrors
that make London today look like paradise**

Map reference: page 21, H5
Tooley Street, London SE1. Tel: 09001-600066.
www.the dungeons.com
Tube: London Bridge.
Daily Oct–Mar 10am–5.30pm/last admission
4.30pm, Apr–Sep 10am–6.30pm/last admission
5.30pm, later in July and August. Entry fee.

Tucked beneath the northern side of London
Bridge Station, this crowded attraction takes
you on a scary journey through the cata-
combs of old London town. The tour begins with an
obligatory photo opportunity – head in the stocks, a
blackened chopper at your neck. The visitor is
plunged into darkness, and it takes a while to adjust
to the gloom. The atmosphere is pretty spooky as
cell after cell reveals an assortment of reprobates in
ever more torturous positions. Blood-curdling
screams issue from mechanical waxwork figures:
an executioner garottes some pathetic soul, while
another vomits blood into an overflowing barrel.

The ecclesiastical section contains the figure of a
kneeling Anne Boleyn muttering prayers and blink-
ing. Because her features have been projected onto
her, this is the most realistic and affecting piece in the
exhibition. Cases display a variety of devices used in
bygone days, such as the chastity belt forced on
women when their God-fearing husbands rode off
to the Crusades. Next comes a trawl through Jack
the Ripper's East End of London, with actors offering the visitor clues to his identity.

The Judgement Day boat trip, a journey through
the Tower of London's Traitor's Gate aboard barges,
is accompanied by cries and screams. Next you are
ushered into the London of the Black Plague, followed by the Great Fire of 1666 (predicted by a talk-
ing head of the prophet Nostradamus), with the
atmosphere re-created by dry ice and an increasingly
stuffy room. Terrified shrieks can be heard in the distance while you are exhorted to run for your life
through a maze of hot corridors, arriving at a rotating
tunnel with a kaleidoscopic array of fiery colours,
before being ejected into fluorescent-lit reality and
the chance to purchase your photograph for a fiver.

*Food and drink: There's an in-house café-bar. Across the
street, Hay's Galleria contains a branch of Café Rouge and
a Balls Brothers wine bar with a good selection of food.*

A subtle
welcome to
the devilish
pleasures of
the London
Dungeon.

London Fire Brigade Museum

**Old firefighting engines and equipment
from a city with a blaze-laden history**

Map reference: page 21, G5
94A Southwark Bridge Road, London SE1.
Tel: 020-7587 2894.
www.london-fire.gov.uk/about_us/
Tube: Borough.
*Admission only by pre-booked tours Mon–Fri
10.30am, 12.30pm and 2.30pm. Admission fee.*

Those with a tendency to follow fire engines
should seek out this specialist museum,
housed in the residence of a 19th-century
brigade superintendant. Several vintage fire engines
are on display in a hall opposite the reception area,

Vintage fire-fighting equipment at the London Fire Brigade Museum.

and the main house has a wide collection of historical items ranging from helmets, uniforms and breathing apparatus to vivid paintings of the World War II blitz. Curiosities include 17th-century hollowed-out tree trunks which carried water beneath main roads (the origin of the term "trunk road").

Fire fighting was important in a city whose rapid growth outstripped the ability of safety regulators. After the 1666 Great Fire, insurance companies employed Thames watermen to extinguish fires in buildings under their cover. The trouble was that, if a brigade employed by a particular insurance company turned up at a burning building not displaying the badge of its employer, it would leave the fire to rage. Many of these badges are on display.

One early brigade chief, James Braidwood, died in the nearby Tooley Street fire of 1861 which raged for two days and smouldered for another two weeks. As a result, the government agreed to set up a publicly funded city-wide fire brigade. The introduc-

tion of modern devices such as thermal imaging cameras is chronologically charted.

Food and drink: Borough High Street, a few minutes' walk away at the end of Marshalsea Road, has a wide range of inexpensive restaurants such as Tas, a Turkish restaurant. Its many pubs include The George, an old coaching inn now owned by the National Trust.

Madame Tussaud's

Classic waxworks, more popular than ever in the age of celebrities

Map reference: page 23, E2
Marylebone Road, London NW1. Tel: 020-7935 6861. www.madame-tussauds.com
Tube: Baker Street.
Daily 9am–5.30pm; Oct–Jun 10am–5.30pm, 9.30–5.30 weekends; entrance fee, timed tickets recommended; combined tickets sold for waxworks and adjacent planetarium.

In an age when computer animation routinely fills cinema screens with the miraculous, what impels 7,000 people a day to stand in line breathing in the traffic fumes of London's Marylebone Road in order to gaze at mute, immobile effigies with glass-fibre bodies, wax heads and glass eyes? Knowing the answer to that question has turned Madame Tussaud's into the top tourist attraction in London, beating the Tower into second place.

A key ingredient in the success is that the models are no longer roped off or protected by glass cases. You can stroll right up to them – an impertinence their bodyguards would never permit in real life. You can give Saddam Hussein a piece of your mind. You can be photographed with your arm around Gérard Depardieu. If you haven't brought a camera, a Tussaud's photographer will invite you on entering the exhibition to be pictured alongside the waxwork of a current celebrity and a print will be waiting for you, at a price, when you leave. Whatever impulse draws crowds to see a minor television personality declare open a supermarket is at work here in overdrive, and the reactions are similar. Is Mel Gibson really that short? Doesn't Joan Collins have at least one wrinkle?

An attraction of Tussaud's has always been the pleasure of passing judgment on the quality of the likenesses. This has improved over the years, and you feel you could almost strike up a conversation with Nelson Mandela. The surprise is that so many

of the moulds are still remarkably unconvincing. James Dean, Marilyn Monroe and Alfred Hitchcock are just about recognisable because of the Hollywood context, and Harold Wilson and Margaret Thatcher bear only approximate resemblances to the prime ministers who animated 10 Downing Street. Often it works out that the more unreal people seem in real life – Richard Branson, for instance – the more authentic they appear in Tussaud's.

The story of the waxworks began in 1789, during the French Revolution, when Marie Grosholtz, trained by a doctor in modelling anatomical subjects in wax, was asked to prepare death masks of famous victims of the guillotine. Although she married a French engineer, François Tussaud, in 1795, she left him in 1802 to spend the next 33 years touring Britain with a growing collection of wax figures. Today those gory beginnings are echoed in the waxworks' Chamber of Horrors, which contains the blade that sliced off Marie Antoinette's head and recreates various none-too-scary tableaux of torture. Vlad the Impaler acts as doorman.

In 1993 the exhibition finally embraced audio-animatronics, populating a "Spirit of London" ride with moving and speaking figures ranging from William Shakespeare ("To be or not to be") to contemporary street hawkers. Visitors are carried past the historical tableaux in miniature sawn-off taxis; the quality of the effects is uneven, but some of the speaking figures are astonishingly lifelike.

If you like the idea of getting close to celebrities

ABOVE:
Tussaud's
version of
the Tudor
monarchy.

LEFT:
The Beatles,
waxing
lyrical.

without the remotest chance of being snubbed or ignored, Madame Tussaud's will probably appeal – but, unless you like queueing, buy a timed ticket in advance or get there when it opens (9.30am in summer, 10am in winter). If, on the other hand, you are interested in the achievements and motivations of human beings, just about any other London museum will provide greater insight.

Food and drink: Phoenix Palace (3–5 Glentworth Street, 020-7486 3515) has reliable Cantonese food, Sir Terence Conran's Orrery (55 Marylebone High Street, 020-7616 8000) has excellent modern European food; expensive.

Woven textiles by Walsh & McCrea, circa 1955.

Museum of Domestic Design & Architecture

Decorative arts for the home

Map reference: page 23, F1
Middlesex University, Cat Hill, Barnet, Hertfordshire.
Tel: 020-8411 5244. www.moda@mdx.ac.uk
Tube: Oakwood or Cockfosters, then a 15-minute walk. From Oakwood, there is a shuttle bus from outside the station straight to MODA. Rail station: New Barnet, then 307 bus to Cat Hill roundabout. Bus: numbers 298, 299 or 307 to Cat Hill roundabout.
By car: from the M25 take exit 24, signposted A111 Cockfosters, drive for 3 miles (5 km) to Cat Hill roundabout. Limited campus parking.
Open: Tues–Sat 10am–5pm, Sun 2–5pm.
Closed: Mon, Easter, Christmas, New Year.

The museum moved in 2000 to a new, glass-and-metal-fronted, lottery-funded building on the Cat Hill Campus of the University of Middlesex. Two exhibitions are on show at any one time – one permanent, one not – and research facilities are available.

There are six collections: that of the Silver Studio, donated when the Silver Studio, a pattern-design practice, closed in 1963 after an influential hundred-year history; the Domestic Design Collection; the Crown Wallpaper Collection, with around 5,000 samples; Sir J. M. Richards Library, donated by one of the 20th century's most noted architectural writers; the Peggy Angus Archive of ceramic and wallpaper designs; and the Charles Hasler Collection of typography and printed ephemera. (Material not currently on display may be viewed by prior appointment.)

The permanent exhibition, *Exploring Interiors: Decoration of the Home 1900–1960*, is located in an airy space on the ground floor and documents how the style of living rooms, dining rooms and kitchens of British homes changed in the six decades after the Victorian age. Displays of wallpapers, fabrics, furnishing catalogues, newspaper and magazine cuttings and photographs are organised chronologically, and there is a separate section on kitchens.

The late-Victorian, Arts and Crafts, Art Nouveau, Art Deco and 1950s styles are well represented. Fact-fans (and those with a tendency to reminisce) will love such snippets of information as how much a home-owner had to earn in the late 1950s in order to afford an average three-bedroom house (£15 a week for a £2,000 residence).

Changing exhibitions, each lasting around four months, take place on the first floor in a similarly lofty space. Previous exhibitions include The Silver Studio Then & Now, featuring original artworks, working records and wallpaper and textile samples from the museum's key archive.

MODA runs an impressive range of workshops and talks, including practical days for children, and a small shop. The only drawback for visitors to London is its suburban location.

Food and drink: There's an inexpensive cafe on the university campus but otherwise there are no obvious recommendable eateries in the neighbourhood.

Museum of Garden History

In a medieval church setting: how popular plants found their way to Britain

Map reference: page 20, D6
St Mary-at-Lambeth, Lambeth Palace Road,
London SE1. Tel: 020-7401 8865.
www.museumgardenhistory.org
Tube: Waterloo, Westminster.
Bus: 507 from Waterloo or Victoria.
Sun–Fri 10.30am–5pm (closed mid-Dec to Feb).
Admission free.

Across the Thames from the Houses of Parliament, at the south end of Lambeth Bridge, the world's first museum dedicated to the history of gardens is an oasis amid heavily trafficked roads. Located in the beautifully restored church of St Mary-at-Lambeth, next to Lambeth Palace, its appeal is not confined to avid gardeners. Amid stained glass and classical music, thoughtfully ordered exhibits are interesting and accessible.

Thematic exhibits include Children and Gardening, Elements of Design, Carter's Tested Seeds, and an impressive selection of Historic Garden Tools, including watering cans and sprayers. Information panels discuss the impact of the medieval church and Islam on the evolution of gardens. Additional displays explore the difficulties faced by adventurous plant hunters transporting new species of flowers, shrubs and trees from Africa, Europe, Russia and North America, to Great Britain in an age where it could take up to three months to cross the Atlantic.

After enjoying the museum's indoor delights, you can wander out into the walled churchyard and into the Tradescant Garden. A replica of a 17th-century Knot Garden, it is designed using geometric shapes based on squares and whole or part circles, and is home to plants from that period. The garden is dedicated to the celebrated 17th-century gardeners and plant hunters John Tradescant (1570–1638) and his son John (1608–62), both of whom are buried here. A gently bubbling garden fountain adds to the hypnotic tranquillity of this magical setting, and the sight and scent of its old-fashioned roses and herbaceous perennials is intoxicating. St Mary-at-Lambeth's rich history is evident in many of its memorials, including one remembering Captain William Bligh of the *Bounty*, who lived locally.

In addition to a vast array of books about gardens and gardening, the museum shop's offerings include hand-made floral based soaps, pretty china, seeds, candles, and cards. A variety of potted plants may also be purchased from Tradescant Garden.

Food and drink: The museum's very reasonably priced café offers sandwiches, soup, excellent cappuccino, and a tempting selection of home-made cakes and pastries.

National Museum of Childhood

How children have lived and played

Map reference: page 23, G2
Bethnal Green, Cambridge Heath Road, E2.
Tel: 020-8980 2415.
www.museumofchildhood.org.uk
Tube: Bethnal Green (Central Line), rail: Cambridge Heath or Bethnal Green; buses: 26, 48, 55.
Sat–Thur 10am–5.50pm, closed Fri.
Free admission. Wheelchair access.

Bethnal Green may seem an unlikely setting for this imposing outpost of the Victoria and Albert Museum. Why here, in the heart of London's East End? In fact, the iron frame and glass roof structure, reminiscent of Victorian market or station architecture, was originally one of a number of temporary structures built for the South Kensington Museum (as the V&A was originally called) in Brompton. It was transplanted here in 1868, initially with the intention that it should be run as a local museum devoted to local industries. However, for many years it was an overspill for the V&A's main collection, including an increasing number of items relating to children. Eventually, in 1974, it became a museum dedicated to childhood.

The downstairs galleries display classic children's toys, such as dolls' houses, train sets, toy soldiers,

Vintage seed box from the Museum of Garden History.

A plastic Magic Man from 1991.

humming tops and pedal cars. On the upper level are optical toys, soft toys, toy theatres, magic sets, board games, and more.

The upstairs gallery also presents a history of childcare and child development through the ages. Displays range from childbirth in the 17th century to adolescent rebellion in the 1960s and '70s. They plot the evolution of nappies and children's underwear (exhibits include the monogrammed underpants worn by a podgy Prince Albert Edward, "Bertie", the future Edward VII), and an extensive section covers children's formal costume, beginning with an exquisite 17th-century christening gown.

The museum is also a mine of sobering facts and statistics: a display on children's health reveals that, in the 18th century, 70 percent of infants died before the age of two. You can find examples of the game Aunt Sally, a crude wooden head on a pole that children would try to topple with stones.

The airy layout and stream of delightful diversions encourage visitors to wander at leisure, experiencing the kind of serendipity associated with childhood. There is also plenty that will appeal to children themselves. A magnificent rocking horse can be ridden; the model railways can be activated; a dressing-up box can be rifled through; an activity corner encourages learning through play. In the basement, a modern "soft centre" (admission charge) allows young children to tumble about without hurting themselves in a fun and colourful version of a padded cell.

Food and drink: The museum has a self-service café offering drinks, sandwiches, cakes and children's lunch boxes. A few minutes' walk away at 242 Globe Road is Wild Cherry (020-8980 6678), one of London's top vegetarian restaurants. It has an imaginative menu, a modern interior and a pretty patio garden. Closed Sat and Sun.

Ragged School Museum

Life as it used to be for London's East Enders

Children from London's Seven Dials district washing before class, 1885.

Map reference: page 23, G2
46–50 Copperfield Road, E3. Tel: 020-8980 6405.
www.raggedschoolmuseum.org.uk
Tube: Mile End.
Wed & Thurs 10am–5pm; first Sunday of the

month 2–5pm; some other Sundays.
Admission free, donations are appreciated.
Wheelchair access: available only on ground floor.
Children: schools events include a Victorian classroom re-enactment and, during school holidays, adults and children can join in with the workshops, treasure hunts and story-telling.

Overlooking the Regent's Canal, three converted Victorian warehouses exist almost exactly as Dr Thomas Barnardo conceived them in 1896. The aim of the Ragged Schools Union, set up in 1844, was to provide free schooling for children of the poor. Besides education, the youngsters received food, clothing and shelter. Part of the aim was to reduce juvenile crime.

The Copperfield Ragged School is reconstructed to provide insights into how poor children lived and learned. The museum's many photographs have been donated by local families, and portray the sense of community in the areas of Limehouse, Wapping, Bow, Bromley and the Isle of Dogs.

The Victorian classroom is designed as it was by Barnardo – in cream and maroon – and is kitted out with slates, chalkboards, wooden desks and an abacus. The "History of the East End" exhibition has displays ranging from a 19th-century shoe-mending kit to a 21st-century place setting, taken from a trendy new Bethnal Green restaurant. It's diverse but the clear theme remains the solidarity shown by working-class East Enders during hard times such as World War II bombing.

Above the classroom is a reconstructed 1900s kitchen, complete with fire range and tin bath for Monday's clothes wash and Friday's bath-time.

Food and drink: The Towpath Café is situated in the basement and sells drinks and snacks.

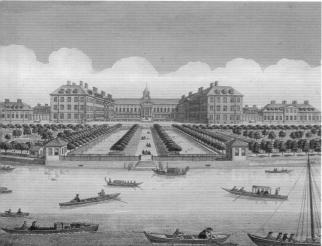

that Wellington lay in state. Decorated with regimental colours, the adjoining Chapel features *Christ Rising from the Tomb*, a fresco by Sebastiano Ricci.

A huge painting of the Battle of Waterloo by George Jones hangs in the entrance to a small museum. It overlooks a 1:300 scale model that, with an audio presentation, illustrates the hospital and its massive grounds in the 18th century.

Display boards relate the institution's history. A mock-up of a residential room, now enlarged to 9 ft (2.7 metres) square from the original 6 ft (1.8 metres) square, reveals how a resident's room might look today. Other displays include Pensioner uniforms, medals and memorabilia.

The extensive gardens, used in spring for the popular Chelsea Flower Show, provide a haven of quiet in busy central London. Tours (to be arranged in advance) are led by chirpy In-Pensioners, and you can chat with residents.

Thomas Bowles's A View of the Royal Hospital and the Rotunda in Ranelagh Gardens, 1751.

Food and drink: *There's no public cafeteria, but visitors can use the café of the nearby National Army Museum.*

Royal Hospital, Chelsea

A home for British war veterans

Map reference: page 40, D3
Royal Hospital Road, Chelsea, SW3 4SR. Tel: 020-7881 5246; www.chelseapensioner.org.uk. Tube: Sloane Square. Buses: 11, 19, 22, 211, 239 Apr–Sept, 10am–noon and 2–4pm, can be closed at short notice; gardens open 10am–12.45pm and 2–4.30pm (later in mid-summer), access restricted before and during Chelsea Flower Show. Admission free. Wheelchair access to all parts.

The historic Royal Hospital, set in beautifully tended grounds on the Chelsea Embankment, is a residential home for some 400 old soldiers, the Chelsea Pensioners. Splendid in their scarlet coats and ceremonial tricorn hats, the Pensioners, all men, are a familiar sight whenever British war veterans are on parade. The In-Pensioners (permanent residents) waive their army pension in return for board, lodging, leisure amenities, clothing and medical care.

Charles II founded the hospital in 1682 as a refuge for British war veterans. James II had architect Sir Christopher Wren enlarge the plans and the hospital finally came into use in 1692. The main buildings, two residential wings linked by the Great Hall and Chapel, were designed in English baroque style. The wood-panelled Great Hall, the dining room, features a vast mural with Charles II on horseback, painted by Verrio. It was in this hall in 1852

The Women's Library

Charting the fight for female equality

Map reference: page 21, J3
Old Castle Street, E1. Tel: 020-7320 2222.
www.thewomenslibrary.ac.uk
Tube: Aldgate East.
Exhibition hall 9.30am–5pm Mon–Fri (until 8pm Thurs), 10am–4pm Sat. Exhibitions free; small deposit needed for Reading Room pass.

A varied collection of suffragette memorabilia and banners, plus magazines, books and badges produced over the years by the women's movement, was rescued from storage in a damp university basement in 2002 and put on show in this converted Victorian bathhouse in Whitechapel, East London.

The archive is comprehensive enough to be an important academic resource, but colourful banners, cartoons and campaigning materials from teacups to card games enliven the exhibition area.

Britannia as a sufragette on a 1911 poster.

Food and drink: *The library's Wash Houses Café serves hot lunches, plus pastries, cakes, coffee and tea all day.*

London has always been a crossroads. English immortals such as Dickens, Keats and Dr Johnson lived here, but so did such celebrated visitors and émigrés as Freud, Handel and Marx. These museums commemorate their lives

Apsley House: Wellington Museum

The residence of the Dukes of Wellington

Map reference: page 20, A5
Hyde Park Corner, W1. Tel: 020-7499 5676.
Tube: Hyde Park Corner.
Tues–Sun 11am–5pm (last admission 4.30pm).
Closed Mon except Bank Holidays, plus Good
Friday, May Day Bank Holiday, 24–26 Dec, New
Year's Day. Limited wheelchair access; sound-
guides for the visually impaired. Admission fee.

It's been said that if a letter were mailed from any-where in the world to "No. 1, London" it would arrive at Apsley House, the first house past the tollgate into the capital from the west. Its fame was also due to its celebrated resident, Arthur Wellesley, the first Duke of Wellington. Wellesley moved into this Robert Adam-designed house at the height of his popularity in 1817, after a dazzling military career in India, Spain and Portugal, which culmi-nated in his victory over Napoleon Bonaparte in the Battle of Waterloo in 1815. In keeping with his sta-tus, the Duke employed Benjamin Dean Wyatt to enlarge and "modernise" Adam's design, principally by adding the spectacular 90-ft (27-metre) long Waterloo Gallery, based on Versailles.

The gallery was the site of the annual banquet given by the Duke for the officers who served him at Waterloo, entertaining them lavishly around a table which held 1,000 pieces of silver. Among the museum's 4,000 objects are table ornaments, gold and silver daggers, and elaborate candelabra.

Equally splendid is the Duke's collection of paint-ings – many from the Spanish Royal Collection. As well as paintings by Rubens, Bruegel, Van Dyck and an equestrian portrait of Wellesley himself by Fran-cisco de Goya (said to have been disliked by the Duke), the gallery features the saucy *The Conjurer* by Caravaggio, and the evocative *The Waterseller of Seville* by Diego Velazquez. Most of the public rooms offer exquisite views of Hyde Park and a clas-sical, masculine interior, Wyatt having replaced Adam's sensual green design with the more formal gold-and-white.

The Duke's correctness was, naturally, inspired by the military: the satin and silk tabaret (wallpaper) in the Striped Drawing Room is said to echo Napoleon's tent room at Malmaison. Such formality is diluted by listening to the hand-held audioguide that takes visitors not only through the house but also allows them to zoom in on specific exhibits or hear more detail by entering sequences of numbers. Some of these audio details are charming – for instance, the present Duke of Wellington reminisc-ing about sliding down the banisters of the Grand Staircase as a boy. These occasional glimpses of a personal life help make Apsley seem more like a home, augmented by glimpses of swings and a see-saw through the windows, proof that the present Duke and his family actually live in the place.

ABOVE: Meissen plate showing Apsley House in about 1818.

A curious aspect of Apsley House is the recurring theme, faithfully reproduced by the curators – the Victoria and Albert Museum – of the Duke of Wellington's arch enemy, Napoleon. Exhibits of the French emperor are everywhere: a plaster cast of his death mask in the Basement Gallery; the fantastic Sèvres Egyptian dinner service presented by Napol-eon to the Empress Josephine; and, most strangely, an 11-ft (3-metre) neo-classical sculpture of Napoleon by the great sculptor Canova. Based on a statue of a Hellenistic athlete, the Duke's adversary looks posi-tively heroic, and dwarfs nearly everything else in his conqueror's home.

Food and drink*: Directly across Park Lane on Hyde Park Corner is the Intercontinental Hotel (020-7409 3131). The Coffee House serves lunch and snacks, while the lobby with views of the park is open to the public and serves light snacks and sandwiches. The original Hard Rock Cafe (7 Old Park Lane, 020-7629 0382) is still going strong.*

Carlyle's House

A writer's home from the 19th century

Map reference: page 40, C4
24 Cheyne Row, SW3. Tel: 020-7352 7087.
Tube: Sloane Square.
Wed–Sun Apr–Oct 11am–5pm.
Entry fee. Free to National Trust members.
No wheelchair access. Museum is on four floors
and there are no lifts.

It was fortunate, one wag remarked, that Thomas and Jane Carlyle married each other, or there would have been four miserable people in the world instead of two. Yet the house to which the dour Scottish essayist and his wife moved in 1834 attracted a coterie of writers and intellectuals, including Charles Dickens, John Ruskin and Alfred, Lord Tennyson.

Carlyle's writings, influenced by his Calvinist background and the works of Goethe, attacked unfettered capitalism, excessive democracy and black people in general. They are, unsurprisingly, not popular today, though they were influential at the time.

The appeal of this narrow house in now fashionable Chelsea is that it has been preserved pretty much as it looked at Carlyle's death in 1881. The ground-floor parlour has its piano (on which Chopin once played), the kitchen has a dresser with a shelf that served as the maid's bed, the first-floor library contains Carlyle's books, and the attic study, lit by a skylight, is where he set down his thoughts on such subjects as Chartism, the French Revolution, and the Negro Question. There's a strong sense of how lives were lived in the house. The paintings, including a portrait of the Carlyles, are interesting, and a restored walled Victorian garden can be visited.

Dickens House Museum

The world's foremost repository of Dickens documentation and memorabilia

Map reference: page 20, E2
48 Doughty Street, WC1. Tel: 020-7405 2127.
www.dickensmuseum.com
Tube: Russell Square, Chancery Lane.
Mon–Sat 10am–5pm. Admission charge.
No wheelchair access. Museum is on four floors
and there are no lifts.

This house, where Charles Dickens and his family lived between 1837 and 1839, was opened in 1925 as a small museum dedicated to the author's life and work.

The exhibits are a collection of letters, furniture and possessions from various stages in Dickens's life, including some from his father's stretch in Marshalsea prison. The walls are adorned with numerous portraits of the author and his eccentric whiskers, as well as many delightful illustrations of his stories. The basement houses a huge collection of Dickens's books, and visitors can watch a video describing both his professional successes and his

LEFT: characters from *Oliver Twist*, a display in Dickens House Museum.
BELOW: stained-glass window by J. Winbolt portraying the elderly Dickens.

troubled personal life, including his strained relations with his wife and children.

The displays on the upper floors illustrate his other great passion, the theatre, where he demonstrated considerable flair as producer, director and actor. The posters, pictures and other memorabilia here give an insight into his life outside his novels and fill out the character of the man, an admired celebrity during his lifetime.

The museum has extensive library and research facilities comprising books, photographs and literary manuscripts; telephone or email for an appointment.

The surrounding streets are lined with fine town houses that evoke the affluence of a smart quarter of Victorian London, even though the area is quiet and dusty now. However, it is difficult to imagine Dickens living in this house because of the rather institutional decor and the arrangement of the furniture. There's not much to amuse children in this quiet place, where the displays are definitely not to be touched. The museum is located in something of a tourist desert between Bloomsbury and Clerkenwell and will appeal mainly to enthusiasts.

Food and drink: There are no bars or cafés in the immediate vicinity, the nearest being along High Holborn.

Dr Johnson's House

The City's oldest remaining residence

Map reference: page 21, F3
17 Gough Square, EC4. Tel: 020-7353 3745.
www.drjh.dircon.co.uk
Tube: Blackfriars, Chancery Lane.
Mon–Sat 11am–5.30pm (till 5pm Oct–Apr).
Entrance fee.
No disabled access; there are several flights of stairs and no lifts.

Tucked away in a maze of winding alleyways off Fleet Street, this was the home of Samuel Johnson (1709–84) from 1748 to 1759, during which time he wrote the first comprehensive dictionary of the English language. The museum evokes this larger-than-life character and his famous wit, his work and his personal life.

In 1911 the house was saved from dereliction by the publisher Cecil Harmsworth, whose family still administers the house, and whose mission in keeping it open is that "the house should never be regarded as a museum or as an emporium of irrelevant 19th-

Dr Samuel Johnson as portrayed in a window of his former home.

century bric-a-brac." A refurbishment in 2001 reinstated authentic colour schemes – chocolate brown woodwork was fashionable in Johnson's day. Most of the furniture is of the period rather than from the house itself. The walls are lined with portraits by Joshua Reynolds, a great friend of Johnson's.

A video takes you through Johnson's life and work. He came from fairly humble beginnings – his father was a tradesman and sheriff of Lichfield – and failed to complete his degree at Oxford University through lack of funds. Yet he rose to become one of London's elite circle of intellectuals; friends included Edmund Burke and Oliver Goldsmith.

The top floor of the house is the Dictionary Garret, whose roof was blown off during the wartime blitz in January 1942. Here, Johnson almost single-handedly carried out the research for his dictionary of 40,000 words. Ruefully, he defined the word "lexicographer" as a "a harmless drudge". Six clerks at a series of long tables copied out his instructions.

A copy of the two volumes can be leafed through on the ground floor. While some words have changed subtly in meaning over the centuries (for example, nice = superfluously accurate; delicate; refined), many of his pithy definitions still fit the bill (for example, fop = a man of little understanding and much ostentation).

Food and drink: Nearby Fleet Street has lots of pubs and restaurants. At No. 15 is Ye Olde Cheshire Cheese, one of Johnson's haunts. Rebuilt after the Great Fire, it still has a medieval crypt beneath it. Inexpensive but can get packed with tourists.

The ultimate psychiatrist's couch.

Freud Museum

The London home of Sigmund Freud

Map reference: page 22, E1
20 Maresfield Gardens, NW3. Tel: 020-7435
2002. www.freud.org.uk
Tube: Finchley Road. Buses: 13, 82, 113.
Open: Wed–Sun, noon–5pm. Admission charge.
Wheelchair access: limited.
Library/Research: Freud's personal library and
an on-site reference library may be consulted by
serious researchers, by prior appointment.
Shop has books and inventive souvenirs.

In March 1938, Austria fell under the yoke of Nazi Germany. Three months later, and long after most of the predominantly Jewish psychoanalytic community had already fled, Sigmund Freud left his home of 47 years in Vienna and moved with his family to London. For the following year, until his death from cancer in September 1939, the father of psychoanalysis lived and worked in a red-brick house in leafy Hampstead, now home to the Freud Museum.

In the move from Vienna, Freud managed to retain a great number of his personal belongings and, once established in London, re-created his old working environment. His study on the ground floor still contains the original famous couch on which his Viennese patients would recline to tell him their dreams and free-associate. Beside it is the green velvet chair in which Freud would sit and take notes.

Decorated with oriental rugs, the room also displays his prized collection of antiquities, including framed Roman frescoes, Greek vases and Egyptian figurines. The bookshelves lining the walls are filled with the leather-bound volumes he was able to bring with him – behind the desk you may be able to see works by Flaubert, Shakespeare and Goethe.

The dining room next door contains exquisitely painted Austrian peasant furniture and photographs of Freud's apartment in Vienna. On the upstairs landing are two portraits of the great man, one by Salvador Dalí, who was introduced to Freud in London. Also upstairs is a room devoted to temporary exhibitions and a room celebrating the life and work of Freud's daughter Anna.

Anna Freud, also a psychoanalyst, never married and lived in the house until her own death in 1982. A bookcase in her room displays family photographs and copies of her publications – she specialised in the psychology and analysis of children. Also here is her own consulting couch, the chair in which she sat and knitted while listening to patients.

To preserve the authenticity of the house, many of the exhibits are given little in the way of explanation. Freud enthusiasts won't mind, but the general visitor may find this a bit frustrating.

Food and drink*: NW3 Café (inside Habitat, 191–217 Finchley Road) has sandwiches, coffee and some hot dishes. Yo! Sushi (O2 Centre, 255 Finchley Road) provides conveyor-belt sushi in modern surroundings; cheap.*

Handel House Museum

Hallelujah! Unto us a museum is born

Map reference: page 20, A3
25 Brook Street, W1 (entrance at rear, in Lancashire Court). Tel: 020-7495 1685.
www.handelhouse.org
Tube: Bond Street or Oxford Circus.
Tues, Wed, Fri, Sat 10am–6pm, Thurs 10am–8pm, Sun & Bank holidays noon–6pm.
Entrance fee. Access for disabled.

On the odd occasions when volunteer musicians are available, live music played on two newly built harpsichords sets the best mood for this immersion in George Frideric Handel. In 1723 he became the first occupant of a terrace house at 25 Brook Street, the upper floors of which have been refurbished to simulate his home, using an inventory of his possessions taken after his death here in 1759. New furnishings are being added as funds permit. The upper floors of the adjoining No. 23 accommodate information panels and temporary exhibitions.

Handel wrote many of his great works, including *Israel in Egypt* and his *Messiah*, in Brook Street. Having made his mark with several opera companies in London, he became interested in church music and attended the newly built St George's in nearby Hanover Square, where his works are now performed in conjunction with the museum.

He owned more than 60 paintings, including two Rembrandts, and the re-creation of his rooms features fine art focusing on musicians and singers who performed his works and on events for which he composed music, such as the Royal Fireworks. Items on display in the adjacent building include a letter he wrote about the *Messiah*, Mozart's handwritten arrangement of a Handel fugue, and early editions of his operas and oratorios. It's a museum for enthusiasts rather than generalists.

Hogarth's House

Homage to the father of political cartoons

Map reference: page 22, C3
Hogarth Lane, Great West Road, W4.
Tel: 0208-994-6757.
Tues–Sun Feb–Oct 1–6pm, plus bank holidays.
Closed Mon. Call for winter hours.
Tube : Turnham Green, plus 40-minute walk.
Rail: Chiswick (from Waterloo), plus 15-minute walk. Bus: E3, 190, 290.
Cars: A4, car park for Chiswick House.
Free admission.

William Hogarth, painter and engraver, was a serious man who loathed injustice. He highlighted his concerns about contemporary society in a series of witty, anecdotal engravings that became best sellers, most famously in *The Rake's Progress* (1733–34) and *Marriage à la Mode* (1743). Perhaps because of his popularity, his standing as a painter has often been undervalued.

Hogarth moved with his family to this three-storey house from busy Leicester Fields (now Leicester Square) in 1749. In a monstrous bit of irony that would not be lost on the satirist, this "little country box by the Thames" now lies by the A4 to Heathrow, its owner immortalised in the thundering Hogarth roundabout. The traffic noise is muted inside the house, though, and a small garden in the back (no chairs) attempts a pastoral charm.

Against the splendour of neighbouring Chiswick House, Hogarth's House is modest and homey, the residence of an artist rather than an aristocrat. But for anyone even remotely curious about painting, stories, engravings or the 18th century, the museum is surprisingly interesting. It's also free.

The collection of beautifully executed engravings (in an otherwise empty house) is extensive. In the dining room is *Hogarth's London: The Four Times of Day – Covent Garden in winter; Soho in spring; Sadlers Wells in summer; Charing Cross in autumn*, as well as drawings depicting the plight of women and blacks. The upstairs parlour, with its attractive Venetian window, contains *The Rake's Progress*. Particularly intriguing are Plates 1 and 2, with two versions of each. Hogarth was constantly refining his work, adding ever more pessimistic details to otherwise humorous drawings, trying to convey to an indifferent public the cruelties he observed around him.

Hogarth is buried in the grounds of Chiswick

LEFT: a bed in Handel House Museum.

Hogarth Painting the Comic Muse – a self-portrait.

Sensuous detail from Hogarth's *Marriage à la Mode.*

church near the Thames, but visiting the grave means crossing the roundabout on foot. From the roundabout, Hogarth's House is signposted, implying that it lies behind the gates of Chiswick House. This is misleading: a more direct route is to head for the larger house's car park, then walk on the pavement parallel to the A4 in the direction of London.

Food and drink: There is no café on the premises. For restaurants, see entry on page 106 for Chiswick House.

Keats House

Where the romantic poet fell in love

Map reference: page 22, E1
Keats Grove, Hampstead, NW3. Tel: 020-7435 2062; www.keatshouse.gov.uk
Tube: Hampstead or Belsize Park. Rail: Hampstead Heath. Buses: 24, 46, 168, C11, C12
1 May–31 Oct, Tues–Sat 10am–noon schools and pre-booked group visits only; Tues–Sun and Bank Holidays noon–5pm open to all. Tours Sat and Sun at 3pm, no booking needed. On Tues–Sat group visits can be arranged, bookable in advance. Admission fee. Tickets valid for unlimited visits for 12 months.

While living from 1818 to 1820 with his friend Charles Brown, the poet John Keats (1795–1821) produced some of his best poetry, including *Ode to a Nightingale*, written sitting under a plum tree in the garden. A new plum tree has been planted to mark the spot. It was also here that he met and fell in love with Fanny Brawne, daughter of his next-door neighbour. They became engaged, but Keats was suffering from tuberculosis, and in the winter of 1820–21 he was advised by his physician to leave England for the warmer climate of Italy. Keats never returned, dying in Rome in 1821 at the age of 25.

When Keats lived here, the house consisted of two semi-detatched dwellings – later converted into one home. Despite the extensive modifications it's still possible to visualise the house as Keats knew it; the knocker on the front door is original, as are most of the fire-grates, shutters and reeded surrounds. The interior, decorated in Regency style, retains much of its original character. The artefacts displayed bring Keats and Fanny Brawne to life. There are locks of the poet's hair, original paintings, facsimiles of his letters and Fanny's engagement ring.

The location, across the road from Hampstead Heath, is a tranquil spot, removed from London's bustle. A visit can be combined with a walk on the

heath and a visit to the village. Keats House is also the venue for frequent literary events, particularly poetry readings, workshops and literary walks.

Food and drink: Polly's Tea Rooms, 55 South End Road (020-7794 8144), round the corner from Keats House, is a friendly café, with table service; cheap. The Magdala, 2A South Hill Park (020-7435 2503) a pleasant gastro-pub, is famous for being the place where Ruth Ellis, the last person to be hanged in Britain, shot her lover.

Marx Memorial Library

An independent subscription library with extensive special collections

Map reference: page 21, F2
37A Clerkenwell Green, EC1. Tel: 020-7253 1485.
www.marxmemoriallibrary.sageweb.co.uk
Tube: Farringdon (also Thameslink rail) or buses 55, 63, 243 and 259.
Mon 1-6pm, Tues–Thurs 1-8pm, Sat 10am–1pm. By appointment only in August. No wheelchair access. Admission free. Membership £8.

For researching the politics of working-class movements, the library's extensive collection of political history, fiction, philosophy and biographies is invaluable. Its agenda is clear from the shelf labels. One shelf begins: "Who built Thebes of the seven gates?" The one below answers: "In the books you'll find the names of kings." And the conclusion a shelf lower: "Did the kings haul up the lumps of rock?"

The agenda continues through the library's special collections. The International Brigades Association's archive contains primary source material on the Spanish anti-fascist war from 1936–39 and attracts scholars from all over the world. The Klugmann Collection documents early radical and Chartist publications. The John Williamson American Labour Movement Collection contains relevant journals and pamphlets from the 1920s to the 1970s. Also held are the J.D. Bernal Peace Collection and a set of the *Daily Worker* (later the *Morning Star*).

John Keats, the romantic poet's romantic poet.

The mural painted in 1935 by Viscount Hastings on a wall in the Marx Memorial Library.

Many come to see Lenin's Room, where the Soviet leader worked to produce the revolutionary newspaper *Izkra (Spark)*. His desk is on display, along with preserved copies of the vital paper he oversaw in London, then had smuggled into Russia and sold underground. The building itself, built in 1737, has long been a centre for many radical movements.

Monthly lectures cover topics such as communist history and feminism. Marx would have approved of such events, but might be less tolerant of the Lenin paperweights, memorial mousepads printed with his face, key chains commercialising 20th-century political placards and the "Revolutionary Take-Away Bags", all on sale in the library.

Food and drink: Any genuine socialist would choose Scotti's Snack Bar (next door to the library) over the trendier places nearby; cheap and cheerful. La Rochetta, on Clerkenwell Green, is a small, good-value Italian restaurant.

Sherlock Holmes Museum

Clues to the fiction's greatest sleuth

Map reference: page 22, E2
221B Baker Street, NW1. Tel: 020-7935 8866.
www.sherlock-holmes.co.uk
Tube: Baker Street.
Daily 9.30am–6.30pm. Entry fee.
Not wheelchair accessible; suitable for children.

The sitting-room of the Sherlock Holmes Museum, and a sketch of the sleuth himself.

Appropriately enough, given that Holmes and his sidekick Dr Watson are fictional characters, the exhibits here don't always make it clear what is real and what isn't. The Victorian policeman or maid at the door will check your ticket, before you pass up the narrow staircase and into an imaginative evocation of the detective's apartment. The more you know about Holmes, the more you can get out of the detailed exhibits, which, right down to the book titles, are all relevant to the stories. Though they may not belong to a "real" Sherlock Holmes, they are all genuine Victorian antiques and refreshingly free of glass cases and "do not touch" signs.

In the bedroom, atmospherically candle-lit, is a make-up case for Holmes's elaborate disguises and, in a corner, the famous violin. On the wall are photographs of notorious (real) Victorian criminals, such as Dr Crippen, who murdered his wife, and Lizzie Borden, who killed her parents with an axe.

A "maid" is on hand in the study to answer questions. She is also willing to take pictures of anyone who wants to sit in the chair with the trademark deerstalker hat and calabash pipe (neither of which feature in the original stories). Also in the study is a chemical kit, a Victorian device for carbonating water and syringes for Holmes's cocaine habit.

The other two floors are full of manikins representing scenes from various stories, one of which moves. The arch villain, Moriarty, also used to turn his head, but was too lifelike, causing piercing screams to echo down the stairwell. Some exhibits explain the stories and artefacts in more detail, but there is no information on Holmes's creator, Sir Arthur Conan Doyle (1868–1952) – a fascinating Scot whose fascination with crime helped him solve real-life mysteries as well as fictional ones. He also wrote well-regarded historical romances and science fiction, and believed in spiritualism and fairies.

As for the building itself, records show that it was a lodging house from 1860 until 1934, that some

maids who worked there were related to a Mr Holmes, and that an artificial teeth maker called Dr Watson lived next door in the 1890s.

Food and drink: Just to the left of the museum is the Volunteer Pub, with French windows open to the road, a wooden interior, slot machines and pub grub. Across the road are two modern cafés, Bar Linda and Croque Monsieur. A few minutes away, the Rasa Singapura (Regent's Park Hotel, 154 Gloucester Place, 020-7723 6740) is a reliable Chinese restaurant.

Wesley's House, Wesley's Chapel and the Museum of Methodism

Documents the history of Methodism and the life of its founder, John Wesley.

Map reference: page 21, H1
49 City Road, EC1. Tel: 020-7253 2262.
Tube/rail station: Old Street; bus routes: 43, 76, 141, 271.
Mon–Sat 10am–4pm, Sun noon–2pm.
Entry fee to the museum and house.
Research facilities available.

An 18th-century lithograph of John Wesley visiting his mother's grave.

Overlooking Bunhill Cemetery on City Road, Wesley's Chapel and John Wesley's House form the headquarters of World Methodism. As well as attracting Methodists from far and wide, who come to see where John Wesley lived and died, the complex presents the history of a religious movement that sowed the seeds of social reform in Britain.

Wesley founded Methodism in 1739. Disillusioned by the corruption and complacency he found in the Anglican Church, he sought to restore the original doctrines of Christ and return to fundamentals – "the love of God and of all mankind". In line with this, he sought to raise the nation's social conscience, and Methodism was soon associated with radicalism. To this day, it is frequently noted that the British Labour Party owes more to Methodism than it does to Marx (an observation first attributed to the Labour Party MP Morgan Phillips).

A tour of John Wesley's House is made considerably more interesting by the audio commentary (45 minutes), told from the point of view of Wesley's devoted housekeeper, Elizabeth Ritchie. It builds a vivid portrait of Wesley, a man who rose at 4am every morning, who valued use more than ornament, was an enemy of waste, display and luxury, and enjoyed simple food and regular exercise. During the summer months, he would take to the open road to preach, covering 5,000 miles (8,000 km) by carriage or on foot. In winter, he stayed at home, where he made up for the sedentary lifestyle this imposed by bouncing around on a "chamber horse", considered a beneficial form of exercise at the time. Yet, in spite of his great sense, Wesley made a bad marriage that ended in separation.

The house contains many of Wesley's personal possessions, including his travelling gown, tricorn hat and travelling case. In the upstairs drawing room is an electric shock machine, for use in shock therapy, an exciting new cure-all which interested him.

Wesley died in 1791, aged 88. His first-floor bedroom is presumed to be the scene of his death, but more significant to many of the pilgrims who come here today is his personal prayer room, dubbed the "powerhouse of Methodism", just off the bedroom.

After touring the house, it is worth visiting the Wesley Chapel (completed in 1778), considered by Wesley to be "perfectly neat but not fine". It contains many monuments to influential Methodists; Wesley's tomb can be found in the garden behind.

Food and drink: The complex has no catering facilities, but opposite it, on City Road, is Flowercity.co.uk, a flower-cum-coffee shop selling light snacks and drinks.

The Arts

Shakespeare may have been born and died in Stratford-upon-Avon, but he staged his plays in London. The city has long been a stronghold of the arts, especially theatre and music, and these museums celebrate that heritage

Design Museum

Where good looks survive mass production

Map reference: page 23, G3
28 Shad Thames, SE1. Tel: 020-7940 8790.
www.designmuseum.org
Tube: Tower Bridge, London Bridge, Bermondsey.
Open: Mon–Fri 11.30am–6pm, Sat–Sun
10.30am–6pm. Admission fee.
Wheelchair access.

Many old warehouses in the Butlers Wharf area have been converted into luxurious apartments, occupied by wealthy and design-conscious people. It's appropriate, therefore, that the gleaming white Design Museum is located at the eastern end of Shad Thames.

Originally a 1950s warehouse, the Design Museum was converted in the modern style by the architects Conran Roche and first opened its doors in 1989. The museum's founder, Sir Terence Conran, whose successful Habitat and Conran home-furnishing shops and series of fashionable restaurants can be found throughout London, originally set up the Boilerhouse design project in the Victoria and Albert Museum; when the V&A declined to make it permanent, a gravely displeased Conran turned his attention to Butlers Wharf. Although he intended to restore the old warehouse, in the end it proved less expensive to strip much of the existing structure down to its steel skeleton and rebuild it.

The Design Museum, whose elegant, layered front commands wonderful views of the River Thames and Tower Bridge, is Europe's first museum dedicated to the exploration and study of modern design for mass production. How an object looks, who it will be used by, what it is made of, its feel, cost and weight, are all elements of design that are explored in detail through the museum's permanent and temporary exhibits.

Make your way up the wide, white marble stairs past the glass brick walls to the Temporary and Exhibition Galleries on the first floor. This simple, white space acts as a blank canvas for temporary exhibits of intriguing subjects such as Bauhaus – one of the 20th century's most influential design schools – and alternative urban housing.

The oak floors of the Design Museum's Collection and Review Galleries, located on the second floor, are bathed in natural light, with high ceilings and vast windows accentuating the tremendous views. Here, visitors can wander amid a series of thematic product displays; these chronicle the evolution of now commonplace articles such as television sets – including a 1969 white, round TV set which heralded the arrival of the "space-age" – cameras, telephones (e.g. the 1895 Skeleton Telephone), and even plastic packaging. Samples of past, present and future design innovations show that function and aesthetics can go hand in hand.

There's an increasing emphasis on contemporary design, with the top floor being given over to it. Recent temporary exhibits have showcased an Aston Martin V12 Vanquish and Nike trainers and a certain amount of sponsorship seems to have been accepted.

The museum shop offers a selection of books as well as entertaining and unusual gift ideas, from analogue cuff-links to glass teapots. There is a lift for disabled visitors, and the shop, café and all exhibits are accessible by wheelchair.

Food and drink: The museum café offers reasonably priced light lunches and, if you're lucky, a seat overlooking Tower Bridge. As a special treat, there's Terence Conran's adjacent Blue Print Café (020-7378 7031), which has elegant but pricey European and Mediterranean cuisine, plus lovely views.

ABOVE: *The Head* by Eduardo Paolozzi, outside the museum.

LEFT: John Galliano design at a Dior show in the Design Museum.

OPPOSITE PAGE: Ellen Terry as Queen Katharine in *Henry VIII* at Stratford-upon-Avon in 1902, from the Theatre Museum's collection.

ABOVE: Fenton House.

RIGHT: the drawing room.

Fenton House

Historical house in Hampstead with an amazing collection of harpsichords

Map reference: page 22, D1
Windmill Hill, Hampstead NW3 6RT.
Tel: 020-7435 3471. Infoline: 01494-755563.
www.nationaltrust.org.uk/thameschilterns
Tube: Hampstead. Buses: 46 and 268.
Open Mar 3–25, Sat and Sun 2–5pm; 31 Mar–4
Nov, Wed–Fri, 2-5pm, Sat, Sun and Bank
Holiday Mondays 11am–5pm. Booked parties at
other times by arrangement with the custodian.
The noteworthy garden is handicap accessible,
but the house lacks lifts or ramps. Stewards on
each floor provide information during opening
times. Admission charge.

You could do a lot worse than visiting Fenton House in the springtime. William Eades, whose father was a bricklayer by trade, wasted no effort in creating this red-brick estate in 1686. While its exhibits of ceramics and antique musical instruments inside will draw many specialists, Fenton House benefits most from its spectacular garden and wonderful setting in old Hampstead.

The garden was created along with the house at the end of the 17th century. It is the largest private garden in Hampstead and, as was the case then, it is maintained by one very ambitious gardener. Still, somehow, he keeps it perfectly groomed for visitors to come out, relax and partake of the "hill air".

The house's ceramic collection may be small when compared to that of the grand museums in London, but its quality is apparent. The Oriental Room houses many early Chinese ceramics bought by Lady Binning, the proprietor who gave the house to the National Trust in 1952. The ceramics are held in beautiful cabinets and some date from 500 AD and include a guffawing Buddha. The Porcelain Room contains 18th-century continental and English porcelain ranging from aristocratic ladies and dancing dandies to cherubs and jesters.

In the various rooms of the house sit the real prizes of this museum: the working harpsichords donated by Major Benton Fletcher. Throughout the spring, concerts are held in the dining room, as classical musicians re-create the style of parlour parties in the 18th century upon authentic, lovingly restored instruments (telephone for details). If you're lucky, you may even hear music students practising for exams in May, providing a grand soundtrack for a grand old house.

Food and drink: Hampstead High Street and Heath Street, just minutes from Fenton House, have a good collection of pubs and eating places. These include:
The Flask. Tucked away on the small and narrow Flask Walk. Its outdoor seating takes up half of the street it presides upon and this moderate pub does the grub and ales you'd expect.
Moroccan Al Casbah. On the corner of Flask Walk and Hampstead High Street. A spicy addition to the corporate chains on the high street, this restaurant serves moderately priced Moroccan cuisine.

Musical Museum

A large collection of automatic or self-playing musical instruments

Map reference: page 22, B3
368 High Street, Brentford, Middlesex, TW8.
Tel: 020-8560 8108.
www.musicalmuseum.co.uk
Tube: Gunnersbury. Bus: 65, 237, 267.
Sat and Sun 2–5pm Apr–Oct, Wed 2–4pm
Jul–Aug. Tour and demonstrations.
Admission fee. Wheelchair access.

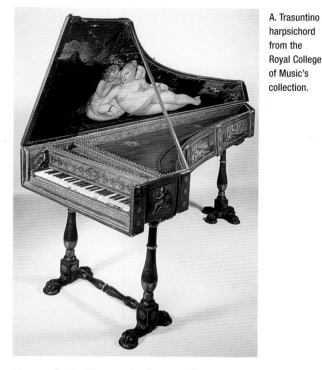

A. Trasuntino harpsichord from the Royal College of Music's collection.

Housed at present in a former church, this museum has a diverse selection of automated instruments (played using devices such as perforated rolls of paper to "programme in" the music). Perhaps the most familiar of these are the player-pianos. Historically important piano rolls of the playing of composers such as Rachmaninov, Gershwin and Debussy still exist, giving useful clues to the interpretation of their piano music. The 20th-century American avant-garde composer Conlon Nancarrow also used piano rolls to compose works with exceptionally complex counterpoint.

There are a number of music boxes (in which the sound is produced by a revolving spiked drum that "plucks" tuned metal prongs), familiar from children's toys. More complex exhibits include the Mills Violano-Virtuoso, a combined automatic violin and piano, and the Phonoliszt Violina that plays three violins simultaneously. The most impressive items are automatic organs, particularly the large Wurlitzer used to entertain cinemagoers in between the films.

The museum will close in late 2002 and re-open in purpose-built building nearby in 2004. Details on the progress of the move can be found on the website.

Royal College of Music Museum of Instruments

More than 600 instruments dating from the 15th century to the present day

Map reference: page 40, B2
Royal College of Music, Prince Consort Road,
SW7. Tel: 020-7589 3643.
www.rcm.ac.uk/places/facilities/museum.html.
Tube: South Kensington. Bus: 9, 10, 52.
Wed 2–4.30pm during term time.
Admission fee.

This museum, located in one of the country's most prestigious conservatories, is devoted largely to the instruments of Western classical music (around 500 items). But there's also a smaller section, of around 100 artefacts, devoted to the instruments from Africa and East and South Asia.

To get to the museum, follow the signs from the college entrance (it's a convoluted route). The ground floor is devoted to Western aerophones (instruments where the sound is produced by the

---

MUSEUM OF THE MOVING IMAGE

Until it closed in 2000, this was one of London's most innovative attractions. Combining a serious look at cinema's history with entertaining hands-on exhibits aimed at children, it neatly complemented the National Film Theatre, its next-door neighbour on the South Bank. The British Film Institute plans to develop this site by 2004, incorporating a new riverside film centre and a regenerated Museum of the Moving Image. For details of progress, the website to watch is bfi.org.uk

LEFT: an Oberlender recorder.

player's breath) and, predominantly English, keyboard instruments. The aerophones are displayed in cases running down the left-hand side of the gallery, and are arranged according to their place in the Western orchestra: flutes (flageolets, recorders and side-blown flutes), oboes (including cor anglais), clarinets and basset horns, bassoons, and assorted brass instruments, including Gustav Holst's trombone and the unusual-looking serpents and ophicleides.

The case at the far end of the gallery contains a clavicytherium (South German, *circa* 1480), the earliest known surviving stringed keyboard instrument – an early forerunner of today's pianos. Among the keyboard instruments that fill most of the floor space are examples of spinets (related to the harpsichord) and square pianos, and an 18th-century Broadwood piano.

The mezzanine floor holds the collection of non-Western instruments, and the cases where the Western chordophones (instruments where the sound is produced by the plucking or bowing of a string held under tension) are displayed. The first cases contain instruments from China (including a sheng, bamboo mouth organ, and a couple of lovely temple bells), Burma/Myanmar (look for the fine example of an arched harp) and India, which includes a beautifully decorated "experimental" vina – a South Indian lute. The free-standing case in the centre has a few African and West Asian instruments, including mbira (a plucked idiophone – where the sound comes from the resonation of the actual body of the instrument) from Zimbabwe, and an 'ud, forerunner of the Western lute, possibly Syrian.

The majority of the cases running along the balcony contain Western stringed instruments, from violins to viols, and lutes to harps. Gems here include an enormas chitarrone (a lute-like instrument) from Venice, dated 1608, a lovely English "division" viol from 1692, and a collection of tiny 18th-century "violins" known as pochettes.

Shakespeare's Globe Exhibition

All the world's a (re-created) stage…

Map reference: page 21, G4
New Globe Walk, Bankside, SE1. Tel: 020-7902
1500. www.shakespeares-globe.org
Tube: Cannon Street, London Bridge.
Daily, including weekends (except Christmas
Eve and Christmas Day) Oct–Apr 10am–5pm,
May–Sept 9am–midnight.
Admission charge.

There are other replicas of Shakespeare's Globe – the one in Tokyo has a glass roof which slides shut when it rains – but the recreation on London's Bankside, completed in 1997, is the most authentic, made from the materials used in the 16th century and open to the elements. Thus the frequent telephone query to the box office – "Is the theatre air-conditioned?" – can truthfully be answered either way. The adjacent exhibition recounts the story of the original

The Bard as he may have looked, and the meticulously re-created Globe Theatre.

theatre and its modern *doppelgänger*, and uses computer technology to explore aspects of Shakespeare's craft.

Entertaining guides begin the tour outside the building, relating how, in 1598, the theatre's founder, actor-manager James Burbage, unable to extend the lease on his site north of the Thames, had the theatre dismantled and carried by night across a frozen river to be reassembled on the south bank, a notoriously libertine area. William Shakespeare (1564–1616) acted here and was a part-owner. The theatre prospered on Bankside for 14 years until a stray piece of wadding from a stage cannon landed on the roof during a performance of *Henry VIII*, setting fire to the thatch. The thatch in today's building has been specially treated to resist fire. Modern fire regulations also limit the audience to a maximum of 914 in the covered galleries and 500 standing in the open area in front of the stage – less than half the number permitted when *Macbeth* and *King Lear* first played.

Except on summer afternoons, when performances are held, the tour continues inside the theatre itself. The guides have a stock of diverting anecdotes (not all easily accessible to foreign visitors) and bizarre facts (the massive oak pillars were given a marble-like lustre by being painted with a mixture of mustard, vinegar, water, pigs' blood and four-day-old dog urine). The tour then moves to the exhibition hall, which visitors can take as long as they like to explore.

In true Shakespearian tradition, the stories are vividly told. Information panels, photographs and video footage recount how the American actor-director Sam Wanamaker fought for decades against indifference and officialdom to realise his dream of reconstructing the Globe close to its original location. Southwark Council was hostile to the redevelopment, arguing that the road sweepers' carts housed on the proposed site would be difficult to relocate, and the council's leader opined: "Shakespeare is tosh."

Some displays are traditional museum fare: 16th-century dog skulls and tavern mugs found when excavating the site, 16th- and 17th-century books such as Holinshed's *Chronicles of England, Scotland and Ireland*, on which Shakespeare based many of his historical plays, and the costume worn in 1997 by the Globe's director, Mark Rylance, when he played the lead in *Henry V*. But a wealth of touch screens and hands-on displays provide the fun element.

You can rehearse one of a number of Shakespearian scenes, reading your character's lines from a screen in response to a recording of actors declaiming the other parts; the whole scene is then played back and your performance is accorded a

There's a close rapport between actors and audience in the Globe.

Edmund Kean as *Richard III* with John Cooper as Richmond in 1814, from the Theatre Museum's Stone Collection.

gratifying round of recorded applause. You can then compare your efforts with those of the famous, playing back, for example, renderings of Hamlet's "To be or not to be" soliloquy by a variety of actors, ranging from a scratchy recording of Herbert Beerbohm Tree to more recent performances such as those by Richard Burton, Peter O'Toole and Kenneth Branagh.

The musically inclined can push various numbers on an on-screen scale to play tunes on such Tudor instruments as a lute, cittern, sackbut or tabor. Other touch screens explain how special effects were achieved in Shakespeare's time – Jupiter taking flight in *Cymbeline*, for instance, or the maimed Lavinia spouting blood in *Titus Andronicus*.

For the Shakespeare enthusiast, more specialist displays explain, for example, how printers chose to punctuate early versions of the plays. You are invited to respond to multiple-choice questions such as "How many typesetters worked on the First Folio?" – a correct answer is greeted with applause and a wrong answer with a chorus of disapproval. It's a clever way of echoing the ambience of the original Globe, where raucous audience participation was expected. For those who wish to take such studies further, various antiquarian books are for sale, such as a 1685 Fourth Folio for £70,000.

Food and drink: *There's a café, open from 10am, and a restaurant, open from noon. Both have good views of the Thames. The nearest pub, a few minutes' walk along the river to the east, is the historic Anchor Inn.*

Theatre Museum

Celebrates the history of modern theatre

Map reference: page 20, D3
Russell Street, WC2. Tel: 020-7943 4700.
www.theatremuseum.org
Tube: Covent Garden or Leicester Square.
Bus to Strand or Aldwych.
Tues–Sun 10am–6pm. Free admission.

Can a museum capture the main attractions of live theatre: the unpredictable interaction between actors and audience, the immediacy of a first night, the sense of creative risk? The Theatre Museum, a branch of the Victoria and Albert Museum, scarcely tries, relying for the most part on traditional displays of costumes and models in glass cabinets, old paintings and playbills, and occasional film clips on video monitors. Given that even the Transport Museum round the corner employs actors to portray yesteryear's bus conductors and Tube tunnellers, you'd think the Theatre Museum might hire a few resting players to stalk the corridors as Hamlet or Archie Rice, enlivening the somewhat solemn atmosphere. Given that the museum has been created in the basement of Covent Garden's old Flower Market, Eliza Doolittle might do nicely.

As it is, a certain sense of theatrical life is provided by various special activities. Make-up demonstrations (daily at 11.30am, 1pm, 2.30pm, 3.30pm and 4.30pm) show how a model's face can be transformed. Costume workshops (daily at 12.30pm and 3pm) are popular with both children and adults,

ALEXANDER FLEMING
LABORATORY MUSEUM

*Discover
Penicillin
just as
Alexander
Fleming
did in 1928*

**St. Mary's Hospital
Paddington, London
The birthplace of penicillin**

"That's funny"

On 3 September 1928 a chance event with momentous consequences took place in a small laboratory in the Clarence Wing of St. Mary's Hospital. Alexander Fleming, Professor of Bacteriology, had recently returned from holiday and was clearing away some petri dishes of bacteria he had been working on for a paper on staphylococcus before going away when he noticed that one of them had become contaminated with a mould. This mould was dissolving the staphyloccoci close to it in the dish. At once he realised that quite by chance he had stumbled on something of importance. Fleming had discovered penicillin.

The Clarence Wing, St. Mary's Hospital where penicillin was discovered

From humble background to world renown

Alexander Fleming was 47 when he discovered penicillin. From humble beginnings on a Scottish hill farm, he studied medicine at St. Mary's Hospital Medical School and became a bacteriologist at the Hospital working for Sir Almroth Wright "the godfather of British microbiology". His experiences with the casualties of the Great War convinced him that most antiseptics then being used were causing more harm than good. In 1921 he discovered the body's own natural antiseptic which he called lysozyme. His discovery of penicillin, one of the greatest medical advances of all times, earned him a Nobel Prize in 1945 and made him a household name before his death in 1955.

Fleming in the laboratory

Dawn of the antibiotic age

The work of a team of scientists in Oxford including Professor Howard Florey and Dr Ernst Chain brought penicillin into use as a lifesaving drug in the 1940s. Penicillin was hailed as the wonder drug. For the first time there was was the possibility of cure for many previously life threatening diseases. But some bacteria were already resistant to penicillin and others developed resistance. A team of scientists from SmithKline Beecham paved the way for a new generation of semi-synthetic penicillins to overcome this problem when they discovered the nucleus of penicillin in 1957. New antibiotics must be constantly developed to continue the ever continuing war against bacteria. Penicillin had shown the way ahead.

The original penicillin culture plate

ALEXANDER FLEMING LABORATORY MUSEUM

The birthplace of penicillin

The laboratory in which Fleming discovered penicillin has now been reconstructed to show it as it would have been in 1928. The accompanying display and video presentation tell the story of Fleming and penicillin. We hope you enjoy your visit.

The Museum is staffed by volunteers and all admission charges are used to maintain the Museum.

The Alexander Fleming Laboratory Museum at St. Mary's Hospital has been made possible by the generous support of SmithKilne Beecham Plc, the Special Trustees of St. Mary's Hospital and the Delegacy of St. Mary's Hospital Medical School.

**The Museum is open
Monday to Thursday
10am - 1pm
Closed Public
Holidays**

**Open at other times
by appointment only
Monday to Thursday
2 - 5pm and Friday
10am - 5pm**

**Individuals and
groups welcome**

**To arrange your visit,
please contact:
The Curator
Alexander Fleming
Laboratory Museum
St . Mary's Hospital
Praed Street,
London W2 1NY
Tel: 020 7886 6528**

allowing them to dress up as, say, Lady Capulet or a mouse from *The Wind in the Willows*. Combined tours of the museum and the neighbouring Theatre Royal, Drury Lane (check times with museum) enable you to explore the backstage and understage areas of a working theatre.

The traditional nature of the museum's permanent exhibits can be traced to the fact that it was created from three major collections: Gabrielle Enthoven's vast collection of programmes and playbills, donated to the Victoria and Albert Museum in 1924, a collection of Diaghilev Ballets Russes costumes, and various British Theatre Museum Association collections such as the Henry Irving archive. To get the most out of these, it would help to have a certain knowledge of theatre in general and British theatre in particular. Likewise, those with an interest in theatrical history will appreciate artefacts such as Sir Christopher Wren's design for a 17th-century playhouse, an early draft of Sheridan's *School for Scandal* (1777), and memorabilia belonging to Lilian Baylis, Noël Coward and John Gielgud.

Occasional video screens remind visitors of the movement that cannot be captured in a glass case. There's a rare mute film of Henry Beerbohm Tree's 1899 production of Shakespeare's *King John*, and scenes are compared between two strikingly different productions of *King Lear*, one by the Royal Shakespeare Company, the other by the Talawa Theatre Company. Performance artists are shown in action at London railway stations.

The wide range of oil paintings might not merit a place in the National Gallery but they do convey the flamboyant acting styles of 18th and 19th-century stars such as David Garrick and Edmund Keen. A 1955 portrait of Richard Burton as Henry V is eye-catchingly lurid.

Coming more up to date, an extended exhibition traces the development of Alan Bennett's 1990 National Theatre adaptation of Kenneth Grahame's children's book *The Wind in the Willows* "from page to stage". Individual displays focus on the writing, casting, rehearsals, sound, lighting and make-up. The ramp leading to the main galleries is lined with the hand-prints of various contemporary stars and celebrities – a Wall of Fame that distantly echoes Hollywood Boulevard's Walk of Fame.

Food and drink: Covent Garden is awash with pubs and restaurants of every description. For history enthusiasts, the Lamb & Flag pub (33 Rose Street) dates back to 1627, and Rules (35 Maiden Lane, 020-7836 5314) is a venerable, though pricey, venue for English roasts and real ale.

Vaslav Nijinsky as the Golden Slave in Rimsky-Korsakov's *Schéhérazade* in 1910.

Mansions and Palaces

Regal power and splendour are reflected in Buckingham Palace, Kensington Palace and Hampton Court Palace, but nobles and wealthy merchants have also left fine houses which portray the past lifestyles of the rich and famous

Banqueting House

Diplomatic entertaining, 17th-century style

Map reference: page 20, D5
Whitehall, SW1. Tel: 020-7930 4179.
www.hrp.org.uk/bh/indexbh.htm
Tube: Westminster, Charing Cross or
Embankment; bus: 3, 11, 12, 24, 29, 53, 77A,
88, 109,159.
Mon–Sat, 10am–5pm (last admission 4.30pm),
sometimes closed at short notice for functions;
access for disabled by prior arrangement.
Admission charge.

Still used for receptions today, the Banqueting House, an Historic Royal Palace, represents a fascinating era in Britain's past. In 1649, Charles I was publicly beheaded here, and it was the only building of the mighty 23-acre (9.3-hectare) Palace of Westminster to survive a devastating fire in 1698. Today it is the Great Hall's splendid painted ceiling, the only complete project by Peter Paul Rubens still *in situ*, that attracts most visitors.

James I, whose reign brought a period of much-needed religious tolerance and diplomatic stability after the Tudors, wanted a prestigious building for the reception of foreign ambassadors. To emphasise his cosmopolitan taste and patronage of the arts, he commissioned Inigo Jones to design a galleried hall in the Palladian style, a radical architectural shift for 17th-century England. The Banqueting House was finished in 1622 and its Great Hall was at first used for masked balls, pageants and theatre.

To celebrate the life and accomplishments of his father, Charles I commissioned the Flemish artist Rubens, who was in England as the King of Spain's ambassador, to paint panels for the ceiling of the Great Hall. After installation of the nine panels in 1635, no more revelry took place here for fear of candle smoke damaging the artwork.

On the theme of the harmony and abundance brought about by his reign, the images show James I – who enthusiastically supported the divine right of kings – surrounded by mythological gods. In the central panel he is being lifted heavenward, while above the entrance door we see the birth of Great Britain as England and Scotland unite, with James appearing as Solomon. Overseas representatives were subjected to a resplendent if unsubtle promotional campaign.

A video shown in the vaults fills in the history,

LEFT:
Ceiling of the Banqueting Hall, finished for Charles I in 1635 by Peter Paul Rubens.

while an audioguide explains in fascinating detail each of the painted panels, the Great Hall's layout and court etiquette of the time.

Food and drink*: Bank Westminster (45 Buckingham Gate, 020-7379 9797) is a brasserie with Zander bar. One-Twenty-One-Two (Royal Horseguards Hotel, Whitehall Court, 020-7839 3400) serves a contemporary menu.*

Buckingham Palace

Where the Queen lives and works in London

Map reference: page 20, B5
Buckingham Palace, London SW1.
Tel: 020-7321 2233. Recorded info: 020-7799
2331. www.the-royal-collection.org.uk
Tube: Green Park, St James's Park, Victoria,
Hyde Park Corner.
Daily Aug–Sept 9.30am–4.30pm (last admis-
sion). Disabled visitors telephone 020-7839
1377. Admission charge: tickets may be bought
in advance or on the day from the ticket office
near The Mall in Green Park or through the
Royal Collection by phone or online.

When the State Rooms of Buckingham Palace were first opened to the public in 1993, the initial reaction of many was disappointment. Lines stretched down The Mall, the admission price was steep, and, rather than being able to take a leisurely peek at Her Majesty's London

OPPOSITE:
a costumed guide welcomes the tourists to a lantern-lit tour of Hampton Court Palace.

The Garden Front of Buckingham Palace.

home, one felt a bit like a sheep being roughly herded. With an eye on public opinion, the Royal Household has, for the most part, sorted out these problems. Timed tickets mean the end of long queues and visitors are encouraged to walk through the rooms at their own pace (although in one direction only). A minimum of two hours is advised.

The building, dating from 1702, was originally the home of John Sheffield, Duke of Buckingham. It was acquired by George III in 1761 as a private dwelling; 65 years later, George IV commissioned architect John Nash to convert it into a full-scale palace. But Nash was constrained by money and politics, and, rather than re-create a residence of "lofty grandeur", had to adapt the existing building. For this reason, many of the 19 rooms on show, although lavishly furnished, are surprisingly small, especially the Throne Room.

Visitors enter the palace from Buckingham Gate, through the Ambassadors' Court, the entrance used on official occasions by diplomats. The first thing of note is the Grand Staircase. Rebuilt by Nash of marble and gilt bronze, it is both dramatic and functional, allowing access to the State Rooms from two directions. Visitors with little time should hurry to the splendid rooms in the west wing which look out over the garden; anyone intending to linger in the east wing will need to buy the meticulously catalogued official guide, as many of the Queen's treasures – such as the Sèvres porcelain vase in the Green Drawing Room (thought to have belonged to Madame de Pompadour) are behind silk ropes and

easily overlooked. Through the Throne Room is the Queen's Gallery, housing just a fraction of the works from the Royal Collection *(see Galleries entry on page 210)*. Particularly striking are the Rembrandt portraits *Agatha Bas* and *The Ship Builder and his Wife*, and *The Farm at Laeken* by Rubens.

Queen Victoria was the first monarch to take up residence at Buckingham Palace. Finding the rooms too small for court entertainments, she sold the Royal Pavilion in Brighton to fund a major expansion in 1853–55. Principal among the new additions was The Ballroom, opened to the public in the year 2000 and used for investitures and official receptions. In a rare showing of informality – for the palace can seem as chilly as a 19th-century museum – a video shows royal events that have taken place in the room, such as a state dinner for Nelson Mandela, and the Prince of Wales's 50th birthday party. Members of the public are also allowed to sit down, the only time on the tour.

The State Dining Room, resplendent with red walls and carpet, contains examples of the silver-gilt dinner services made by the Crown goldsmiths. The table sits only around 20 people; when more space is required, banquets are held in the Ballroom or in the Picture Gallery. Adjoining the dining room is the Blue Drawing Room, one of the finest in the palace. Divided into bays by giant Corinthian columns, the ceiling, with great billowing coves, is Nash at his opulent best. A feature often overlooked amidst the splendour is the 1790 astronomical clock, designed by Jean-Antoine Lépine.

The Grand Staircase (LEFT) and Blue Drawing Room at Buckingham Palace.

The Music Room is one of the most delightful in the palace, a gold and white confection whose ceiling, parquet floor and glittering, semi-circular proportions give one the feeling of being in the middle of the sun. Five windows look out over the garden; six mirrors reflect and intensify the view. The Queen's three eldest children were baptised here in water brought from the River Jordan.

The final State Room is the White Drawing Room. It looks and feels French, with Gallic-inspired wall decoration, George IV's French furniture, fine white-marble chimney-pieces and a secret door from the Royal Closet, through which the Royal Family enters on formal occasions.

The Ministers' Staircase leads through the Marble Hall to the Garden, open to the public. Although the 1,500-ft (450-metre) walk offers only a tantalising glimpse of the grounds, the route does curve around the lake several times, offering wonderful views of the palace's rarely seen western façade.

In 1825, George IV appointed William Townsend Aiton of the Royal Botanic Gardens at Kew to oversee their development. The 19th-century 3-acre (1.2-hectare) lake was fed from the overflow of the Serpentine in Hyde Park, and now provides a nesting site for some of the garden's 30 types of birds.

With the sound of geese and the scent from more than 350 kinds of wildflower, the palace garden truly is a "walled oasis in the middle of London". Never is this more evident than when exiting the grounds onto traffic-filled Grosvenor Place, where the roar of traffic and the hurly-burly of Victoria

Station are inescapable reminders that one is only a commoner, after all.

Food and drink: Email your friends about your royal experience at Café Internet (22–24 Buckingham Palace Road, 020-7233 5786). The Goring Restaurant (Beeston Place, 020-7396 9000) is English, dignified, expensive.

Burgh House/ Hampstead Museum

One of the finest Queen Anne residences

Map reference: page 22, E1
New End Square, Hampstead, NW3.
Tel: 020-7431 0144.
www.london-northwest.com/burghhouse
Tube: Hampstead, bus: 46, 268. Rail:
Hampstead Heath Station, South End Green.
Wed–Sun noon–5pm, bank holidays 2–5pm,
Sat by appointment only.
Free admission (donations welcome). Research library can be visited by appointment, guided tours by arrangement.

Along with his "vitriolic" wife, the Reverend Allatson Burgh (1822–56) was so unpopular that his parishioners petitioned Queen Victoria to have him removed. By contrast, the house named after the family is an exceptionally friendly little museum.

Tucked away among the quiet, countrified lanes

of Hampstead, this is the area's second oldest house. It was erected in 1703 for a Quaker family, the Sewells, and former residents have included friends of Keats, and the daughter of Rudyard Kipling. At one point it was used as an officers' mess for the Hampstead Militia. Having fallen into disrepair, it was saved from redevelopment by the local community in 1979. Its doors are open to casual visitors, wedding parties and cultural events of all kinds. It hosts regular musical recitals (varying from classical to Latin American beat), meetings, concerts, art exhibitions, talks and poetry readings. Bridge and Scrabble clubs meet in the afternoons and Thursday is Hindu and Buddhist night.

The award-winning garden, lovingly maintained since 1979, embroiders the grounds with well over 100 varieties of plant, including the purple creeper which garlands the stair rails and porch. The garden is "informal... from force of circumstances and from choice" and the volunteer staff are similarly unaffected and welcoming.

Through double doors on the left is the lovely Music Room, which despite its 18th-century wooden panelling and fireplace, is an extension from 1925. A piano sits in front of the shallow bay window, and a watercolour depicts Hampstead Heath in 1896, when it was still a wild moor. Further along the hall, on the left, the bright little art gallery holds rolling exhibitions by local artists. On the right is the pea-green library refurbished in the "style of the Georgian Period".

On the first floor, the Hampstead Local History Museum depicts the area's development from prehistory. There is always a display on Constable, a one-time resident of the area, plus original works by Helen Allingham. Oddities include the country's oldest Boy Scouts banner (1910) and some eccentric furniture made by Marcel Breuer for the famous Isokon Flats on nearby Lawn Road. Designed in the 1930s for "minimal living", they housed creative types such as the sculptor Henry Moore and the detective novelist Agatha Christie.

The best reason to visit Burgh House is to sit outside on the terrace afterwards on a sunny day, consuming a cream tea or other home-made food from the basement Buttery and watching the butterflies dance from flower to flower.

The richly decorated Gallery of Chiswick House.

Food and drink: *The house has a Buttery (11am–5.30pm). The alley of Ginsberg Yard, to the left of Hampstead Tube station includes an exotic Moroccan restaurant, Al Casba (moderate), on the corner with the High Street and, further along, the Flask pub, with some seating outside.*

Chiswick House

Romantic 18th-century villa and gardens built around classical Italian themes

Map reference: page 22, C4
Burlington Lane, W4. Tel: 0208-995 0508.
Tube: Turnham Green (District line), plus complicated 40-minute walk. Rail: Chiswick (from Waterloo), plus 15-minute walk. Bus: E3, 190, 290. Cars: A4, small car park.
Apr–Sept 10am–6pm (last admission 5.30pm); 1–28 Oct until 5pm; 29–31 Oct until 4.30pm; 1 Nov–31 Mar Wed–Sun until 4pm. Closed 24–26 Dec, 1–16 Jan. Gardens (free) open daily, dawn to dusk.
Admission fee includes 50-minute audio tour.

Chiswick is a grand house in miniature, exquisitely positioned and perfectly formed. It was designed by Richard Boyle, the Third Earl of Burlington (1694–1753), the foremost architect of his time, who wanted to create the kind of house and gardens that might have been found near ancient Rome. Modern visitors are often surprised to discover there is little or no furniture in the house, but this was always so. Lord Burlington built it as an

View from the Cascade Terrace by George Lambert shows Chiswick House's gardens in 1742.

adjunct to another building (now demolished), and linked the two together. The older house was for living in, the neo-classical addition was for ceremonies, parties, and for displaying the Earl's fine collection of paintings, many of which remain.

Lord Burlington was particularly influenced by the 16th-century Italian architect, Andrea Palladio. To the left of the house's front entrance is a statue of Palladio, complete with frilly garter; to the right is a statue of Inigo Jones, chief architect of the gateway. The shallow-stepped dome which gives Chiswick House its graceful, distinctive shape is modelled on Rome's Pantheon; the columns of the portico are copied from the Temple of Jupiter Stator. The tapering form of the chimneys is unique in England.

The ground floor is plainly furnished, as in Burlington's time, and houses an introductory film and an exhibition. The grand rooms are reserved for the first floor, which has a very unusual structure: in the centre of the building is an octagonal room with a lavish domed ceiling – the tribune or saloon. This was the architectural heart of the building and the setting for gatherings and *conversazioni*. The northern part of the house is divided into three small rooms: the western one is circular, the central one is rectangular with semi-circular apses, and the eastern room is octagonal. Their small scale and rounded edges are intimate and sensual, with the overall symmetry heightened by framed views of the gardens through the doorways of the interconnected rooms.

The most sumptuous of the Green, Red and Blue Velvet rooms, so-called because of their intricate wallpaper, is Lord Burlington's study, elegantly adorned in blue. The room's tiny dimensions and rich colours convey an impression of standing inside a jewel box, or inside a Fabergé egg.

The grounds are historically important, for it was here that the idea of the "natural style" of gardening – one of England's main contributions to European culture – was conceived. Burlington began the grounds 10 years before the villa, creating a formal "lake" (canal) and a series of radiating walkways ending in classical buildings. He brought in a protégé, William Kent, to soften the gardens and create a romantic, horticultural world. There is an abundance of statuary, a classical bridge, an Ionic temple, and a waterfall.

Look out for "Lilly's Tomb", a stone monument with a Latin inscription, marking the grave of a pet dog. If possible, avoid coming at 5pm, which is rush hour in the sky as planes cruise incessantly overhead towards Heathrow airport.

Food and drink: *Anyone arriving by train or bus will have to be content with the café in the grounds, where the food (sandwiches on ciabatta bread, jacket potatoes) is slightly better than the utilitarian block that houses it. Best bet is breakfast, served 10am–noon. Those arriving by underground fare better. Between the station and Chiswick House are several adequate chains (Café Rouge, Wok, Wok), plus Zizzi (tel: 020-8747 9400), a spacious, open-plan restaurant serving wood-fired pizzas.*

Ham House

An unusually well preserved Stuart House

Map reference: page 22, B5
Ham, Richmond TW10. Tel: 020-8940
1950. www.nationaltrust.org.uk
Tube or train to Richmond Station,
then 371 bus. By car: the house is at
the river end of Ham Street, off the
A307, between Richmond and
Kingston. Access for pedestrians along
the tow-path; a ferry operates
10am–6pm from Marble Hill House,
Twickenham daily Apr–Oct, weekends
only Nov–March.
House open Apr–Oct, Sat–Wed 1–5pm. (Note
the house is closed Thur and Fri). Gardens
open all year Sat–Wed 10.30am–6pm (or dusk
in winter). Admission charge.
Wheelchair access to all floors of the house.
Guided tours by arrangement.

ABOVE: the North Front of Ham House.

BELOW: portrait of an unknown man by Nicholas Hilliard (1547–1619) at Ham House.

Ham House was built in 1610 for Sir Thomas Vavasour, Knight Marshal to James I. In 1626 it became the home of William Murray, a childhood friend of Charles I, who fought for the Royalists during the Civil War and was given the title of the 1st Earl of Dysart.

The earl's daughter, Elizabeth, inherited the house and also took the title Countess of Dysart. The new Countess was well educated and described as "a woman of beauty", but was also extravagant and ambitious. She married Sir Lionel Tollemache, a wealthy squire in 1648. Even before Sir Lionel's death in 1669, Lady Dysart was rumoured to have formed an attachment to John Maitland, 1st Duke of Lauderdale, whom she married in 1672. It was during this time that Ham House was extended and refurbished into one of the most splendid houses in the country, suitable for one of the most powerful ministers to Charles II.

After the Duke's death in 1682, legal wrangling among his relatives forced the Duchess to pawn her pictures and jewellery. She died penniless, at Ham, in 1698. The house, neglected, remained in the family, until William, 9th Earl, in 1884 took responsibility for repairs, and installed heating and electricity. It was given to the National Trust in 1948.

The ground and first floor and the basement are open to the public. A tour starts in the Great Hall with its chequerboard floor is part of the original 1610 building. The chapel was first the family's living room, before being converted in 1672. The Great Staircase is a show-piece, with its military decorations, installed in 1638, just before the Civil War. The first floor has the State apartments, the finest rooms in the house.

Although many rooms are worth noting, the Long Galley, the Library and the Green Closet are particularly rich in decoration. The ground floor has the Duke and Duchess's apartments. The Duchess's bedroom was originally designed for the Duke, hence the military pictures above the doors.

The basement has the kitchen, pantry and the Duchess's bathroom. The kitchen is dominated by the table and the fireplace behind, and has many utensils and equipment dating from the 17th century.

The gardens are a delight. The lawns on the south side of the house lead down to a wilderness area, which is semi-formal with hedges enclosing areas of grasses and wildflowers. The Dairy has a video display showing a short history of the house.

Events range from Easter egg hunts and gardening demonstrations to evening concerts.

Food and drink: *The Orangery in Ham House is a tea room serving light refreshments (Apr–Oct 11am–5pm, and some winter weekends).*

Hampton Court Palace

Majestic building, great gardens and vivid memories of Henry VIII

Map reference: page 22, A6
Richmond, Surrey. Tel: 020-8781 9500.
www.hrp.org.uk
Rail: from Waterloo to Hampton Court Station (32 minutes). Tube to Wimbledon and then by train, or Tube to Richmond and then bus R68 from station. Bus: R68, 111, 411, 216, 501, 440, 513, 726, 267 (Sun only). Thames River Launch: from Westminster, Richmond or Kingston (summer only).
Late Mar–late Oct, Mon 10.15am–6pm, Tues–Sun 9.30am–6pm; late Oct–mid-Mar, Mon 10.15am–4.30pm, Tue–Sun 9.30am–4.30pm; Last admission 45 minutes before closing. Closed 24–26 Dec. Admission charge. Joint ticket with Tower of London available. Wheelchair access.

This is one of the most popular days out in London, and it will take several hours to see and do everything. Surrounded by 60 acres (24 hectares) of magnificent gardens on the banks of the Thames, the palace dates from the reign of Henry VIII (reigned 1509–47). It is enormous, with several sections dedicated to different periods in its history. Get your bearings on the introductory Welcome Walk through the courtyards. Costumed guides give entertaining tours of some parts of the palace at regular intervals, and the audio tours are informative. All tours are included in the admission price, but group sizes are limited, so it's prudent to register at the information centre in Clock Court. There are also activities for children.

The earliest Tudor section of Hampton Court was built around the Clock Court in the early 16th century by Cardinal Thomas Wolsey, chief minister to Henry VIII. He presented it to the king in 1525. Henry spent much time here, but after his death the palace was little used until William and Mary (reigned 1689–1702) came to the throne. They demolished most of

Henry's grand state apartments, but the Great Hall and Chapel Royal – the most striking rooms – survive. During their reign, Sir Christopher Wren began rebuilding the king's and queen's apartments on the south and east sides. Work continued under Queen Anne (1702–14) and George I (1714–27).

The last monarch to use Hampton Court as a residence was George II (1727–60), but after his wife Queen Caroline died in 1737, the royal court never returned to the palace. Over the next century it was maintained and restored, and in 1838 Queen Victoria opened Hampton Court to the public. In 1986, the King's Apartments were devastated by a fire, but were well restored over the next six years.

Six routes take you through the palace and explain how it was used by the different monarchs. You enter Henry VIII's State Apartments through the Great Hall, the last of the English medieval great halls to be built. It was used as a dining hall for the court and is the largest room in the palace, measuring 106 ft (32 metres) long, 40 ft (12 metres) wide and over 60 ft (18 metres) high. The magnificent hammer-beam roof with its cantilevered beams and richly carved decoration is original. The Flemish wall tapestries, woven in the 1540s, tell the story of Abraham.

Catherine Howard, Henry VIII's fifth wife who was beheaded for alleged adultery, is said to roam the Haunted Gallery. This leads to the Chapel Royal which, more than anything else in the palace, displays full Tudor glory. The Royal Pew looks down into the chapel, and provides the best view of the stunning vaulted ceiling, painted bright blue with

The baroque East Front of Hampton Court Palace.

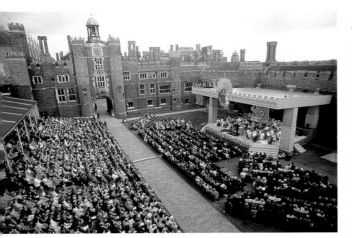

carved and gilded pendants. The huge oak reredos (altar screen) was carved by Grinling Gibbons and installed in the 18th century. The chapel has been in use for more than 450 years and visitors can attend Sunday services.

The Tudor Kitchens – a palace favourite – are the most extensive of their kind in Europe. They are laid out as if in preparation for a feast in Henry VIII's time, with massive fireplaces and cooking pots, food and utensils, a butchery, larder, ovens and wine cellars. The audio tour gives a fascinating insight into the enormous job of feeding the king's court, including their favourite foods and recipes for Peacock Royal and other feasting dishes.

A visit to the splendid King's Apartments is most enjoyable on a guided tour, during which you'll hear anecdotes from the days of William III for whom the rooms were built in the late 17th century. Highlights include the King's Staircase, painted by Antonio Verrio; the King's Guard Chamber, with more than 3,000 arms arranged in huge wall displays; the King's Great Bedchamber; and the King's Privy Chamber, the main ceremonial room. The Privy Gardens were designed to be seen from this room.

The Wolsey Rooms are thought to have been the Cardinal's private lodgings. Two of the smaller rooms are lined with the 16th-century linenfold panelling which once graced much of the Tudor palace, so-called because it was meant to mimic the effect of draped fabric. The other rooms form the Renaissance Picture Gallery, displaying a selection of the palace's 16th- and 17th-century paintings by German, Flemish and Italian artists.

The Georgian Rooms, once the private rooms of George II and Queen Caroline, are set up as they were during the final days of the royal court in 1737. The Queen's Bedchamber, Dressing Room and Bathroom, and her Private Oratory give an intimate glimpse into her private life. The Queen's State Apartments were used by Caroline for entertaining. Its principal room is the Queen's Drawing Room, designed by Wren to align with the long canal and provide a superb view of the park, whose long avenues of trees converge on this room.

Allow time to enjoy Hampton Court's magnificent gardens. On the south side of the palace, leading down to the river, is the flower-filled Privy Garden, built for William III as his private garden. Alongside are the box hedges of the Knot Garden and the sunken Pond Gardens. The Lower Orangery houses Andrea Mantegna's *Triumph of Caesar* series, one of the greatest works of the Italian Renaissance. In the glasshouse next door is the Great Vine, the oldest known vine in the world, which was planted by "Capability" Brown in 1768. It still produces 500–700 lbs (220–320 kg) of grapes annually.

The Maze, planted in 1702, is all that remains of the original Northern Gardens. This leafy labyrinth covers a third of an acre and contains a half-mile of paths. The Tiltyard Gardens were formerly used by

The Hampton Court Palace Music Festival.

The King's Staircase, the State Apartments of William III.

Henry VIII for jousting tournaments. The East Gardens are laid out in a great semi-circular parterre. Beyond is Home Park, with a deer park and great canal. Near the palace, the Royal Tennis Court dates from the 1620s and is still in use today.

Food and drink: The Privy Kitchen, set inside the palace near the Tudor Kitchens, serves morning coffee, tea and pastries; light lunches, soup, sandwiches and cakes; and afternoon tea. The Tiltyard Tea Room, in the Northern Gardens, is self-service, has a coffee bar, outside terrace and children's menu. Both are cheap and open 10am–4pm in winter, 10am–5pm in summer. The restaurant and brasserie of the Carlton Mitre Hotel (opposite the palace, 020-8979 9988) have good views over the Thames.

Kensington Palace

Home to some members of the royal family

Map reference: page 40, B2
Kensington Gardens, W8.
Tel: 020-7937 9561. www.hrp.org.uk
Tube: Queensway or High Street Kensington
Bus routes: 12, 94 (Bayswater Road) or 9, 10, 33, 49, 52, 52A, C1 (Kensington Road).
Mar–Oct 10am–6pm; Nov–Feb 10am–5pm; last entry one hour before closing; closed 24–26 Dec and 1 Jan.
Admission charge includes an audioguide.
Wheelchair access: limited.

Kensington Palace was the childhood home of Queen Victoria, Britain's longest reigning monarch. Diana, Princess of Wales moved here after her marriage to Prince Charles in 1981 and lived here until her death in 1997. Her former apartments and the parts of the palace that are still home to other (mostly minor) members of the royal family are off limits, but the State Apartments have been open to the public since 1898.

Built as a relatively modest country house in 1605, the old Jacobean mansion was bought by William and Mary after they came to the throne in 1689. They hired Sir Christopher Wren to re-model and enlarge it for their royal residence. William's successor, Queen Anne (1702–14), greatly enlarged the gardens and constructed the Orangery. Much rebuilding took place during George I's reign (1714–27), and the new rooms were lavishly decorated by the painter William Kent. Queen Caroline, wife of George II (1727–60), created one of the first English landscape gardens to the east of the palace, which forms the basis of Kensington Gardens today, including the Serpentine.

The South Front of Kensington Palace.

After 1760, Kensington Palace ceased to be the seat of the reigning monarch and was used as a residence for George III's children and their families. Queen Victoria was born here in 1819, and lived at the palace until her accession to the throne in 1837. Her statue stands in front of the much-photographed East Front of the palace. This simple facade best portrays the character of Kensington Palace: that of a domestic residence rather than a state showpiece. However, the South Front, built for William III in 1695, is the main exterior feature of the palace and it was here that thousands of mourners laid tributes of flowers after Diana's untimely death.

To reach the entrance on the northeast side, you pass one of the palace's most delightful features, the Sunken Garden, with its flower-lined formal terraces and fountains. Inside, you can tour the Royal Ceremonial Dress Collection and State Apartments, and a temporary exhibition is generally on show. The former is more interesting than you might expect. Every item of dress had its own symbolism and significance, and was a passport to court. Along with exhibits of court dress and ceremonial uniforms which explain the strict protocol, the ground-floor rooms contain a tailor's showroom and dressmaker's workshop, plus a collection of dresses worn by the Queen. Downstairs, the glamorous attire of the palace's most famous clothes-horse, Princess Diana, is on permanent display.

The highlight of the King's Apartments is the Cupola Room, designed by William Kent in 1722. With its coffered dome, gilt chandeliers and statues

Above: the King's Gallery.

Right: the Royal Ceremonial Dress Collection.

Return to the Privy Chamber to enter the Queen's Apartments. These rooms were used by Queen Mary, and are much plainer than those in the rest of the palace. Queen Mary's Bedchamber, where she died of smallpox in 1694, is the most interesting room. It has the original elm floorboards, while the bedspread and hangings belonged to James II.

Queen Mary's Gallery was much more ornate in her time, when it was filled with fine furniture as well as her extensive porcelain collection. It leads to the Queen's Staircase, plainly decorated and designed by Sir Christopher Wren to give access to the gardens.

Spend some time exploring the gardens and visit the Orangery, built for Queen Anne in 1704–05 to house plants during the winter months. Its design, attributed to Nicholas Hawksmoor and modified by Sir John Vanbrugh, has classical features such as white panelling, cornice and 24 Corinthian columns. The wood carvings above the arches are by Grinling Gibbons. It is now a café and restaurant.

Food and drink: *The Orangery, Kensington Gardens (Mar–Oct 10am–6pm, Nov–Feb 10am–5pm. Lunch 12–2.30pm, teas 3–6pm), serves morning coffee, light lunches and afternoon teas. Children's menu. Cheap.*
Wagamama, 26 Kensington High Street (tel: 020-7376 1717). Fun, minimalist noodle canteen serving healthy Japanese food, and fruit and vegetable juices. Long shared tables. Cheap–moderate.

of Roman gods and emperors set in niches, the decor aimed to link the English monarchy to the grandeur of imperial Rome. The huge plinth in the centre of the room holds a rare musical clock. Queen Victoria was christened in this room in 1819.

The King's Drawing Room, the focal point of court life where the king held public days, has a magnificent view over Kensington Gardens and a striking painting of Venus and Cupid by Giorgio Vasari. It caused a royal quarrel when Queen Caroline, who hated the picture, had it removed during George II's absence, but upon his return the king demanded that his "fat Venus" be restored.

The most charming room in the palace is Queen Victoria's Bedroom, where she was awakened at the age of 18 to be told she had become Queen. It contains her original bed, writing desk, an ornate cradle and other mementoes. The Ante Room and the Duchess of Kent's Dressing Room lead to the King's Gallery. It measures 96 ft (29 metres) and displays some of the finest pictures in the Royal Collection. Above the mantle is a wind dial made in 1694 for William III. William Kent remodelled the room in 1725, giving it its crimson walls and ceiling paintings which depict the story of Ulysses.

Kenwood House

Showcase for the Iveagh Bequest

Map reference: page 22, E1
Hampstead Lane, NW3. Tel: 020-8348 1286.
www.english-heritage.org.uk
Tube: Northern Line to Archway or Golders
Green, then 210 bus; or Northern Line to
Highgate, then a 1-mile walk.
Apr–Sept: daily 10am–6pm. Oct: daily
10am–5pm. Nov–Mar: daily 10am (10.30am
Wed & Fri) to 4pm. Closed 24–26 Dec and 1
Jan. Free admission. Gift shop and bookshops.

Pieter van den Broecke by Frans Hals, 1633. part of the Iveagh Bequest at Kenwood House.

Standing proud over the northern slopes of Hampstead Heath like a dazzling white wedding cake, Kenwood House is one of the flagship buildings of English Heritage, and home to one of the world's finest art collections, the Iveagh Bequest. The magnificent works include a Rembrandt *Self Portrait*, Vermeer's *Guitar Player* and Gainsborough's *Mary, Countess Howe*, plus superb pieces by Reynolds, Turner, Hals and Van Dyck.

The present stuccoed villa was remodelled between 1764 and 1779 by Robert Adam in neoclassical style, adding to the original brick building that dates from around 1700. Kenwood House was the residence of the 1st Earl of Mansfield during its redevelopment, but today it is presented to the public primarily as an historic building containing an art collection rather than as a furnished family home.

The vast majority of the original 18th-century furniture has disappeared, but some items have been recovered, as well as some fine contemporary pieces from other Adam houses. The rooms have all been beautifully maintained in their original style, with some, such as the spectacular Library, lined with gilt panelled walls and splendid ceiling murals of classical mythological themes. Low lighting and shaded windows protect the paintings and furniture, while the bare wooden floorboards enhance the elegance of Adam's architecture.

Upstairs rooms are usually reserved for special exhibitions, but the one small public gallery contains an exquisite collection of cameos, intaglios (incised brooches and seals) and ornate belt buckles.

A visit here provides a popular highlight to a walk through Hampstead Heath, which spreads out southwards and around three sides of the house. Ponds, grassy meadows and wooded enclosures form a suitably pastoral scene with views of central London.

Food and drink: Adjoining the house, in the Service Wing, the Coach House restaurant serves a pricey but tempting selection of hot and cold meals, snacks and sandwiches, with tables outside in a pretty walled garden. Alternatively, there are several pubs dotted around the edge of the Heath: Spaniards' Inn is a few minutes' walk away on Spaniards Road, and The Flask is about 20 minutes' walk down the east side of the Heath on the edge of Highgate Village.

Kew Palace

The country retreat of George III and family

Map reference: page 22, B4
Royal Botanic Gardens, Richmond, Kew, to the
left of the Brentford Gate entrance.
Tube: Kew Gardens. Rail (from Waterloo): Kew
Bridge, Kew Gardens.
The palace is closed for interior renovation until
2003–4. Normally open 9.30am–dusk daily
except 25 Dec, 1 Jan. Entrance fee for gardens.

Kew Palace was originally built for a Dutch merchant, Samuel Fortrey, and was known as the Dutch House until 1827. The date of construction, Fortrey's initials and those of his wife

Kew Palace, known as the Dutch House until 1827.

can be seen above the doorway. The palace is the only survivor of a number of royal residences in Richmond dating from medieval times. The Dutch House was leased to Queen Caroline in 1728 as an annexe to the White House at Kew Green for "the rent of £100 and a fat Doe" and the future George III spent much of his childhood there.

The "Old Palace", as the house had become known, was bought by George III in 1781 and helped him keep out of the public gaze during his first period of madness in 1788. After Queen Charlotte died in the house in 1818, it stayed empty until 1899, when her granddaughter, Queen Victoria, opened it and, a few years later, the grounds to the public.

Measuring just 70 by 50 ft (21 by 15 metres) this is Britain's smallest palace and was described by the London *Times* as "an out-building, on the scale of a small country-box". Before its first restoration in 1973, it had no electricity or direct water supply apart from that of a well in the Tudor vault which traditionally never runs dry. The unusual brickwork of the palace, laid in Flemish bond style, has been renovated using traditional techniques and is now closer to the original intentions of its builders. Research into the history of the palace's interior is ongoing and, after renovation, a clearer impression may be given of how the royal family lived during the 18th century.

The Queen's Garden, behind Kew Palace, was opened in 1969. Laid out in

George III by Thomas Gainsborough, *circa* 1781.

the style of a 17th-century garden, it contains a parterre (a formally patterned flower garden), sunken garden, gazebo, pleached alley and a "mount" with a rotunda on top. The plants are restricted to those that would have been grown at the time and include herbs used for cooking and medicine.

Leighton House

A Victorian artist's oriental fantasy

Map reference: page 40, A2
12 Holland Park Road, W14. Tel: 020-7602 3316.
www.rbkc.gov.uk/leightonhousemuseum
Tube: High Street Kensington; buses: 9, 10, 27, 28, 33, 49, 328.
Wed–Mon 11am–5.30pm, closed Tues; guided tours Wed and Thurs noon. Free admission; charge for guided tour. No disabled access.

The rather plain red-brick exterior of this west London house conceals one of the most extraordinary interiors in the city. The home of the Victorian artist Lord Frederic Leighton from 1866 until his death in 1896, it is a mix of lavish orientalism and conventional Victorian comforts, a private palace done out in intense, jewel-like colours.

Leighton was a popular artist during his own lifetime. His career took off when Queen Victoria purchased *Cimabue's Madonna carried through the Streets of Florence*, the first of his paintings to be exhibited at the Royal Academy. Dashing and talented, he became President of the Royal Academy. However, by the 1920s and '30s, Victorian art was deeply unfashionable, and when Leighton's most famous painting, *Flaming June*, was sold in the 1960s it fetched just £50.

Leighton's house, designed by his friend and fellow Royal Academician George Aitchison, was an integral part of his quest for beauty. The *pièce de résistance* is the Arab Hall (1877–9), on the left past the entrance. Inspired by a Moorish palace in Palermo, it was originally conceived as a setting for Leighton's collection of Damascene and Isnik tiles, many given to him by the traveller Richard Burton.

The Dining Room and the Drawing Room have views over the gardens and are hung with many of Leighton's paintings *(see entry in Galleries section, page 207)*. Upstairs, beyond the Silk Room with its zenana overlooking the Arab Hall, is Leighton's studio, where he not only worked but also held soirées. The ante-room off the studio contains a small fireplace inset with Chinese porcelain, where Leighton's models warmed themselves as they changed.

Though he regularly held parties, Leighton did not encourage overnight guests, and so had only one bedroom built in the house. Functional compared with the other rooms, it is simply furnished with one single bed. The ultimate aesthete, Leighton lived for art and beauty and was reputedly celibate.

Food and drink: No refreshment facilities. Round the corner, at 270 Kensington High Street, is Café Tarte for good sandwiches, coffee and pastries. There is a branch of the pizza/pasta parlour ASK at 222 Kensington High Street (tel: 020-7937 5540).

Leighton House, an ornate curiosity in west London.

Museum of Fulham Palace

Where the bishops spent their summers

Map reference: page 22, D4
Bishops Avenue, SW6. Tel: 020-7736 3233.
Museum open Mar–Oct Wed–Sun 2–5pm;
Nov–Feb Thur–Sun 1–4pm, including Bank
Holidays. Gardens open daily; tour of palace
twice a month, usually the second Sunday.
Tube: Putney Bridge. Rail: Putney. Wheelchair
access. Children will love the gardens.

It bills itself as "London's Best Kept Secret" but this isn't strictly true: the museum itself, a series of exhibits detailing the life and times of the bishops who lived here from AD 704 to 1973, is mainly for enthusiasts, and the palace itself – an irregular blend of architectural styles – is curiously devoid of character. This is probably because almost every bishop not only remodelled the palace to better reflect his personal image and status, but at the end of his appointment, carted off the worldly chattels, condemning the rooms to a bare and chilly existence.

The palace's gardens, a well-kept secret, meander along the River Thames. They roll back to reveal herb gardens, a giant oak from 1550 and a beautiful wisteria pergola (flowering in May) before disappearing in romantic abandon for 13 acres

Fulham
Palace,
"London's
best-kept
secret".

(5 hectares) to wrap itself around almshouses and Gothic gatehouses of Hansel and Gretel proportions. Once enclosed by the longest moat in England, the gardens became famous in the 17th century when Bishop Compton imported rare species, such as magnolia, and grew them in Europe for the first time. Against this magnificent backdrop, the almost abandoned palace takes on a certain dignity.

The hour-long tour, conducted twice a month, begins in the Tudor courtyard, takes in the Great Hall, the oldest room in the palace (1480), and includes the Dining Room – where a Palladian ceiling is undergoing restoration – and the Georgian Dining Room. The most interesting room is the Chapel, unfortunately modernised in 1950, but with pleasing frescoes painted by Brian Thomas, an artist known for mixing biblical and contemporary dress.

The museum, in two early 19th-century rooms, helps to put the story of the palace and the fabulously wealthy bishops – they were said to have at one stage presided over, not only London, but "all the Americas" – into perspective. Particularly useful is a replica of the building colour-coded to show each architectural era. Other exhibits include paintings, Roman finds, and Bishop Winnington-Ingrams' cope (cape), resplendent with semi-precious stones.

The museum will continue to develop as funds are raised, and all admission fees go towards restoration work and better exhibits. But the real attraction is a stroll through the gardens, which recall the past so evocatively.

Food and drink: Jackie's Cottage Café is tucked away in the grounds at the entrance to the palace. It serves cheap and cheerful fare like scampi and chips and all-day breakfasts; next to the outdoor tables is an aviary filled with birds. The Eight Bells pub close by at 89 Fulham High Street serves food, but even better is the Golden Lion at 57 Fulham High Street.

Osterley Park House

Robert Adam-designed summer residence for the founders of the Child & Co bank

Map reference: page 22, A3
Jersey Road, Isleworth, Middlesex.
Tel: 020-8232 5050.
www.nationaltrust.org.uk/thameschilterns.
Tube: Osterley.
House and Jersey Galleries open 31 Mar–4 Nov Wed–Sun and Bank Holidays 1–4:30pm. Grand Stables: Sun afternoons in summer. Park and Pleasure Grounds: daily 9am–7.30pm or sunset. Wheelchairs or shuttle bus from the car park; self-drive electronic vehicles Wed, Thur and Sun afternoons in summer, plus indoor wheelchairs in house.
Admission fee. Free to National Trust members.

Visiting Osterley Park House is similar to a day out in the country, and needs to be planned accordingly. A long journey (one hour from Green Park tube, plus a 25-minute unsigned walk from Osterley station – turn left out of the station, walk to the traffic lights, turn left again) and eccentric opening hours mean Osterley is not a place to be visited on a whim. Once there, though, visitors are rewarded with views of grazing ponies, towers, ponds, swans, a Bluebell Trail (flowering in May) and a handsome landscape of curving lakes and undulating fields. The only thing to mar the tranquillity of this classically English scene is the stream of planes on the flight path to nearby Heathrow.

The present house dates from 1761, when Robert Adam transformed a crumbling Tudor mansion into an elegant neo-classical villa. Its unmodernised appearance both inside and out classifies it as one of Britain's most complete examples of Adam's work, while the 16th-century Grand Stables are largely intact and still in use. Osterley's location and lack of nearby attractions means the house is seldom crowded, and the 375-acre (150-hectare) estate, with its forest, landscaped parks, Doric temples and Pleasure Grounds (all free), have a local, neighbourhood feel – albeit on a grand scale – allowing one to idle away the morning until the house opens at 1pm.

When Robert Adam was hired by Francis Child, Lord Mayor of London, to create a retreat for himself and his family, Adam was the most fashionable architect in the capital, famous for remaking houses from top to bottom, designing not only the facade, but also the interior and furniture. His task at Osterley was complex: to design a comfortable family house that was also grand enough in which to entertain (and influence) prominent guests. His solution was to design a mixture of "show rooms" on the ground floor, and "family rooms" upstairs. And yet, perhaps because of Osterley's rural location, even the show rooms have an informality and sensuality not normally associated with state apartments – a testament to Adam's ability to impress and seduce in equal measure.

The entrance into the house is through the courtyard and the East Front, which, curiously, Adam wanted to demolish (one of the few times Sir Francis won out over the architect). The Entrance Hall was built to dazzle, with decorative plasterwork of Roman arms, and statues of Hercules and the harvest goddess Ceres in the niches at either end. The grandest rooms are the three which form the State Apartment, and were conceived as a sequence of different styles – French, English and Italian – and different colours – red, green and blue, which allude to the elements of fire, earth and air.

The Antechamber, also called The Tapestry Room, is warm and vibrant, ruby-red with wall-to-wall embroideries custom-made in Paris. Furniture, rather than wall decoration, is the focus in the Bedchamber, in particular the huge, double-columned four-poster bed. The bed's crowning touch looks, in the words of

a noted chronicler of the time, like "a dome designed by a milliner", a gold-painted head-dress affair adorned with artificial flowers.

By contrast, the Dressing Room is light and airy, its pale sky-blue walls embellished with an "Adam special" – Etruscan designs in black and rust thought to be "unlike anything hitherto practised in Europe". It was one of eight Adam-designed "Etruscan rooms", and the only one remaining.

The family rooms upstairs are also of interest, although a few have no furniture. National Trust volunteers in every room can, however, occasionally be overpowering in their enthusiasm. The Jersey Galleries, which are in a separate building on the grounds, have changing exhibitions unrelated to the house.

ABOVE: Robert Adam's drawing room at Osterley Park.

BELOW: *Vulcan and Venus*, Gobelins tapestry panel from 1775.

Food and drink: The attractive Osterley Tea Room with its walled tea garden is located in the stables. Produce is often from Osterley's own grounds. Thornbury Road, which leads up to Osterley's gates, has three eating places: Memories of India, an upmarket, reasonably priced Indian restaurant (closed 3–6pm, but open all day Sunday); Osterley Cottage, an airy Chinese place, open all day; and Gallery Patisserie, serving sandwiches, espresso and cakes.

Prince Henry's Room

Recalling the diarist Samuel Pepys

Map reference: page 21, E3
17 Fleet Street, EC4. Tel: 020-8294 1158.
Tube: Temple.
Mon–Sat 11am–2pm. Free admission.

This is a room rather than a palace, but gains a royal connection through its use by Prince Henry, James I's elder son, who died of typhoid in 1612, aged 18. As Duke of Cornwall, he used the room as an office from which to run the duchy. Today the house is one of London's few surviving 17th-century timber-framed buildings, though its exterior was rebuilt in the early 20th century.

The room has an elaborate plasterwork ceiling and fine wood panelling and contains artefacts and paintings relating to Samuel Pepys (1633–1703), Secretary to the Admiralty but better known as the diarist who vividly chronicled the Great Plague and the Great Fire of London. The room's leaded light windows look out on the traffic jams of Fleet Street, once the centre of Britain's national newspapers but now frequented mainly by lawyers and accountants.

A German silver-gilt, gold, gems and mother-of-pearl partridge, circa 1600, from the Gilbert Collection.

Food and drink: To maintain the mood, one can visit Ye Olde Cheshire Cheese (Wine Office Court, 145 Fleet Street, 020-7353 6170), a tavern which was rebuilt after the 1666 Great Fire. Although now a bit touristy, it retains its character and has been a literary haunt for centuries.

Somerset House

Rare treasures in a grand building

Map reference: page 20, E4
The Strand, WC2.
Tel: 020-7845 4600.
www.somerset-house.org.uk
Open: daily 10am–6pm (house), 7.30am–11pm (courtyard). Tube: Charing Cross, Temple, Waterloo, Blackfriars. Bus: 13, 91, 68, 91, 168, 188. Wheelchair access (tel: 020-7836 8686 to reserve disabled parking). Shops. Waterloo Bridge access from 8am. Admission fee to galleries.

A Swiss snuffbox, circa 1812, from the Gilbert Collection.

Tucked away between the north bank of the Thames, Waterloo Bridge and the busy bus lanes and London University buildings of the eastern end of The Strand is Somerset House, a magnificent example of neoclassicism, designed in the 18th century by the Swedish-born British architect Sir William Chambers. Located on the site of a former 16th-century Renaissance palace, Chambers' noble edifice was originally built to house several government offices, including the Navy Board, and the three main learned societies of the United Kingdom: the Royal Academy of Arts, the Royal Society and the Society of Antiquaries.

By the early 20th century the building was principally used as the headquarters of the Inland Revenue and the Registry of Births, Marriages and Deaths. By the 1970s, however, it was decided that the House should be returned to public use. After major renovation, it opened in 2000 as the new home of The Gilbert Collection and the Hermitage Rooms, in which items on loan from the monumental St Petersburg museum are shown in temporary exhibitions.

The central courtyard was renovated and is now a fabulous space, complete with choreographed fountains and, in winter (sponsorship permitting), an outdoor ice-rink. The terrace alongside the river is now used as a showcase for outdoor sculpture, with past exhibitions featuring large-scale work by British sculptor Tony Cragg. Also within the complex is the Courtauld Institute of Art *(see pages 179–80).*

Hermitage Exhibition

Housed in the south wing are five rooms devoted exclusively to the show of works on loan from St Petersburg's Hermitage. Impressively furnished in grand Russian imperial style, with marquetry floors, smoked-glass chandeliers and rich swathes of curtaining, the rooms are intended to give the visitor the impression of having been whisked off to a hidden corner of the Hermitage. The suite of rooms is quite small, however, and there is not much to see for your money (this is the most expensive section of Somerset House), so it's advisable to go along only if the exhibition really grabs your attention. Past shows include "Treasures of Catherine the Great" and "French Drawings and Paintings: Poussin to Picasso".

The Gilbert Collection

Also in the south wing is the exceptional collection of silver, gold and micro-mosaics (intricate pictures made from coloured stone or glass), donated to the British nation in 1996 by the London-born real-estate millionaire, Sir Arthur Gilbert.

On the ground floor, highlights include a glittering pair of 18th-century silver-and-iron church gates, commissioned by Catherine the Great, and, in the "Indian Palace furniture" section, a lavish howdah (a chair for riding on an elephant).

On the upper floor, look out for a tiny Viennese 19th-century crown and six gem-encrusted boxes from the collection of Frederick the Great. It's worth saving some time and energy for the final room, where a breathtaking body of silver tableware is shown, including works by mastercraftsmen Paul de Lamerie and Paul Storr.

Food and drink: The complex includes The Admiralty (020-7845 4646), Oliver Peyton's exclusive restaurant serving French regional cuisine. The licensed Introductory Gallery Café has light snacks, the Deli has sandwiches and snacks, and in summer the River Terrace Café serves up light meals and great views of the Thames.

Spencer House

How aristocratic life was lived

Map reference: page 20, B5
27 St James's Place, SW1. Tel: 020-7499 8620.
www.spencerhouse.co.uk
Tube: Green Park.
Sundays only (except Jan & Aug) 10.30am–5.30pm. Timed tickets available on the day; no advance booking. No children under 10. Admission fee.

One of London's earliest examples of neo-classical architecture, this private palace was built in 1756–66 for the Spencer family (of which Diana, Princess of Wales was the most celebrated recent member) and has been renovated to its late 18th-century appearance. It provides both a classical showcase and, with eight state rooms, a sumptuous setting for receptions.

Master carvers replicated the original architectural detail and the state rooms contain period furniture, paintings and sculpture, some on loan from sources such as the Royal Collection and Tate Britain. The garden is also being restored to its original 1798 appearance, with plants and shrubs such as Eryngium agavifolium and Hosta sieboldiana elegans.

The Spencers have not lived in the house since 1926 and offices now occupy part of the building.

Food and drink: Just St James (12 St James's Street, 020-7976 2222) offers a Modern British menu. Moderate.

The forecourt of Somerset House is turned into a skating rink for several weeks each winter.

War and Conflict

There are swords, guns, tanks, fighter planes and even a warship on display, but many of these museums focus on the social costs of war and attempt to portray in sound-and-light "experiences" the human suffering it entails

British Red Cross Museum and Archives

Caring for people in time of crisis

Map reference: page 40, D2
9 Grosvenor Crescent, SW1 Tel: 020-7201 5153.
www.redcross.org.uk
Tube: Hyde Park Corner.
10am–4pm Mon–Fri. By appointment only.
Admission free.

By concentrating on the consequences of war, this permanent exhibition provides an effective counterpoint to the other museums in this section, with their emphasis on bombs and bullets. Since its creation in 1863, the Red Cross has dedicated itself to humanitarian relief. Some of the collecting boxes it has used over the years to raise funds are displayed here, along with old posters, photographs, food parcels sent to prisoners of war, and various types of medical equipment.

A popular exhibit is the Changi Quilt, sewn by women interned in Singapore during World War II; having incorporated their names in the quilt, they sent it across to the male section of the prison as a way of announcing to their menfolk that they were still alive.

An extensive reference library, photographic collection and video library is available to researchers.

Cabinet War Rooms

The underground bunker from which Churchill directed Britain's war effort

Map reference: page 20, C5
Bottom of Clive Steps (at end of King Charles Street, which runs off Parliament Street), SW1.
Tel: 020-7930 6961. www.iwm.org.uk
Tube: Westminster.
Daily from 9.30am Apr–Sept, 10am Oct–Mar, last admission 5.15pm. Admission charge.

The appeal of this wartime nerve centre lies in its authenticity. It's not some Disney-style reconstruction: these are the actual claustrophobic corridors along which Britain's political and military leaders walked, the rooms in which they worked, ate and, often, slept for the six years of the war. Many of the 21 rooms were simply abandoned in 1945 and were left untouched until the museum opened in 1984; many that were cleared out have been meticulously restored to their wartime condition, "down to the last paper clip", using old photographs for reference, and more are being opened.

A government storage basement was secretly adapted as a secure inner sanctum in 1938, when war seemed inevitable. Viewed initially as a temporary expedient, the rooms became essential in 1940, when intensive bombing raids on London began. A concrete slab 3 ft (1 metre) thick was then placed over the rooms to protect them against a direct hit. But there is no evidence that Hitler ever learned of the existence of such a desirable target.

Today's sandbagged entrance is new, since the rooms were originally accessed from the government offices above. The initial gallery, once a coal bunker, sets a wartime mood with displays of newspaper front pages, identity cards and ration books, plus a real 50-kg (110-lb) bomb. A hand-held audio guide provides a commentary in eight languages (English, Dutch, French, German, Hebrew, Italian, Spanish and Swedish), and punching in codes at various points provides additional information, such as reminiscences by secretaries who worked in the bunker or extracts from some of Winston Churchill's most memorable speeches.

The Cabinet Room is set up as it would have been for a meeting in 1940, with the red box used to carry State papers sitting in front of Churchill's distinctive chair at the top table. A waxwork officer arranges the agenda on the table but, like a scattering of other mannequins around the museum, it emphasises

OPPOSITE: the Imperial War Museum

BELOW: the pose that led Hitler to brand Churchill as "a gangster"

The Central Map Room of the Cabinet War Rooms.

the cramped conditions rather than diluting the authenticity. The thick red girders made the site appear more impregnable than it probably was.

The long corridor linking the rooms is reminiscent of a Victorian hospital or barracks and was packed with storage cupboards and map chests. A sign on the wall told the occupants what the weather was like outside their cocoon; traditionally, "windy" meant that an air-raid was in progress. Heavy sealed doors and rifle racks are a reminder that an imminent Nazi invasion was a real possibility in late 1940 and early 1941.

The Map Room and the rooms that served as round-the-clock typing pools illustrate forcefully the gulf between communications in the 1940s and today's VDU-filled world. Marker pins moved round a large map of the Atlantic indicate the success or failure of convoys in surviving enemy submarines, and blackboards show the chalked-up aircraft casualties of the previous night. Banks of colour-coded telephones connected to manually operated switchboards provided the latest good news, or bad. One archaic Gestetner copier did little to lessen the burden of typing and retyping top-secret documents on manual typewriters. and the air-conditioning can scarcely have coped with the pall of smoke from the staff's cigarettes and Churchill's cigars.

Churchill's bedroom/office, virtually papered with maps, is grander than those provided for other senior figures, but only marginally so. A custom-made table placed on his bed enabled him sit up in bed "looking like a pink cherub", as one staffer recalls on the audio commentary, and read the latest reports before getting up. He used microphones on his desk, connected to the BBC, to make several wartime broadcasts. His chamber pot sits by the bed.

One converted broom cupboard, on show to visitors today, remained a mystery to most of the Cabinet War Room staff. They thought it might contain the cellar's only flushing toilet, reserved for the prime minister – chemical toilets were standard. In fact, it housed a pioneering "hot line" to the White House, enabling Churchill to have confidential talks with President Franklin D. Roosevelt. The massive equipment needed to scramble and decipher the conversations was concealed in the basement of Selfridges department store in Oxford Street and connected by cable to the War Rooms.

Displays at the end of the tour include a selection of weapons owned by Churchill and selections of the letters and telegrams that flowed between him, Roosevelt and Stalin. Copious handwritten amendments to typed drafts of his speeches show how much he polished them. His reactions to losing the 1945 general election and photographs of his 1965 funeral conclude the exhibition, but the former mess-room is now a shop selling CDs and videos, Churchillian keyrings and toy bulldogs.

A tour of the Cabinet War Rooms, which are run by the Imperial War Museum, takes about an hour, and is compelling enough to have attracted two American presidents, Bill Clinton and George W. Bush.

Food and drink: Government offices dominate the area. There's a small pub, the Red Lion, in Parliament Street, but the best bet is to stroll up Whitehall to Trafalgar Square.

Firepower

The Royal Artillery Experience at Woolwich

Map reference: page 23, J3
The Royal Arsenal, Woolwich, London SE18.
Tel: 020-8855 7755. www.firepower.org.uk
Daily 10am–5pm, closed Christmas Day.
Tube to North Greenwich then 161, 422 or 472 bus. Direct, frequent trains from Waterloo East, Charing Cross, London Bridge and Cannon Street. By bus 53 from central London, 472, 161, 180, 380, 422, 54, 53 locally.
Fully wheelchair accessible with nearby parking and drop off at the door. There are braille signs for the artillery exhibits.

A very different style of military museum, this lively venue, located in the historic Royal Arsenal at Woolwich on the River Thames, is full of audio-visual and interactive exhibits. The aim is to tell the story of artillery. The centrepiece is the ground-shaking "Field of Fire", which puts viewers in the midst of battle. Bombs and shells whizz overhead, guns roar and smoke fills the room. The thoughts, feelings and actions of those involved in campaigns in the second half of the 20th century are captured through film, music and words.

The ultimate wastefulness of warfare is made clear enough through the experience, and care is taken not to glorify conflict. There is also a large two-level gunnery gallery which has an impressive display of artillery, and "have a go" simulators allow visitors to realise and experience the danger of being a gunner in the field of war. The upper tier is a history gallery with many interactive displays, and there is a separate medals gallery.

The opening of Firepower was the culmination of almost 15 years of fundraising and planning and has been financed partly by the Heritage Lottery Fund. The museum is fittingly located in the historic Royal Arsenal site, which is open to the public for the first time since the Royal Artillery Regiment was established in the early 18th century.

Adjacent to the main museum building are several historic buildings including the former Military Academy, purportedly designed by Nicholas Hawksmoor, which have also been renovated to house some of the larger parts of the collection.

Food and drink: The museum has a café serving snacks.

Artillery on show at Firepower.

Absorbed by "The Field of Fire".

Guards Museum

Starring five regiments of the Foot Guards

Map reference: page 20, C6
Wellington Barracks, Birdcage Walk, SW1. Tel:
020-7930 4466 ext. 3271. www.army.mod.uk
/ceremonialandheritage/museums
Open daily 10am–4pm including weekends and
Bank Holidays. Closed Christmas and all
January and some ceremonial days.
Tube: St James Park (Petty France exit).
Victoria Station with services from the south
via Connex and Gatwick Express is nearby.
Disabled access is possible but visitors must
call in advance.

Situated within Wellington Barracks, 200 yards from Buckingham Palace, the Guards Museum represents the history of the five regiments which, together with the Household Cavalry, the Life Guards and Blues and Royals, form the Household Division of the Army. The regiments are the Grenadier Guards, Coldstream Guards, Scots Guards, Irish Guards and Welsh Guards.

The Guards play a central role in London's ceremonial.

The museum has a well-displayed mixed collection recounting the military history of the Foot Guards, and much of it is shown at child's-eye level. A good proportion is based on one individual's experiences of a particular battle or event. It is intended to be about the people from all classes of society, their sacrifices and their glory, a social history in uniform. Before the museum was opened in 1988, the collection had rarely been seen by the soldiers and never by the public.

Like many regiments of the Army the Guards have their origins in the English Civil War (1642–49), which ended with Charles I's execution. Following the restoration of the monarchy in 1660, they were formed from a regiment of Oliver Cromwell's Model Army and two regiments of the exiled King's Body Guard. The collection includes items from this time on and of particular interest are the uniform and shako which belonged to the Duke of Wellington and the collection of medals for valour, including many Victoria Crosses. They also have a fine collection of the orders and decorations of Adolphus, 1st Duke of Cambridge (1774–1850), the youngest and favourite son of George III, and his son the 2nd Duke (1819–1904).

The museum shop (closed Mon) is a collector's paradise. It is a specialist shop offering an extensive range of modern and antique model and toy soldiers, as well as military souvenirs and music.

A visit could be combined with watching the Changing of the Guards at Buckingham Palace.

Food and drink: The museum has no café but there are lots of fast-food joints in nearby Victoria Street. Quilon, an upmarket Indian restaurant, is in the St James's Court Hotel (41 Buckingham Gate, 020-7821 1899).

HMS Belfast

The work of a 20th-century warship

Map reference: page 21, J4
Morgans Lane, Tooley Street, SE1.
Tel: 020-7940 6300. www.hmsbelfast.org.uk
Tube: London Bridge.
Mar–Oct 10am–6pm, Nov–Feb 10am–5pm,
closed 24–26 Dec. Admission charge.
Disabled access on two of the nine decks.

Moored just upstream from Tower Bridge, this is Britain's only surviving example of the big-gun armoured warships built during the first half of the 20th century. Now part of the Imperial War Museum *(see next entry)*, it gives a fascinating insight into the work of a warship and the strains of life on board. Launched in Belfast in 1938, the vessel was in active service until 1965, and served in World War II and the Korean War (1950–53). As a "cruiser", or flagship, it played an important role in leading convoys.

The recommended tour (free map provided) begins on the quarterdeck, proceeds via the boatdeck to the bridge and gun turret "A", then descends via the living quarters to the boiler and engine rooms. Gun turret "A" is one of four such turrets, each of which would have been manned by a team of 27 highly trained men able to launch eight rounds of shells a minute from each gun. The guns could be used against land and sea targets up to 14 miles (23 km) away – the ones in turret "A" are currently trained on a service station 12 miles (20 km) up the M1 motorway. It is worth venturing down into the heavily armoured shell room below the gun-turret, where a further 22 men would have sent the shells up to the gun room by mechanical hoist. A secondary battery of anti-aircraft mountings located on either side of the ship could be used against enemy planes up to 39,000 ft (11,900 metres) away, supported by the massive Bofor guns on either side of the bridge.

At the height of its career, the *Belfast* accommodated 950 men. It was refitted in the 1950s, and life for the sailors improved dramatically, with the addition of showers, proper bunk beds, a laundry and a modern kitchen with the same fittings as on the royal yacht, *Britannia*. Most of what you see belongs to the 1950s revamp, but a portion has been returned to its original, commissioned state, with cramped messes slung with hammocks only 21 inches (52 cm) apart.

As the "mother" ship in the fleet, the *Belfast* was equipped with an operating theatre, a dental surgery and hospital beds, as well as extensive food and ammunition stores, a butcher and bakery, where a team of six bakers would keep the fleet in fresh bread. All these facilities are on display, with wax dummies, sound effects and plenty of props. But what really brings the boat to life is the archive footage of the *Belfast* in action. This includes the moving story of the destruction of the German battlecruiser *Scharnhorst* in the Battle of North Cape in World War II, when only 36 out of the 1,963 Germans on board survived, and an account of the *Belfast*'s role in the Normandy Landings of 1944.

Food and drink: Hay's Galleria, close by, has a selection of chain-style restaurants and a Balls Brothers wine bar under its high vaulted roof. A few minutes away, just past Tower Bridge, are several Sir Terence Conran restaurants – see food listing on page 61 for Tower Bridge Experience.

Imperial War Museum

Chronicling a century of conflict

Map reference: page 21, F6
Lambeth Road, SE1. Tel: 020-7416 5439.
www.iwm.org.uk
Tube: Lambeth North.
Daily 10am–6pm. Free admission.

This stately building opened in 1815 to house the Bethlem Royal Hospital for the insane, popularly known as Bedlam and an inspired choice for a museum chronicling the horrors of modern warfare. After the hospital moved out of London in the 1930s, the central block of the building, whose wings had been demolished, was turned over to the Great War collection of the Imperial War Museum, previously housed in South Kensington. After World War II – during which, ironically, the museum was damaged in air raids – it also began to gather material from this and later conflicts, and three smaller sites, including the warship *HMS Belfast (see previous entry)*, were acquired to accommodate it.

There's so much to see that this is an ideal outing for a rainy afternoon: you need two to three hours to explore the main part of the museum, and at least another hour to see the Holocaust Exhibition. Over the past 10 years, the Imperial War Museum has expanded its remit from the purely military to include a rolling programme of exhibitions covering many aspects of modern history, often only loosely connected with conflict – from code breaking and refugees to fashion and sport. Many of these exhibits are aimed at the young – see the leaflets *What's On* and *What's On for Children* for details.

HMS *Belfast* with a backdrop of the Tower of London and Tower Bridge.

down to the human level. Official material, such as Field-Marshal Bernard Montgomery's papers, Hitler's will and the overoptimistic "piece of paper" that prime minister Neville Chamberlain waved on his return from meeting Adolf Hitler in Munich in 1938, are interspersed with the letters, diaries, sketches and interviews of ordinary soldiers, civilians, prisoners of war, conscientious objectors and refugees. Also on show are manuscripts of war literature, such as Siegfried Sassoon's *Memoirs of an Infantry Officer*, and a room full of Victoria and George Crosses awarded for heroic deeds.

The Blitz and Trench "experiences" may appeal more to children than adults. There is no queue at the Trench, but you can see why: it's inexplicably dark and not especially realistic, though the sense of smell is quite effective: an unpleasant musty odour gives way to the sharpness of disinfectant as you pass the hospital tent. You may have to queue for the Blitz Experience, which works better than the Trench. The darkness in which you wait for air raids is atmospheric and recorded announcements help to create tension. You even get a healthy dose of dust from collapsed buildings.

Upstairs is an extension of the Large Exhibits Gallery. On the right as you come up the stairs is an aeroplane fuselage that you can walk

An array of weaponry at the Imperial War Museum.

The museum also includes a cinema, which shows newsreels and wartime films.

As you enter the main hall, the direction you take will depend on where your interest lies. The stairs at the back of the Large Exhibits Gallery lead down to exhibitions on the two world wars. Here, physical artefacts, art, photography, film and sound recordings weave an atmosphere as close as possible to the mood of the time, while interactive screens give access to further information.

All this film and sound can be quite an assault on the senses. It is better to settle on a particular section and absorb the small details. Looking at a letter informing a father of his son's death brings it all

through. The Secret War exhibit on counter-intelligence is also on this floor. Juxtaposed with the glamour of fictional spies is the harsh reality of espionage. Of six female World War II spies featured in one display, only one survived the war. There's a cyanide capsule, to be taken if captured – this one was handed in by an agent who luckily didn't have to use it.

The second floor holds one of Britain's leading collections of 20th-century art – the World War I gallery is to the right; World War II to the left. Many of the works were officially commissioned for propaganda purposes, including the famous painting *Gassed* in the John Singer Sargent room. The London Blitz drawings by Henry Moore are very fine.

The Holocaust Exhibition

Occupying the next two floors is the Holocaust Exhibition, the largest display of its kind in the world outside Israel and the United States. It will take you a good hour to look around and to listen to the large amount of video and film available. Be warned: this is an intense and harrowing exhibition and it is not advisable to bring children (there is a lower age limit of 13, but it's not always strictly enforced). It is built around the testimonies of a selection of survivors who tell of their experiences chronologically from the origins of anti-Semitism through to its horrific manifestation in the Holocaust.

Film footage accompanies the stories, as does rare and important historical material. Larger items include a section of a deportation railcar, the entrance to a gas chamber, a dissection table, shoes collected from victims of the gas chambers and a large model of part of Auschwitz. Especially poignant are personal belongings such as the letters of an eight-year-old Austrian boy, Georgy Halpern, who hid in an orphanage until he was betrayed and deported to Auschwitz. After he was gassed, his mother's last letter to him, also on display, was returned to her marked "No longer at this address". Equally chilling are the logbooks of concentration camp killings, meticulously kept by Nazi bureaucrats, and the original plans for the gas chambers.

The Holocaust Exhibition marks a change of emphasis for the museum, from documenting the mechanics of warfare to exploring the effects on the victims, but even so punches had to be pulled. "We had to strike a balance between accessibility and sheer horror in order to ensure that the exhibition is endurable," said its director, Suzanne Bardgett.

The Imperial War Museum caters for scholars as well as casual visitors. The dome above the entrance hall houses a large reference library, which is open to the public; however, because the reading room is small, a place must be booked two weeks in advance. The museum doesn't hold personal service records – these are held by the Public Record Office – but if you want to find out about a family member involved in one of the wars, you're free to do independent research and the library staff will point you in the right direction.

The museum holds the world's largest sound archive (32,000 hours) and the oldest film archive (120 million ft of film from as early as 1917), as well as more than 6 million photographs, 30,000 international war posters and substantial collections of maps. Many items are displayed in the exhibits, but if you're looking for something in particular, you can have free access to the archives by appointment. Programme makers seeking footage for television documentaries on the world wars provide a useful source of revenue.

In order to digest what you've seen in the museum, you might wish to relax in the delicately symmetrical Peace Garden, opened by the Dalai Lama in 1999. It's to the right of the manicured flowerbeds as you exit the museum.

Food and drink: Perdoni's is a popular no-nonsense café at 18–20 Kennington High Road (020-7928 6846), dishing up everything from pasta and roast beef to omelettes.

National Army Museum

From swords to heat-seeking missiles

Map reference: page 40, C4
Royal Hospital Road, Chelsea, SW3.
Tel: 020-7730 0717.
www.national-army-museum.ac.uk
Daily 10am–5.30pm except 24–26 Dec, 1 Jan, Good Friday, and the Early May Bank Holiday. Tube: Sloane Square, then 5-minute walk. The 239 bus (not Sundays) stops outside the main entrance, and the 11, 19, 22, and 211 stop on the King's Road nearby.
Admission free.
All galleries are accessible to wheelchairs; visitors with special needs can telephone 020 7730 0717 extension 2210 for advice and assistance.

One of London's most attractive buildings, Sir Christopher Wren's elegantly proportioned Royal Hospital, shares its Chelsea address with one of the city's ugliest, the National Army Museum. But behind the anonymous and forbidding concrete and brick exterior lies a comprehensive and superbly presented collection of British Army artefacts.

There's a lot to see, with glittering medals, uniforms, and swords galore, as well as the very latest in military technology. You can feel the

Memories of the British Army's colonial campaigns.

The General
Wladyslaw
Anders Room
in the Polish
Institute and
Sikorski
Museum.

weight of a Tudor cannonball, try on soldier's helmets – from those of Cromwell's New Model Army to that of today's squaddie – and test your military skills on a range of computer-aided challenges.

The galleries chart the campaigns of the British Army from the Middle Ages through 18th- and 19th-century colonial and European adventures, two world wars and more recent conflicts in the Falklands and the Gulf. Portraits by Gainsborough, Reynolds, and lesser artists crowd the walls, Dress swords in the Cut Thrust and Swagger gallery in the basement are works of art in their own right. Here you will learn that military science perfected the sword as a weapon in 1908, just at the time that it became obsolete.

The Road to Waterloo exhibit, which includes an accurate topographical model of the battle, complete with 70,000 model soldiers, displays Wellington's shaving mirror, the bullet that killed General Picton, and the skeleton of Napoleon's horse, Marengo, preserved minus two hoofs, which were made into commemorative snuff boxes.

Lifelike and life-sized models ranging from Henry V's archers to an SAS trooper are shown mostly as mudcaked, wounded, and exhausted, and the replica World War I trench is a place for quiet reflection.

The museum shop sells souvenirs, books, postcards, and a huge range of model soldiers.

*Soldiers in
the Crimea
are shown
receiving a
food parcel
from home in
John d'Albiac
Luard's A
Welcome
Arrival.*

Food and drink*: The café offers a well-made if limited
range of sandwiches, salads, and cakes. Gordon Ramsay
(68–69 Royal Hospital Road, 020-7352 4441) offers
reliable haute cuisine, appropriately priced.*

Polish Institute and Sikorski Museum

How the Poles helped win World War II

Map reference: page 40, C2
20 Princes Gate, SW7. Tel: 020-7589 9249.
By appointment only; open Mon–Fri 2–4pm,
first Saturday each month 10am–4pm.
Tube: South Kensington. Bus: 14, 45a, 49, 74,
349, C1. Admission free.

The Sikorski Museum was set up by members of the exiled Polish community in London who choose not to return to their Soviet-dominated homeland at the end of World War II. This is a specialist museum, named after the war hero and leader of the Polish government-in-exile General Wladyslaw Sikorski (1881–1943). Even so, visitors without knowledge of Poland's role in World War II can take an English-language guided tour (exhibits are labelled in Polish) and get a sense of the struggle of ordinary people during that period from the many everyday items displayed.

The main collection comprises over 10,000 military items contained in rooms dedicated to each of the armed forces, while decorating the museum's main staircase is a collection of paintings and drawings. Star exhibits include an Enigma ciphering machine, the encoding of which was cracked by Polish mathematicians, and the flag of the Second Polish Corps from the victorious Battle of Monte Cassino. General Sikorski personifies Poland's national spirit and his writing desk, part of a collection of his personal and military effects, is a popular photo spot with Polish visitors. Young visitors will enjoy the full-size model of Wojtek, the "soldier bear", adopted by Polish soldiers as a travelling mascot.

The archives of the Polish Institute document the wartime period and are used for academic research in this field.

Food and drink: The nearest Polish restaurant is Wódka (12 St Alban's Grove, 020-7937 6513), 15 minutes' walk away. Reliable, modern cooking, moderate prices.

Royal Air Force Museum

The UK's largest array of military aircraft

Map reference: page 22, D1
Grahame Park Way, Hendon, NW9.
Tel: 020-8205 2266.
www.rafmuseum.org.uk
Tube: Colindale (15-minute walk). Bus 303, from Edgware to Ealing Broadway, stops in front of the museum.
Daily 10am–6pm (except 1 Jan, 24–26 Dec).
Admission free.
Shop, disabled access, baby-changing facilities.

For anyone who has ever fantasised about being a superhero flying ace – from Biggles to Buzz Lightyear – the Royal Air Force Museum is a place of dreams. RAF Hendon, in north London, was one of the earliest centres for pioneer aviators. Claude Graham White, of the Royal Naval Air Service, witnessed Louis Blériot's historic flight across the English Channel in 1909, and was inspired to set up a training school in Hendon in 1910. Throughout both world wars, the developing aerodrome at Hendon served as a military base, and remained in use until 1969. In 1972, the museum was opened here, based in two hangars built in 1917, during World War I.

Here, you can wander among some of the most famous aeroplanes in the history of aerial combat, from the Battle of Britain's Supermarine Spitfire and Messerschmidt Bf109, to the enormous Lancaster and B-17 Flying Fortress bombers.

The scope of the museum incorporates the entire history of flight, with the upper floor of the Main Aircraft Hall dedicated to the earliest experiments to conquer the skies. With due respect paid to Leonardo da Vinci's far-sighted designs for a prototype helicopter, it was the Montgolfier brothers from France who are credited with the first aerial transportation of living creatures. In September 1783, before the Court of King Louis XVI and Marie Antoinette, the Montgolfiers' hot air balloon took to the air in Versailles, carrying as its passengers a sheep, a duck and a cockerel. A few weeks later, heartened by this success, the Montgolfier brothers themselves made mankind's first flight – a 20-minute journey in a balloon over Paris.

It's the aeroplanes down in the cavernous halls, however, that capture the imagination of most wannabe top guns. Some of these, such as the enormous Sunderland flying boat, are opened up to allow you to clamber aboard, to the accompaniment of a recorded audioguide. You can even jump into the cockpit of a small Provost trainer jet and have a go at the controls, though if you're expecting G-force thrust and roaring engines, you may be disappointed, as it remains quietly stationary.

For a virtual aerial experience (small fee), you can have a go on one of the famous Red Arrows stunt planes inside a Flight Simulator, thoughtfully located next to the Engine Bay Café, where you can come down to earth over a light snack. There is also a small cinema, in a section dedicated to RAF recruitment, where you can watch a computer simulated aerial attack scenario (though maybe not for bloodthirsty video-game addicts – the targets here are strictly "non-collateral", in military jargon).

Although the majority of the planes are either bombers or fighter jets – this is the RAF Museum after all – the tone of the place is not excessively militaristic. Due attention is paid to civilian life during peace and war-time. The Battle of Britain Hall re-creates life in Britain during

Classic fighters on show at the RAF Museum.

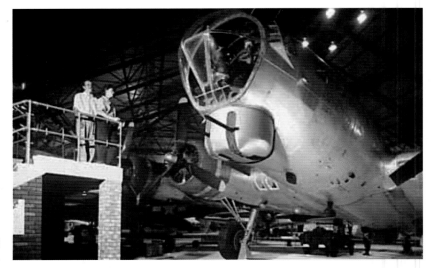

A four-engined Sunderland flying boat.

World War II, with tableaux of scenes such as the evacuation of children from threatened cities, householders' air raid shelters at the bottom of the garden, and the perilous work of bomb disposal crews and air-raid wardens.

The figures in the tableaux are eerily brought to life by video faces projected onto them, so they can talk and sing us through the dramatic goings-on. Even Winston Churchill gives us a very wooden interpretation of his famous war declaration speech.

One of the museum's most lovingly preserved exhibits is another boat plane resurrected from a marsh in the Thames estuary, the surviving hull of which now gleams with beautifully polished woodwork and thousands of brass rivets.

Particularly popular with children visiting the museum is the Fun & Flight section, with some imaginative activities such as throwing balls in air jets to measure wind speeds, eye tests, a light laser game to learn about sound waves, and an aerial load-dropping target game.

Regular special events and demonstrations are held at the museum, including a mock-up of a World War II period classroom, with pupils hiding under desks during an air raid, and writing name tags and ration books in preparation for evacuation.

Food and drink: There are two places to eat – the main restaurant, serving hot meals, in the Battle of Britain Hall, or the Engine Bay café, in the Bomber Command Hall, which serves hot and cold drinks, sandwiches and cakes. If you bring your own food, the only place to eat is in an outdoor picnic area. There are no other nearby places to eat or drink.

A Fusilier in the uniform of the 1790s.

Royal Fusiliers Museum

The story of an illustrious regiment

Map reference: page 21, J4
Tower of London, London EC3.
Tel: 020-7488 5610. www.army.mod.uk/ ceremonialandheritage/museums
Tube: Tower Hill. Buses 15, 42 and 78.
9.30am–5.30pm Mon–Sat 10.30am–4.30pm Sun in summer and 9.30am–4.30pm Mon–Sat, 10.30am–4.30pm Sun in winter. Closed Christmas Day and New Year's Day. No disabled access.
It is not possible to visit the museum without paying the steep entry charge for the Tower of London and there is a small additional charge.

In the centre of the Tower of London, just past the building where the Crown Jewels are displayed, is the modest but elegantly housed Royal Fusiliers Museum. Opened in 1962, this small museum describes and illustrates the long and mostly illustrious history of the Fusiliers.

These fighting men are easy to spot because of the distinctive feathered "hackle" they wear on their caps. This originated in 1778 when, following the defeat of the

French at the Battle of St Lucia, the Royal Northumberland Fusiliers took the white plumes from their enemies' head-dresses and wore them in their own caps as a battle honour. The red tip was added later to distinguish the Fusiliers from the Guards.

The Tower is the regiment's traditional home, The Fusiliers were created there in 1685 by George Legge, Lord Dartmouth, and formed from the existing Tower Guard. King James II required them to guard the Ordnance Train and they were soon styled at the King's pleasure "Our Royal Regiment of Fuzileers". The regiment took its name from a new type of musket, which had a covered flash pan to minimise the risk of sparks igniting the gunpowder.

The museum's displays follow the regiment's campaigns from its first battle for William of Orange against the French in Walcourt up to its present-day peacekeeping involvement in the Balkans and Northern Ireland.

There is also an impressive selection of medals – 20 members of the Royal Fusiliers have been awarded the Victoria Cross – as well as paintings, uniforms and one of the regiment's most prized possessions, the Myers miniature, which commemorates the officers killed in the Peninsula War of 1809–14. Another display describes the regiment's less glorious involvement in the American War of Independence, culminating in the disastrous battle of Cowpens in 1781 that all but destroyed it.

Food and drink*: Within the Tower of London complex, the New Armouries Café, housed in a 1663 storehouse, serves hot and cold dishes. There are also several Prêt à Manger sandwich shops.*

Winston Churchill's Britain at War Experience

How Londoners lived during the blitz

Map reference: page 21, H5
64–66 Tooley Street, SE1. Tel: 020-7403 3171.
www.britainatwar.co.uk
Daily from 10am; last admission 4.30pm
Oct–Mar, 5.30pm Apr–Sept. Admission charge.

World War II hit Southwark worse than most areas of London because German bombers targeted the docks and warehouses around London Bridge. This underground museum tries to re-create the sounds and smells of the blitz through special effects, illustrating what life was like in an air raid shelter and showing the aftermath of a bombing raid.

Wartime news is projected in an underground cinema, and there are lots of wartime posters, magazine covers, newspaper cuttings and extracts from Sir Winston Churchill's speeches. Clothes, radios, toys and toilet paper from the 1940s conjure up an exotically different age, and retired GIs may view a Wurlitzer jukebox and Varga pin-ups with a certain nostalgia. In a wrecked draper's, tailors' dummies are cunningly used to suggest carnage without having to portray real mutilation. School parties have great fun trying on helmets and gas masks, but children might benefit most from the exhibition if, before visiting, they were given a quick briefing about the war.

Food and drink*: There are pleasant fast-food places in Hay's Galleria, opposite the museum. For something different, try Fina Estampa (150 Tooley Street, 020-7403 1342), London's only Peruvian restaurant; prices moderate.*

A lithograph shows Fusilier officers in the uniform current during the Crimean War.

A child tries on a gas mask at the Britain at War Museum.

Ranging from the claustrophobia of a 16th-century galleon to the splendour of a coronation coach, these museums show how an island race navigated round the world and how Londoners tried to keep the capital's traffic moving

Cutty Sark

Recalling the golden age of the tea clipper

Map reference: page 23, H3
King William Walk, Greenwich, SE10.
Tel: 020-8858 3445. www.cuttysark.org.uk
Apr–Sept Mon–Sat 10am–6pm, Sun and Good
Friday noon–6pm; Oct–March Mon–Sat
10am–5pm, Sun and Good Friday noon–5pm.
Entrance fee.
Shop; guided tours by volunteers in costume.

In the heyday of maritime trade, clippers like the *Cutty Sark* ruled the oceans. Life on board was tough and dangerous, yet seafarers would fight for a place in a clipper crew to participate in the competitive races to and from China and Australia. They were prestigious ships to skipper. If a captain steered his ship to victory, his reputation and fortune were made.

Like all the finest clippers, the *Cutty Sark* was designed and built in Scotland, but her solid teak (as opposed to pine) decks and additional "'tween deck" gave her the edge over her rivals by increasing her rigidity without ruining her sleek lines. In her eight years as a tea clipper, from 1869 to 1877, the *Cutty Sark* performed well, but it was in the wool trade that she became invincible. After the opening of the Suez Canal, steam ships were able to reach China in half the time, but it was an unsuitable passage for sailing ships, and their owners looked to Australia for new business. The ocean road to the antipodes was the hardest of all, but the *Cutty Sark*, undaunted by the stormy weather of the Roaring Forties, proved her strength time and again. In 1885, the return journey from New South Wales took just 72 days, a record that was never beaten.

Eventually, however, even the wool trade was taken over by steamships. By 1895, *Cutty Sark* could no longer turn a profit and was sold to the Portuguese. She spent the next 30 years sailing between Lisbon and Rio, and the subsequent war years back under the English flag as a training ship. In 1954, a severely damaged *Cutty Sark* limped up the Thames as far as Greenwich. She was manoeuvred into dry dock and three years later, restored to her former glory, the ship opened as a museum.

The two lower decks, which would once have been packed with cargo, now house the ship's museum. You enter at the "'tween deck" level laid out with a good old-fashioned words-and-pictures display telling the history of the ship, beginning with the origin of her curious name. It was taken from the Robert Burns poem, *Tam O'Shanter*, whose hero was chased by a young and beautiful witch, called Nannie, scantily clad in a "cutty sark" (short shift). The ship's figurehead is of Nannie holding the tail of Tam's horse (traditionally a piece of old rope), which she tore off as he fled. The figurehead on the prow is a copy of the original which stands just inside the entrance.

One section of the deck is taken up by a reconstructed cargo of tea chests, stowed as they would have been by Chinese stevedores in Shanghai – their expertise was highly valued because a badly stowed cargo could cause a ship to founder. Among the few exhibits interspersed between the panels is a model of the *Cutty Sark* in full rigging.

The lower deck, which would also have been a cargo space, is lined with a colourful collection of figureheads from merchant ships, but more compelling is the video display of archive film of life on board the great square riggers in the 1920s and '30s.

Up on the main deck, visitors are free to wander from the forward end, or fo'c's'le, equipped with giant winches used to raise and lower the anchor

OPPOSITE: one of London Transport's striking posters from the early 20th century.

BELOW: the *Cutty Sark*.

RIGHT: an actor
welcomes
visitors to the
Golden Hinde.

BELOW: the
ship's prow.

and load and unload cargo, to the poop deck and the ship's wheel. Between them, the three masts held 34 sails which were controlled by 11 miles (18 km) of rope. When fully set, with a favourable wind the ship could maintain a steady speed of 17 knots (nearly 20 miles/32 km per hour). All accommodation was on the top deck and you can peer into the cabins, peopled with models of sleeping (and snoring) seamen. There were never more than 28 crew members, most of whom slept in the cramped forward deckhouse cabins, next to the galley and carpenter's shop. The Master, Mate and Second Mate had superior quarters just below the poop deck. The officers' saloon, all maple and teak, was used both as a dining room and navigation room, where charts could be spread out on the table.

Back outside, take one last look at the ship from under the prow. Looking down to the hull and up to the towering masts, you cannot help but marvel at the engineering skill and craftsmanship it took to create such a robust, yet graceful vessel.

Food and drink: The Admiral Hardy (College Approach, Greenwich Market; restaurant bookings tel 020-8858 6452), sister pub to the Trafalgar Tavern (see National Maritime Museum entry, page 38), serves reasonably priced bar snacks downstairs, with a pricier seafood restaurant upstairs. Very busy on weekends. Its shop, stocked with fresh seafood from Billingsgate, homemade pies and cheeses is a good source of deluxe picnic food.

Golden Hinde

How Drake sailed around the world in 1577

Map reference: page 21, H4
St Mary Overie Dock, Clink Street, SE1. Tel: bookings 08700-118700. Tube: London Bridge. 9am–sunset. Admission charge.

A few hundred yards east of Shakespeare's Globe on Bankside, at the end of Pickfords Wharf – built in 1864 for storing hops, flour and seeds, and now an apartment block – is a full-size replica of Sir Francis Drake's galleon, the *Golden Hinde*. The Devon-built ship, launched in 1973, toured Britain and North America as a travelling museum until it came to rest here in 1996, and is the only replica to have completed a circumnavigation of the globe. It has thus clocked up more nautical miles than the original, in which Drake set sail in 1577 on the greatest piratical voyage in Eng-

lish history. During his three-year marathon, he allegedly claimed for Queen Elizabeth I the territory now known as California.

Climbing aboard and moving through the replica (minding your head on the ceilings, which are less than 6 ft/2 metres high to keep the ship's centre of gravity low), it's easy to imagine life at sea on such a vessel. Particularly striking are the cramped and harsh conditions endured by the sailors. They spent their lives either at work or asleep on the bare decks, which were often under an inch of water; they had only one set of clothes and no privacy or personal possessions. Answering the call of nature was a hazardous procedure, involving clambering down onto the beakhead at the bow of the ship, and tying yourself to the ship to avoid losing your grip as the beakhead went under water.

Diet was poor and many men perished at sea, although Drake was ahead of his time and supplemented their meagre and festering rations with fruit whenever possible. For this reason, survival rates aboard his ships were better than average, which probably helped his recruiting.

In return for committing themselves to this unenviable lifestyle, the sailors would receive a share of the treasure that Drake plundered. The booty was divided up between Queen Elizabeth I, the sponsors of the voyage, Drake himself, the officers (usually second sons of the aristocracy who needed to find themselves an income) and finally the crew, with even the lowliest receiving a substantial sum of money. During his three-year circumnavigation of the globe, Drake accumulated too much booty to fit in the hold, and he had to replace the ballast (the rocks in the bilge that kept the ship stable) with gold. The *Golden Hinde* thus earned the reputation of being the only ship whose ballast was worth more than the vessel itself.

St Mary Overie Dock, which was noted in the *Domesday Book*, William the Conqueror's 1086 property survey, was named after a monastery that stood here until dissolved by Henry VIII in 1534.

Food and drink: A few yards to the west on Park Street, Cantina Vinopolis (tel: 020-7940 8333) serves moderately priced "Modern British" food and has more than 200 wines by the glass. Opposite it, at 34 Park Street, the old Anchor Inn (0870-700 1456) is a maze of quirky rooms with a reasonably priced restaurant upstairs.

London Canal Museum

The ebb and flow of Britain's waterways

Map reference: page 23, F2
12–13 New Wharf Road (behind King's Cross station), King's Cross N1. Tel: 020-7713 0836;
www.canalmuseum.org.uk
Tues–Sun 10am–4.30pm and bank holidays, last admission 3.45pm. Admission charge.
Good wheelchair access.

Tucked behind King's Cross station, and abutting Battlebridge Basin, this delightful museum covers the history and *modus operandi* of the capital's navigable waterways, particularly Regent's Canal. Constructed in 1862, the building originally housed an ice warehouse – there are two cavernous (42-ft/13-metre deep) ice wells, one of which can be peered into, cleverly lit and oozing water.

An exhibition documents the ice trade in this building, operated by a Swiss-Italian immigrant called Carlo Gatti, who rose from humble beginnings in classic rags-to-riches style to import ice from Norwegian lakes on a grand scale in the days before refrigeration. He saw a niche in the market that needed filling, and ice-cream became his next, successful, venture.

The central plank of the museum's exhibits is *Coronis*, a butty or unpowered boat. Attached is *Corona*, a diesel-engined motorboat, which towed the butty. In all, the narrowboat measures 72ft x 6ft 10 inches (22 x 2 metres). *Coronis* was constructed in Woolwich, London, by Harland & Wolff, and rescued and restored by employees (the museum is a registered charity, and all staff are volunteers and enthusiasts). The cabin is a reconstruction, and visitors are encouraged to squeeze inside to see how cramped conditions were for the folk living and working the canals, and also to inspect the ingenious designs used to maximise the space available.

Right up until the 1960s, until the harsh winter of 1963, families shared these tiny spaces. One or other of them could be seen mopping the outside of the cabin on a daily basis, not because of an

Detail from an 1823 engraving of the Regent's Canal by Thomas Shepherd.

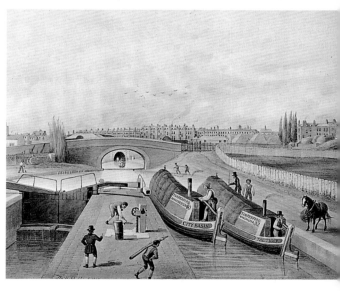

obsessive tendency towards cleanliness but to counter the effects of the wood drying out: the planks shrank with the heat of the cooking stove inside, leaving gaps and crannies where wind could pierce and whistle through.

Children too young to work were tethered by rope to the roof in clement weather and were frequently seen dangling over the edge having taken a crawl too far. There is a rack of typical "lace-work" plates – generally rather gaudy, and gaily painted

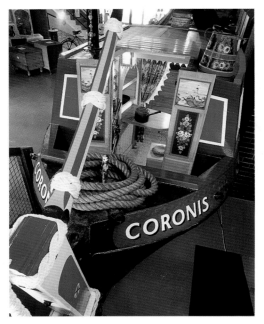

A restored boat in the London Canal Museum shows how cramped the living quarters were.

A charming little film, *Barging through London* (1924), charts a canal worker's lot on a trip from Limehouse to Paddington in vintage Charlie Chaplin-style. The film is for sale on video in the museum shop, which also stocks a good range of material on waterways, including books, maps, postcards and vividly decorated reproduction pottery.

The museum can be hired out by artists and theatre production companies for shows on a grand scale in the airy upper floor, and the museum is also a popular venue for wedding receptions, with guests arriving by narrowboat to a rearranged museum space bedecked with balloons and streamers.

Informative display boards throughout the museum are easy for children to understand, and there's tons of stuff kids will enjoy, such as graphically displayed instructions on knot-tying. There are interactive tools, too, such as the touch-button screen inviting visitors to question Gatti on his life and work (this is interwoven with social history). A quiet area with colouring books and cushions is set aside for children who may be too young to join in the fun.

Food and drink: Not an area noted for its cuisine. The nearby railway termini have lots of bars and snack bars.

hardware, such as buckby cans (coal scuttles) on view inside the boat.

Families usually travelled to and from London and Birmingham, often exchanging part of their cargo (say, coal) for something being carried by a fellow canal worker (perhaps potatoes), although a calibrated barge pole put paid to any notions of spiriting away part of the produce.

The museum is fully glazed and so the building is flooded with light, To its rear, the canal laps the walkway. It is here on the canal itself that the museum's floating exhibition, the 21-ft (6-metre) "pusher" tug *Bantam IV*, is moored. The tug has undergone further restoration, in readiness for once again sailing the waters. In 1995, the museum won a Transport Trust award for its restoration work on the *Bantam IV*.

The basin is home to a range of wildlife, including a clutch of duck and geese species and the occasional heron. There are four terrapins, often seen sunning themselves on the towpath.

Working horses were stabled on the upper floor, where a horse's stall, along with equine paraphernalia are displayed. This floor also houses a library for academic purposes, many information boards, and an education room used by schools; the children usually arrive by boat, and are given tasks such as working out how long a narrowboat takes to pass through a series of locks.

London Transport Museum

Traces the growth of mobility in London for the past 200 years

Map reference: page 20, D4
Covent Garden Piazza, WC2.
Tel: 020-7565 7299. www.ltmuseum.co.uk
Daily 10am–6pm (Fri 11am–6pm). Admission fee (free for accompanied children under 16). Tube: Covent Garden, Leicester Square or Holborn. Bus to Strand or Aldwych.
Lots to interest children. Baby-changing room.

Given the run-down state of much of today's Underground system, the London Transport Museum, housed in the 1871 glass-roofed cathedral that was Covent Garden's Flower Market until 1974, is likely to provoke heartfelt nostalgia in older Londoners who can remember the days when the city could be proud of the innovation and efficiency of its public transport.

But the museum's appeal extends well beyond the charms of old trams and trains, for it traces the social history of modern London, whose explosive growth – from 1 million people to 6½ million between 1800 and 1900 – was driven by new and affordable forms of transport.

The creativity that devised inventive ways of driving tunnels through London's clay extended to devising a classic series of posters encouraging people to change their lives by using the new methods of transport. A 1908 poster for Golders Green – "a place of delightful prospects" – shows an idyllic house and garden in what was then a village surrounded by fields; within 20 years it had been turned into yet another north London suburb as people began to commute further to work. A poster produced during World War I reads: "Why bother about the Germans invading the country? Invade it yourself – by Underground and motor-bus."

A sophisticated design policy, which reached its peak in the 1920s and '30s, married the functional with the aesthetically pleasing, influencing everything from station architecture and signage to vehicle design and upholstery fabrics. For that reason, the restored vehicles don't dominate the museum – you find yourself turning from a gaily painted trolleybus to admire an elegant 1930s uplighter, designed to illuminate Underground escalators.

The vehicles, of course, are the main attraction. From models of an 1800 Thames rowing skiff and an 1820s stagecoach, you pass rapidly on to full-size horse

buses (1830s), horse-drawn trams running on rails (1870s), electric trams (1890s), trolleybuses (1930s) and motor buses (which appeared in an early but unreliable form in 1910 and eventually superseded all their rivals).

Various coaches trace the development of Underground travel, the earliest being an 1890 "padded cell", so called because the builders saw no need to provide windows, there being nothing to see in a tunnel. A 1923 car dramatically belies its age – perhaps because it was still standard stock on the District Line until 1975.

Although the transport enthusiast may find much of interest in the traction pole finial, generator synchroscope and train describer combinator, the casual visitor's attention is drawn to the social consequences of transport innovations. The question of pollution, for example, is addressed – from the 1,000 tonnes of dung deposited on the roads each day in 1900 by the system's 50,000 horses to today's partially successful attempts to minimise air pollution from buses.

Taped interviews with retired staff recall working conditions in the past, and it is recalled that women were not given a chance to drive buses or trains until the 1970s. Tomorrow's world is fancifully previewed, with displays of levitating trains and a fan-assisted tube along which cyclists could be propelled with the aid of compressed air.

Facilities for children are excellent. Fourteen hands-on displays – with buttons to

Yesteryear's horse power from the London Transport Museum.

The Transport Museum is sited in a former Covent Garden warehouse.

push, wheels to turn – provide a "learning route" through the museum. At each of these displays, children are encouraged to stamp a "KidZones" card provided at the ticket booth – a clever incentive for them to complete the tour.

There are also extensive play areas, as well as simulators allowing children to try their hand at driving a tube train and a gallery where they can try on a bus conductor's cap and jacket. Actors playing the part of an early tunneller or a 1930s ticket clerk pop up at various points to describe yesteryear's working conditions.

Video screens show rare vintage footage, and touch screens throughout the museum provide old photographs relating to adjacent exhibits, with captions in all the main European languages.

● For those who want more, the museum has opened The Depot, a purpose-built working museum store at 118–120 Gunnersbury Lane, Acton Town, West London. It houses 370,000 objects that the Transport Museum could not accommodate, including rare vehicles, station furniture and much original artwork and engineering drawings. It holds open days on three weekends a year, as well as pre-booked guided tours once a month. For details, ring 020-7379 6344 or check the www.ltmuseum.co.uk website.

Food and drink: There's an in-house café. The Covent Garden area is awash with pubs and restaurants of every description. For history enthusiasts, the Lamb & Flag pub (33 Rose Street) dates back to 1627, and Rules (35 Maiden Lane, 020-7836 5314) is a venerable, though expensive, venue for traditional English roasts and real ale.

Royal Mews

Carriages and riding stables fit for a Queen

Map reference: page 20, B6
Buckingham Palace Road, SW1.
Tel: 020-7839 1377.
www.royalresidences.com/royalmews.htm
Tube: Green Park or Victoria.
Mon–Thurs 10.30am–4.30pm Aug–Sept;
Mon–Thurs noon–4pm Oct–July; last entry half-hour before closing. As the Royal Mews is part of a working palace, opening hours and displays may change at short notice.
Wheelchair access. Admission charge.

When her son, later Edward VII, brought the first motorcar to Buckingham Palace in 1901, Queen Victoria was not amused. "I hope you will never allow any of those horrible machines to be used in my stables," she said. That wish has been pretty much respected. Although there is one gorgeous Rolls-Royce Phantom VI on display, the Royal Mews remains firmly equestrian.

It was in 1762 that King George III established the stables in their present site, after buying Buckingham Palace, and in 1825 the Royal Mews was redesigned by the renowned architect John Nash.

The mews is a charming place, tucked away to the side of Buckingham Palace near Buckingham Gate. Less formal than the palace and less touristy than the Changing of the Guard, it provides an insight into the workings of the Royal Household, full of quiet details such as the weight of a coachman's red-and-gold livery (16 lbs/7 kg) and the news that on State occasions everyone rises at 5am.

Entrance is through the small riding school, the oldest part of the mews, where the horses are exercised every day. Along one side of an inner courtyard are the gleaming State coaches, notable among them the "Glass Coach" used for royal weddings. Its interior is tiny – a fact one might think would have been considered before Lady Diana Spencer emerged at St Paul's Cathedral in 1981, radiant in a crushed wedding dress.

The Gold State Coach (1762), commissioned by George III for his wedding and coronation, is in a separate room at the far end of the mews. So ornate is this vehicle – Cinderella-like with paintings, gold leaf and large tritons (mythical creatures) – that George was already married and crowned by the time it was finished. The gargantuan vehicle is ornate in the extreme, every inch richly gilded with mouldings. Trumpeting tritons seem to haul the coach by means of hefty Moroccan leather harnesses, while eight swaying palm trees frame the bodywork. The coach panels, painted by the Florentine artist Cipriani, depict scenes symbolising Britain's victories. Eight horses, nowadays Windsor greys, are ridden by postilions. The state coach proceeds at walking pace, while the other coaches in the royal fleet– 16 in all, although not all of them are kept in London – are driven at a trot.

Each coach and landau – all of which are exquisite in their own way – has its peculiar function. The Irish State Coach, built in Dublin, is used mainly for the State Opening of Parliament. The Scottish State Coach bears the royal arms of Scotland and

the insignia of the Order of the Thistle in place of the usual royal arms of England and insignia of the Order of the Garter. And the Glass Coach is almost always used for royal weddings, including the Queen's own marriage, to Prince Philip, in 1947.

The spotless stables accommodate as many as 30 horses, mostly named by the Queen (among them are, for example, Barbados and Dresden). Mainly Cleveland bays and Windsor greys, they are sent to Windsor to "holiday" when not being used for state occasions.

Above the stables, the married grooms' and chauffeurs' living quarters add a splash of colour and domesticity, with pots of blooms spilling over the balconies in spring and summer.

Just past the stables is a room devoted to liveried uniforms and harnesses, beautifully displayed in glass cases reminiscent of those of an old apothecary, with a card attached to every item explaining on which occasion it was – or still is – used. Many of the handsome uniforms still bear the names of coachmen and positions from the Victorian age.

ABOVE: high-class horses in the spotless State Stables.

BELOW: the State Gold Coach.

Food and drink: The Goring Hotel (15 Beeston Place, Grosvenor Gardens, 020-7396 9000) serves stately British food in a slightly stuffy ambience. Christopher's (Thistle Victoria Hotel, Buckingham Palace Road, 020-7976 5522) serves modern American food in a spacious dining room.

Science and
Technology

The pioneering scientists of the Victorian Age tunnelled
under the earth and trained their telescopes on the stars.
These museums show how their discoveries revolutionised
human knowledge and changed the way people lived

Brunel Engine House Tunnel Exhibition

Commemorating the world's first underwater thoroughfare, the Thames Tunnel

Map reference: page 23, G3
Brunel Exhibition, Railway Avenue,
Rotherhithe, London SE16.
Tel: 020-7231 3840. Infoline: 020-8806 4325.
www.museumweb.freeserve.co.uk/brunel.htm
Tube: Canada Water or Rotherhithe.
Open: Apr–Oct, Sat & and Sun 1–5pm;
Nov–Mar, Sun 1–5pm. Admission fee.

This tiny museum, housed in the original engine house for the steam engines that drained the 19th-century tunnel under the Thames, is tucked away in a quiet back street in Rotherhithe, southeast London. It is an historic landmark well worth half an hour or so if you're exploring the Thames riverside, or if you're an engineering student or a tunnel enthusiast.

The tunnel was built between 1825 and 1843 by Sir Marc Brunel, father of the better known Isambard Kingdom Brunel, whose great engineering feats characterised the glory days of the British Empire. When his father fell ill, I.K. Brunel took over and completed this, his first project. Marc Brunel, however, was the originator of the systems employed in this complex work, devising a unique tunnelling shield, which enabled the workers to dig through the soft sediment under the river, a method that pioneered the techniques used in modern tunnel building. Although originally designed for pedestrian and road traffic, with two parallel tunnels, today the tunnel is used by underground trains on the East London line, linking nearby Rotherhithe station with Wapping, on the north bank of the Thames.

The museum's collection of illustrations and models explains the literally ground-breaking creations of Marc Brunel, and also includes a working horizontal V steam pumping engine built by John Rennie, who also built engines for the tunnel project. The engine, although not the original, is a highlight of the museum, with its silently sliding pistons, which are known to keep engineering enthusiasts transfixed in awe. Illustrations also depict the project's struggles and mishaps, which included several floodings and accidents, as well as celebrations, such as a grand banquet held inside the tunnel on 10 November 1827.

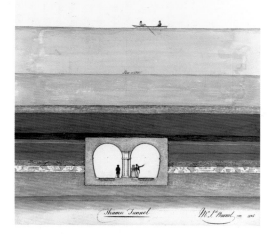

OPPOSITE: the Royal Observatory in the 19th century.

LEFT: a sectional view of Brunel's tunnel.

Educational tours are available, as well as study workshops and local history group events. There is a small selection of related souvenirs and literature on sale, but no refreshments.

Food and drink: *A few minutes' walk away is the 17th-century Mayflower Inn, with a riverfront patio and upstairs restaurant, serving meals Tues–Sat, 6.30–9.30pm.*

Kew Bridge Steam Museum

London's only living steam museum and home to the world's oldest waterworks

Map reference: page 22, B3
Green Dragon Lane, Brentford, Middlesex. Tel:
020-8568 4757. www.kbsm.org
Open daily, 11am–5pm, all year (except for the
week before Christmas). The engines run at
weekends and on holiday Mondays, and the
railway operates on certain weekends between
Mar and Nov (enquire for dates).
Tube: Gunnersbury. Train: Kew Bridge, then 10
minutes by foot.
Car: small car park on the premises

Housed in the original premises of the former Grand Junction Water Works, overlooking the north end of Kew Bridge, this museum is a homage to the power and uses of water.

Open to the public since 1975, the Kew Bridge

into a rather eccentric bathroom centre. The walls are lined with an array of plumbing paraphernalia through the ages: brass and lead pipes, sinks, wooden washing dollies, scrubbing boards, top-loading wash-tubs and foot baths, urinals, pressure gauges, car wash brushes and even a diving board.

The Water for Life Gallery is a display of the history of London's water supply, from Roman times to the Thames Water Ring Main. Here, you can discover how the essential stuff comes out of the taps, via a mock-up sewerage tunnel and bubbling tanks that show the modern processes of filtration and quality control. You can even put on a pair of industrial rubber gloves and plunge your hands into a tank of murky gunge to pick out flotsam and jetsam sometimes found in sewage pipes. Among the more unwelcome residents in London's water system is the red-eared terrapin (Pseudemys Dorbicny), a descendant of unwanted household pets flushed down the toilets, and allegedly capable of inflicting a nasty bite if provoked.

In addition to watching the engines in action, on certain weekends you can also ride on the museum's narrow gauge railway around the grounds, and throughout the year there are various special events, such as the "Magic of Meccano Show".

Food and drink*: A café inside the museum is open weekends only, serving hot and cold meals; at other times, there is a vending machine available outside the café.*

Kirkaldy Testing Museum

A 19th-century workshop for testing building and industrial materials

Map reference: page 21, F5
99 Southwark Street, SE1 (entrance in Prices Street). Tel: 01322-332195. Visits by appointment only, though unarranged visits may be accepted on the first Sun of the month (ring the bell). Admission fee.
Tube: Southwark. Bus route: 381.
Mainly for specialists. Not suitable for children.

While walking through Southwark in 1974, a Dr Dennis Smith stumbled upon an impressive industrial building inscribed with the words "Kirkaldy's Testing and Experimenting Works". Smith, a civil engineer, was intrigued and, finding the door ajar, walked inside. There he discovered a fully equipped but deserted engineering testing station, its tools and machinery

An 1846 Cornish Beam Engine.

Steam Museum contains some of the world's oldest functioning Cornish Beam Engines, so called because they were originally used to drain the deep mines of Cornwall. The engines were brought to the waterworks in the 19th century in order to pump water from the Thames, which was filtered and then supplied to much of West London. Today, the lovingly maintained engines are still run at weekends and on Bank Holiday Mondays, converting the main Steam Hall into an entrancing auditorium of gently hissing pistons and rhythmically driving crankshafts.

Steam engines were the key driving force of the Industrial Revolution, and some of the beam engines kept here are the finest to be found anywhere. The oldest in the museum is the Boulton and Watt "West Cornish" Engine, built in Birmingham in 1820, while the Grand Junction 90-inch engine is the world's largest beam engine in working order.

Your first impression on entering this museum, however, may be that you've mistakenly walked more or less in working order save for a sprinkling of dust. In the centre of this industrial Marie Celeste was a massive 19th-century hydraulic testing machine designed to measure the strength of building and industrial materials.

The building had been the premises of a family business started by the machine's designer, an ingenious Scotsman called David Kirkaldy, in 1866. Dr Smith quickly realised that it should be preserved as a museum and eventually secured it as the headquarters of the Greater London Industrial Archaeology Society, which now meets here twice a month.

Visitors are shown a short film and then given a guided tour. The star attraction is Kirkaldy's 74-ft (23-metre) multi-purpose hydraulic testing machine, weighing 120 tons and exerting pressure of 1 million lbs (453,600 kg); one of only two such machines ever to have been made, it could test for bending, punching, compression, tension, bulging, shear and torsion on everything from bricks and concrete to aluminium and steel. It was used to test the steel in Sydney Harbour Bridge and in Comet jet aircraft.

Food and drink: Tate Modern (see page 194), with its café and restaurant, is a short walk along Sumner Street, off the north side of Southwark Street.

Michael Faraday Laboratory & Museum

Celebrating the "father of electricity"

Map reference: page 20, B4
The Royal Institution, 21 Albemarle Street, W1.
Tel: 020-7409 2992.
www.ri.ac.uk/history/MFL&M.html
Tube: Green Park. Buses: 8, 9, 14, 19, 22, 38.
Open: Mon–Fri, 9am–5pm (Note: the museum is often closed for filming, so try to call first.) Wheelchair access. Not suitable for small children. Fee. Guided tours bookable in advance.

This small museum celebrates the career of Michael Faraday (1791–1867), one of the foremost scientists of the 19th century and often described as the father of electricity. Among his greatest discoveries were the principles behind the electric motor, the transformer and the generator. Life today would be immeasurably different without these insights – all power stations, from coal-fired leviathans to futuristic wind farms, still generate electricity using Faraday's fundamental principles.

The museum and laboratory are housed in the basement of the Royal Institution, a centre for scientific research and education, founded in 1799. Faraday joined the institution in 1813, and it was here that he conducted most of his pioneering work. The laboratory you see today is a reconstruction of his original work space, based on contemporary paintings and situated in exactly the same location in the building. Set around the room are pieces of Faraday's original apparatus, including a large electromagnet, a vacuum pump and jars of chemicals.

Next door, the one-room museum traces Faraday's most important achievements, notably in the field of electromagnetism. The early exhibits include various machines for generating discharges of static electricity. One such, the so-called Great Cylinder Machine, is accompanied by an insulated stool, presumably to prevent the scientist experiencing the discharge through his own body. Also here are some of the earliest batteries in existence.

Three exhibits commemorate Faraday's greatest contributions: a reconstruction of the apparatus in which he first saw the principle of the electric motor (a wire carrying electrical current was seen to rotate around a magnet); the first transformer ever made; and the first electrical generator (a magnet passed in and out of a coil of wire produced electrical current in the wire). All three inventions are still fundamental to the way electricity works today.

Other highlights include a sample of Benzene

Michael Faraday, the blacksmith's son from Surrey who became the greatest experimenter in the physical sciences.

(which Faraday discovered), a so-called electric egg, used for studying electrical discharge in gases, and some of the great man's personal possessions – an engraved watch, a dressing case and an array of medals received in recognition of his work.

Temporary exhibits covering other historical aspects of the Royal Institution, and the museum may expand to cover other scientists. An overhaul would also be welcome, since more interactive and dynamic exhibits would make the slightly fusty displays more accessible to non-experts and children.

Food and drink: Cucina Express, 30b Dover Street. Coffee, sandwiches and daily specials, including pasta concoctions. Cheap. Mash, 26B Albemarle Street. Retro-chic bar and restaurant serving Mediterranean and Asian food. Moderate. The Fountain, at Fortnum & Mason, 181 Piccadilly. Famous English tea, with superb cakes, pastries and ice-cream, but you may have to queue. Expensive. Alloro, 19–20 Dover Street. Elegant, modern Italian restaurant and bar. Expensive.

Royal Observatory

The centre of world time

Map reference: page 23, H4
Greenwich, SE10. Tel: 020-8858 4422.
www.rog.nmm.ac.uk
Rail: Maze Hill, Greenwich (regular trains to/from London Bridge).
Docklands Light Railway: Greenwich.
Open daily 10am–5pm, until 6pm Jun–Aug and weekends in late May and Sept. Last admission 30 minutes before closing. Free.

Founded by King Charles II in 1675 to solve the problem of determining longitude at sea, the Royal Observatory in Greenwich was the centre of astronomical and other scientific research for the best part of three centuries. In the 1950s, with London's street lights and polluted air obscuring the night sky, the observatory moved out to rural Sussex. The Greenwich site was opened as a museum in 1960.

The hill above Greenwich was chosen partly because of its commanding position over the Thames (the site was previously occupied by Greenwich Castle), but also because this was the fashionable part of town in the late 17th century. It remains an undeniably

A mean time-keeper at Greenwich

fine setting, overlooking the green swards of Greenwich Park framed by the classical buildings of the National Maritime Museum *(see page 35)*, with the meandering Thames beyond. These days the scene is dominated by the Manhattan-esque skyline of the Docklands area, and the great white mound (great white elephant to some) of the Millennium Dome on the right. To the left, the view extends to the City of London and St Paul's Cathedral.

The first thing to do when you enter the courtyard is to cross the meridian line into the western hemisphere, or at least to have your photograph taken with one leg in the east and one in the west. On the roof of Flamsteed House you can see a large ball – this was lowered at precisely 1pm each day to enable the ships on the Thames to set their clocks accurately before departing on their voyages around the world. Why not midday? Apparently, staff were too busy taking solar observations at this time. By 1852, with the invention of the electric telegraph, the time was transmitted by a series of bleeps on the hour, and by the 1920s this was broadcast over the radio. The "one o'clock ball" is still lowered at 1pm each day.

Flamsteed House, designed by Sir Christopher Wren (himself a keen astronomer) dates from the founding of the observatory and is named after Sir John Flamsteed, the first Astronomer Royal. In the first room, panels and exhibits look at the history of astronomy from its earliest origins in the ancient civilisations of Sumeria and Egypt. Items on display include a Chinese sundial and a lodestone, a naturally occuring ore used for magnetising compass needles. Continue through a series of rooms depicting Flamsteed's life, before climbing the stairs to the beautifully light Octagon Room, with its tall windows used for observing comets and eclipses.

Go back downstairs to the *pièce de résistance* of the Royal Observatory: its complete collection of John Harrison's sea clocks, designed to remain accurate through the heat and cold, humidity and constant motion experienced on a ship at sea. These were the timepieces which allowed mariners finally to determine their position east or west – an achievement that saved countless lives and was chronicled in Dava Sobel's best-selling *Longitude*.

The earlier clocks, named H1, H2 and H3, are wonderfully ornate examples of precision craftsmanship, in total

RIGHT: the Observatory from the air, including Flamsteed House at the bottom right.

BELOW: historical instruments on show in the Royal Observatory's octagonal room.

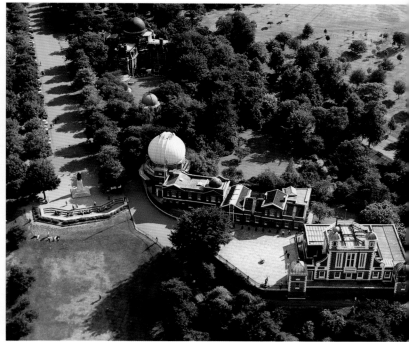

contrast to the simple (and much smaller) design of H4, the timepiece that eventually won the persistent Harrison, a joiner's son from Lincolnshire, the coveted £20,000 prize from a previously sceptical Board of Longitude. His story, which involved much political intrigue, is retold by costumed actors daily at noon, 1.05pm, 2pm and 3pm.

Other displays catalogue the development of marine chronometers, from Harrison's breakthrough designs to those of the 20th century; it is notable how little the design changes from Harrison's – things have only moved on with the recent use of GPS satellite technology.

On your way out of Flamsteed House, pass the caesium fountain clock. This manages to remain accurate to within less than one second in 15 million years and is therefore even more reliable than Harrison's H4. Not quite perfect, but getting there.

The Meridian Building, across the small garden, houses an array of bulky star-gazing equipment. At the far end is the Airy Transit Circle, named after the 7th Astronomer Royal, Sir George Biddell Airy, who used it to define the Greenwich meridian in 1851. In 1884, it was agreed among those nations attending the International Meridian Conference in Washington DC that this would henceforth be the Prime Meridian of the World.

Upstairs in the Arthur Weller Gallery there are displays on modern astronomy, illustrating just how far this science has come in recent years. Computer terminals give hands-on information on planets, stars, comets and other astronomical facts. One model shows the planets in relation to the sun. They are not to scale; if they were, the remotest of them, Pluto, would be the size of a pinhead and would be situated somewhere in the vicinity of Canary Wharf.

Ascend a spiral staircase to reach the large 28-inch refractor telescope. This is still in use, and is open for public viewings on two evenings a month from late November to mid-March (£6 or £8 depending on time; tel: 020-8312 6608 for more details).

A short distance from the main complex is the South Building, which houses a planetarium (shows Mon–Fri 2.30pm; weekends various times, phone 020-8312 6608 for details; admission charge).

LEFT: John Harrison, whose clock allowed sailors to calculate their longitude.

***Food and drink**: The Park Café, opposite the South Building, is open 8am–7pm in summer (until 3 or 4pm in winter) and serves the usual sandwiches and burgers. It has an attractive outside seating area. Down the hill in Greenwich are trendy cafés, noodle bars and restaurants.*

Museums of Medicine

Triumphs and traumas are depicted in these museums, from the breakthroughs of research pioneers and the efforts of nuns and nurses to provide medical care to the gruesome surgical procedures of past centuries

Alexander Fleming Laboratory Museum

Marking the ground-breaking discovery of penicillin

Map reference: page 22, E2
St. Mary's Hospital, Praed Street, W2.
Tel: 020-7725 6528.
www.medicalmuseums.org/museums
Tube: Paddington. Buses: 7, 15, 23, 27, 36.
Open: Mon–Thur 10am–1pm, guided tours on the hour, last tour at noon; closed public holidays; other times by appointment only. Admission fee. Unsuitable for wheelchair users or those with limited mobility. Souvenir shop.

OPPOSITE: an engraving shows Florence Nightingale tending the wounded in 1854 during the Crimean War.

LEFT: the room where Alexander Fleming discovered penicillin.

The highlight is the actual room in which Alexander Fleming (1881–1955) discovered penicillin on 3 September 1928. As professor of bacteriology at St Mary's Hospital, Fleming built on his experience as an army doctor in World War I, when he had observed the anti-bacterial powers of substances occurring naturally in the human body.

The small laboratory has been restored to how it looked then, complete with a newspaper and original books displayed alongside pieces of medical equipment. A volunteer guide, often a retired member of medical staff who knew Fleming personally, will explain how the discovery was made. An informative 10-minute video outlines the Ayrshire-born scientist's work, the story of penicillin and its progression into modern-day medicine.

The exhibition has display boards which detail Fleming's achievements, the breakthrough in developing penicillin into a lifesaving drug, and the clinical trials carried out by a team of scientists at Oxford in the 1940s. The information is enhanced by reproductions of photographs, diagrams from Fleming's notebooks, press cuttings and a 1940s American comic strip featuring the story of penicillin. Fleming's earlier discovery of the body's own antiseptic, Lysozyme, is illustrated by a cartoon of children being caned to produce tears for use as antiseptic.

***Food and drink**: Ishafan (3–4 Bouverie Place, 020-7460 1030) is an inexpensive Persian restaurant. Lots more Middle East cuisine around the corner in Edgware Road.*

Florence Nightingale Museum

How healthcare standards were improved

Map reference: page 20, D6
2 Lambeth Palace Road, SE1. Tel: 020-7620 0374.
www.florence-nightingale.co.uk
Tube: Lambeth North, Waterloo, Westminster.
Rail: Waterloo. Buses: 12, 53, 77, 159, 211, 507.
Mon–Fri 10am–5pm, Sat, Sun, Public holidays 11.30am–4.30pm, last admission 1 hour before closure; closed: Good Friday, Easter Sunday, 24 Dec–2 Jan.
Admission fee. Shop. Wheelchair access.

The museum is situated appropriately within the complex of St Thomas' Hospital, where the Nightingale Training School for Nurses was set up in 1860. A guide explains how determination, commitment and strength of character influenced Florence Nightingale's choice of career and reformed nursing throughout the world.

A 20-minute audio-visual presentation in the small comfortable cinema covers her life, ambitions and achievements. The well-designed exhibition area has factual display boards, many giving personal quotations, alongside accompanying exhibits. The early years cover Nightingale's family homes, depicted in drawings and watercolours by Parthenope, her sister. Souvenirs from travels include coin and shell collections, a "sheikh's pillow" presented by the Beys of the Cataracts in Egypt, and a selection of books in Hebrew and German with Nightingale's annotations.

During 1837, Nightingale believed God called her to His service. In 1851, she persuaded her reluctant parents to allow her to undertake three months training in the nurses' school at Kaiserswerth; nursing was not considered the work of a respectable young woman in those days. On her return she worked as Superintendent at the Hospital for Gentlewomen during Illness. Furniture, a prescription book and handwritten case notes are displayed.

Her work during the Crimean War is covered by

Florence Nightingale in the Military Hospital at Scutari, an 1855 lithograph by J.A. Benwell.

nurses' contracts, press cuttings from *The Times* newspaper, Nightingale's personal medicine chest and – the most famous – a Turkish lantern, the type used at Scutari and which inspired the title "The Lady with the Lamp". A ward reconstruction shows soldiers being nursed, while in the background a scene illuminates to reveal a surgeon amputating a soldier's injured leg. A small diorama shows the wounded making their way uphill to the Barrack hospital in Scutari, pushing buttons lights up locations of battle and hospital sites on a board, and a projector displays slides of the battles.

On her return to England, Nightingale received many gifts, amongst which are a set of cutlery, a

writing case and a replica of a jewel designed by Prince Albert and presented to her by Queen Victoria. On show are a selection of writings, 200 books, pamphlets and articles, and 13,000 handwritten letters expressing Nightingale's views. She produced reports and statistical charts on army health reform, and diagrams can be seen alongside a reconstruction of an Indian Army Officers' tent.

The Nightingale Training School for Nurses was formed after £44,000 was raised for the Nightingale Fund. This benefited all aspects of nursing and midwifery. Photographs of St Thomas' Hospital and nurses during the early days of the training school can be seen. Displays include gifts from Nightingale to the nurses and a uniform *circa* 1896 belonging to Helena Riddick, a nurse at St. Thomas'. A spot-the-difference model adds an element of fun, showing a sick room before and after the visit of a district nurse.

The drawing room of Nightingale's final home at South Street has been re-created using original furniture. Display cases containing personal belongings, Nightingale's bodice and skirt (*circa* 1859) and some of her honours and religious books, followed by a graphic panel showing the influence of her work throughout the world, conclude the tribute.

Food and drink: *There's a branch of fish! at 3B Belvedere Road (020-7234 3333). The Four Regions in County Hall (020-7928 0988) has okay Chinese food but great views.*

Museum of the Order of St John

From Crusaders to first aiders

Map reference: page 21, F2
St John's Gate, St John's Lane, EC1.
Tel: 020-7324 4070.
Tube: Farringdon.
Mon–Fri 10am–5pm, Sat 10am–4pm; closed Sun and all weekend when Bank holidays occur. Tours (obligatory for visiting the Priory and Gate) on Tues, Fri, Sat at 11am and 2.30pm, or by arrangement. Admission free. Wheelchair access to museum only.

Founded in order to care for weary pilgrims and Crusaders, the Knights Hospitallers under the Order of St John were given land in Clerkenwell in 1140 to establish a priory as their English headquarters. Based on Jerusalem's Holy Sepulchre, the church has been rebuilt over the centuries (it was damaged during the 1381 Peasants'

Revolt and in World War II) but stands over its original Norman crypt. Today it is decorated with banners of the Knights of the Order and used for investitures and services.

The Priory's gatehouse was rebuilt in the 16th century. Its wood-panelled halls and rooms – decorated with crests, the Order's important artworks and antique furniture – still serve as working chambers for the Order (and so may be closed at short notice for meetings, so ring beforehand). The small library contains some of the museum's world-renowned archive of reference works on the Knights Hospitallers, the Knights Templar and the Crusades, but viewing of these archives is by appointment only.

Adjoining the gate, an annexe houses the museum's collection of art, documents, coins, silverware and armour, along with several large, centuries-old pharmacy jars. During the Order's long history, the Knights were obliged to resettle in various bases around Europe, notably Malta and Rhodes, and the Order's hand-illustrated, early 16th-century Rhodes Missal is on display. Here, too, is the first ever book on falconry. The knights were skilled falconers and gave one bird a year to Emperor Charles V of Spain in exchange for tenure of the island of Malta (not a golden, jewel-encrusted model as claimed by Dashiell Hammett in his captivating novel, *The Maltese Falcon*). However, some of the exhibits could benefit from a more imaginative layout and clearer labelling.

A section of the annexe is devoted to the St John

Ambulance, covering its formation in 1877 as a first-aid training organisation for Victorian industry through to its role in the community today. Antiquated uniforms, equipment, photos and memorabilia are exhibited, while interactive displays show old footage of first-aiders in action, and what today's volunteers – adults and children – gain from joining.

Food and drink: The area has several good restaurants. such as the excellent St John (26 St John Street, 020-7251 0848). Close to the museum is a trendy bar, Dust (27 Clerkenwell Road, 020-7490 5120).

Museums of the Royal College of Surgeons

Contains the Hunterian Collection and the Odontological Museum

Map reference: page 20, E3
35–43 Lincoln's Inn Fields, WC2. Tel: 020-7869 6560. www.rcseng.ac.uk/museums
Tube: Holborn.
Open: Mon–Fri, 10am–5pm. Admission free.
Free tour 2pm Wed, group tours on request.
Wheelchair access. Cafeteria.

John Hunter (1728–93) was a pioneer in anatomy and surgical practice, inspiring many of the great names in medical history. His vast collection of preserved specimens, both human and zoological, was bought after his death by the British government, and a museum opened in 1813. Additions were made by its conservators until, by the end of the 19th century, more than 70,000 specimens had been accumulated. Two-thirds of the collection was lost when the College was hit in a World War II bombing raid, but around 3,500 of Hunter's own preparations were saved. The present Hunterian Museum was opened in 1963 within the building of the Royal College of Surgeons.

Although the collection is best understood by academics, there are enough offerings and oddities to appeal to anyone with an interest in the history of medicine, and, while many of the exhibits are time-consumingly referenced to a catalogue, the more

intriguing pieces are well labelled. Among the more remarkable (and sometimes repellent) items on display are the results of Hunter's experiments in bone growth, frozen animation and transplantation; foetuses at various stages of development; the carbolic acid spray invented by Joseph Lister in 1865; and the skeleton of Charles Byrne, the "Irish Giant" who stood at 7ft 7 inches (2.32 metres). Zoological exhibits include the skeletons of the extinct moa, dodo and great auk.

Paintings in the collection include famous human and animal studies by Stubbs and Hodges. There is also a picture of the eight-year-old "Sicilian Dwarf" Caroline Crachami, whose 21-inch (53-cm) skeleton is displayed along with tiny personal effects.

The adjoining Odontological Museum – quite drab, but there are plans to renovate both museum spaces – is devoted to teeth. Here, you will see historical dentures, tools for the filling and extraction of teeth, and endless displays of human and animal gnashers.

Food and drink: Bank Aldwych (1 Kingsway, 020-7379 9797) serves modern European food in the dramatically large space of a former bank. Good but expensive.

The courtyard of St Bart's Hospital in the 18th century.

Museum of St Bartholomew's Hospital

More than 800 years of medical practice

Map reference: page 21, F2
West Smithfield, EC1. Tel: 020-7601 8033.
Tube: Barbican, Farringdon, St Paul's.
Open: Tues–Fri 10am–4pm.
Admission free. For a fee, tours of the whole site are run Fri at 2pm. Wheelchair access.

This interesting little museum forms an integral part of St Bart's hospital complex and documents its origins, history and role in the community. Story boards and original documentation chart the major landmarks in the hospital's long and distinguished life.

St Bartholomew's, like many early hospitals, was founded in the 12th century as a monastery offering "hospitality" to pilgrims and the needy. The care provided was initially a combination of shelter, comfort, food and prayer, and only in later centuries evolved into medical treatment. Patients were tended by monks and nuns (hence the term "sister" still in use today).

When, in 1539, Henry VIII declared himself head of the church in England and dissolved the monasteries, appropriating their land and possessions, it left the sick poor with few to care for them. Henry later recognised this fact and, shortly before he died in 1547, he reinstated St Bart's as a hospital.

The current layout of four main buildings around a courtyard was established in the mid-18th century, and the hospital was transformed by the innovations of antiseptic and anaesthesia in the 19th century, and by the foundation of the National Health Service in the 20th. Even so, there has been talk of closure.

As well as the usual displays of grisly surgical instruments such as amputation equipment and lunatic restrainers, there are audio tapes graphically describing life as a nurse, doctor, surgeon or apothecary, illustrating how their roles have changed through the ages.

The exhibits clearly place the hospital in its historical context, although the story boards are quite small and difficult to see if the place is busy. The museum fits in very well as a real part of the hospital and its community, and many of the visitors are relatives and friends of staff and patients. One feels it would benefit – like hospitals themselves – from more generous funding.

The museum is suitable for adults and older children, especially those with an interest in medicine, and can be combined with a visit to St Paul's Cathedral or the Museum of London, which are nearby. (Smithfield meat market, also a long-established fixture, is close to the museum, but carries out its business very early in the morning.).

Food and drink: St John Street, on the other side of Smithfield Market, has some notable restaurants. St John (26 St John Street, 020-7251 0848) favours carnivores. At East One (175–179 St John Street, 020-7566 0088), you pick the Chinese ingredients, which are cooked in front of you.

A finely carved statue of a wounded man in the Museum of St Bart's Hospital.

Old Operating Theatre and Herb Garret

A gruesome look at 19th-century surgery

Map reference: page 21, H5
9A St Thomas Street, SE1. Tel: 020-8806 4325,
recorded information 7995 4791.
Open daily 10.30am–5pm.
Tube: London Bridge.

This is the only part of St Thomas' Hospital to survive on its original site near London Bridge station after the hospital moved to its new location in Lambeth in 1871 (today, the area is dominated by Guy's Hospital). Owing to pressure of space in a rapidly expanding part of London, the operating theatre was located in the attic of the church next to the herb garret.

As the only surviving 19th-century operating theatre in the country, it offers a gruesome but fascinating insight into both the social history of Southwark and the sometimes fearsome medical techniques of the day. The most commonly performed operations here were amputations following breakages or wounds. Road accidents were a frequent cause of injury, with wounds often becoming infected as a result of insanitary living conditions and the filth and manure covering the busy streets.

The female patients were sometimes brought in from the wards blindfolded to relieve them of the ignominy of being exposed inelegantly before an audience of male medical students packed into the theatre "like herrings in a barrel, but not so quiet".

As all operations were done without anaesthetic, the patients had to be physically restrained. Only the poor would be operated on here (the wealthy would be treated at home, usually on their kitchen table). Although the surgeons were skilful enough, they were unaware of how infection was spread, and 30 percent of the patients died within three days of an operation.

The operating theatre was in use at the same time as the church below, and a cavity between the operating theatre floor and the church ceiling was filled with sawdust to prevent blood dripping onto the worshippers.

The adjacent Herb Garret is more soothing. Here there are displays of the herbs and equipment used in the preparation of medicines in the 19th century. The apothecary, one of the most important people in the hospital, would use herbs from the hospital's

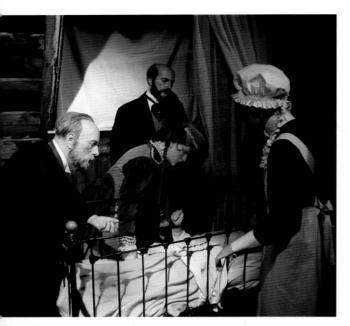

Sir Alex Lasdun and opened in 1964, provides a splendid setting for this collection of portraits and other medical memorabilia.

The RCP itself dates back to 1518, when Thomas Linacre was granted a charter by Henry VIII, and is the oldest medical institution in England; the original stone coat of arms is on the wall behind the main reception desk. The portraits and sculptures depicting the presidents of the college (plus a few heavyweights from medical history, such as William Harvey) are displayed through the main hall and first-floor gallery, as well as in some of the side rooms. To the right of the main hall is the Censors' room, entered through a vestibule. On display here is the Caduceus – the silver rod used in the presidential swearing-in ceremony – and a Mace (similar to that found in the House of Commons) and the President's robe. The Censors' room itself features a bust of Richard Mead by Rubilliac, and a fine collection of 17th-century Spanish oak panelling.

The portraits on the upper level gallery include an imperious-looking Sir Henry Halford set in a colossal gilt frame. At the far end of the gallery, enter the Osler Room to see Holbein's portrait of Henry VIII, and a 19th-century pastiche in which William Harvey demonstrates the circulation of the blood to King Charles I – whose beheading in 1649 was to provide a more direct demonstration – and to the future Charles II.

The Dorchester Library leads off from the other end of the gallery. This impressive collection was bequeathed by the Marquis of Dorchester to replace the one destroyed in the Great Fire of 1666, on the

Re-creating the past in the Old Operating Theatre. herb garden or buy them in from outside. This little museum is suitable for children, but equally interesting for adults, and the two curators are very willing to share their considerable knowledge with visitors. Note that entry to the museum is via a narrow spiral staircase – with no access for the disabled.

Food and drink: The Bunch of Grapes at 2 St Thomas Street is a bright, welcoming pub serving two Young's ales plus pub grub. At the back is a higgledy-piggledy garden. The George Inn at 77 Borough High Street is a unique galleried inn, owned by the National Trust.

Royal College of Physicians

Doctors' portraits and a notable library

Map reference: page 20, A1
11 St Andrew's Place, Regent's Park, NW1.
Tel: 020-7935-1174 ext. 312.
www.rcplondon.ac.uk/college/about_history.htm
Tube: Great Portland Street, Regent's Park
By appointment only. Guided tours (group fee, individuals free) Mon–Fri 9.30am–5pm
Library/research facilities. Wheelchair access.

An 1848 oil by Robert Hannah in the Royal College of Physicians shows William Harvey telling Charles I how the blood circulates.

Unusually for a grade-one listed building, the home of the Royal College of Physicians dates from the the 1960s, now regarded as the architectural equivalent of the Dark Ages. Yet the supremely light and airy structure, designed by

condition that all of the volumes remained in their original order. On one wall are the remarkable "Anatomical Tables", human arteries and veins removed from cadavers, then stuck and varnished onto wooden boards in their natural configuration.

The main library can be visited, but to look at any particular texts it is worth enquiring in advance as many are lent out to other museums and galleries. Landmark volumes in the large collection include one of only 18 remaining copies of the first book ever printed in English (by William Caxton in 1473), *The History of Troy*, and a copy of *Vesalius* (1543), the first modern anatomy – which remained the standard text until *Gray's Anatomy* was published in the 19th century.

As with many of London's specialist museums, this collection is housed in a working building and from time to time certain exhibits may be off-limits.

Food and drink: A Prêt à Manger sandwich bar and two pubs can be found by Great Portland Street Tube station.

Wellcome Trust

Showing the progress of medical research

Map reference: page 20, C1
The Wellcome Trust, 183 Euston Road, NW1.
Tel: 020-7611 8888. www.wellcome.ac.uk
Two10 Gallery Science and Art Exhibitions,
210 Euston Road, NW1. Tel: 020-7611 7211.
Tubes: Euston or Euston Square.
Opening times:
● *The Wellcome Trust Information Service,*
Mon–Fri 9am–5pm, Sat 9am–1pm.
● *History of Medicine Library, Mon, Wed, Fri*
9.45am–5.15pm; Tues, Thurs 9.45am–7.15pm;
Sat 9.45am–1pm.
● *Medical Film and Video Library, Mon–Fri*
9.15am–5.30pm (by appointment only).
● *Medical Photographic Library, Mon–Fri*
9.30am–5.30pm (by appointment only).
● *Two10 Gallery: Mon–Fri 9am–6pm.*
Free admission to both buildings.

The Wellcome Trust is the world's largest medical research charity, established in 1936 by the bequest of Sir Henry Solomon Wellcome, the US founder of the giant Burroughs-Wellcome worldwide pharmaceutical enterprise. The Trust has several buildings and medical exhibitions dotted around London (and one in Manchester), including

the hi-tech Wellcome Wing at the Science Museum in South Kensington *(see page 45)*.

The main Wellcome Building, at 183 Euston Road, houses a vast medical library, which includes History of Medicine, Medical Film and Video, and Medical Photographic libraries and a Medical Information Service, all of which are open to the public. Across the road, at 210 Euston Road, is the Two10 Gallery. This is a small display area in the foyer, where an ongoing series of exhibitions is staged throughout the year, aiming to show the overlap between the fields of biomedical science, art and culture.

If you have a general interest in medicine, the Wellcome Wing of the Science Museum is the place to go. The Two10 Gallery and the libraries are more useful for serious medical researchers, doctors and the like. However, the Wellcome Trust has grand plans to amalgamate all their London offices under one roof, on a site already under development, also on Euston Road. When this project is completed, the original Wellcome Building is expected to house all the Trust's public facilities, including libraries and medical science exhibitions. Its website has the latest information.

Food and drink: No food or drink is available at either building. The nearest place for a snack is Euston Station, which has a range of bars, take-away kiosks and cafés.

Part of a New Anatomists exhibition at the Wellcome.

Museums of Sport

Lord's Cricket Ground

The ancestral home of cricket

Map reference: page 22, E2
St John's Wood Road, NW8 (entrance through
the Grace Gate). Tel: 020-7432 1033.
www.lords.org
Tube: St John's Wood. Buses: 13, 82, 113, 139, 189
To visit the ground and the on-site MCC
Museum you have to take the 90-minute tour
(Apr–Sept: daily at 10am, noon, 2pm; Oct–Mar:
daily at noon, 2pm). No tours on important
match days or preparation days – phone ahead
to check. On match days, ticket holders can
visit the museum only (open 10am–5pm).
Admission charge.
Wheelchair access: whole tour accessible except
upstairs in museum and the Real Tennis court.

Every cricket-lover in the world has heard of Lord's. It is the game's ancestral home and England's premier venue for international and domestic matches. Even more importantly for some, it is home to the Marylebone Cricket Club ("the MCC"), the most prestigious of its kind in the world, recognised by its famous yellow and red ("egg and bacon") colours. Lord's and the MCC were born together in 1787, the brainchildren of wine merchant Thomas Lord and his sponsor, the ninth Earl of Winchilsea. However, the ground has occupied its present celebrated site only since 1813 – construction of the Regent's Canal had forced a move from nearby Lisson Grove.

Tours of the ground begin at its centrepiece, the red-brick pavilion, built in 1890. As the MCC's clubhouse, the pavilion is normally open to members only, and before the club rules changed in 1999, no women were allowed to enter its hallowed corridors. The highlight of the pavilion is the venerable Long Room, through which competing cricketers must walk on their way to the field, and through which they must also return, successful or not. To compound their performance anxiety, portraits of swashbuckling cricket luminaries such as Don Bradman and W .G. Grace stare down at them from the walls.

The Long Room also contains memorabilia from games gone by, but the best pieces are held in the MCC Museum, in a separate building behind the pavilion. Pride of place here goes to the Ashes, competed for in Test Matches between England and Australia. A surprisingly small urn supposedly containing the ashes of a bail. The trophy was first presented to the England team after they had beaten Australia in Sydney in 1883. The previous year England had suffered their first defeat to Australia at home and the *Sporting Times* had published a mock obituary to English cricket, announcing that "The body will be cremated and the ashes taken to Australia." A copy of the obituary is on display.

The rest of the museum traces the game's 450-year history. The early days are evoked by curved bats, two-stump wickets (wide enough to let the ball pass straight through) and a 1744 copy of the Laws – the earliest surviving – handwritten on a pocket handkerchief. More recent pieces include a pith helmet used by the MCC on their tour of India in 1933, Don Bradman's diminutive white boots and the bat used by Graham Gooch to hit 333 runs at Lord's in 1990, the highest test score at the ground. The only disappointments are that some of the displays are rather crowded and that many of the exhibits are not labelled.

Photographs and caricatures complement the bats, balls and pads, and upstairs, large portraits commemorate recent heroes such as Michael Atherton

OPPOSITE: John Wisden, compiler of cricketing statistics, painted by William Bromley in 1850.

BELOW: the legendary W.G Grace in action in 1893.

and Alec Stewart. Also on the upper level is the smallest victim of fast-bowling, a sparrow, struck by a speed-merchant in 1936 and stuffed for posterity. The most unusual exhibit, however, is a diorama of an MCC member having a picnic. (Remember that cricket always stops for lunch.) There he sits in his blazer and club tie relishing the plastic smoked salmon and strawberry tart on the rug before him.

The informative tour also takes in the Real Tennis court, where MCC members play each other at this archaic game, a bit like a cross between squash and tennis; the futuristic, aluminium-and-glass Media Centre, built in 1999 and resembling a UFO on legs; and finally the Lord's Shop, where all manner of souvenirs are on sale. Don't try to buy any club regalia, though; it's restricted to members only.

Food and drink: Lord's Tavern (St John's Wood Road, part of Lord's). Pleasant pub with Thai and traditional English food. 10 percent discount with tour ticket. Harry Morgan's (31 St John's Wood High Street). Traditional Jewish food served in a modern restaurant in the heart of St John's Wood. Moderate.

Museum of Rugby

A behind-the-scenes look at Rugby Union

Map reference: page 22, A4
Twickenham Stadium, Rugby Road,
Twickenham.
Tel: 020-8892 8877. www.rfu.com
From Twickenham railway station, turn right,
keeping left, walk down Whitton road, then
cross the A316 and continue to Rugby Road.
Tues–Sat 10am–5pm (on match days open to
ticket holders only). Stadium tour is available
only on non-match days Tues–Sat at 10.30am,
noon, 1.30pm and 3pm; Sun at 3pm only.
Admission charges for both museum and tour.
Wheelchair access to all areas by lifts.

Since the museum is housed in the English Rugby Football Union's (RFU) headquarters at Twickenham, it comes as no great surprise that it focuses on the English teams. The entrance is through one of the turnstiles in use until 1981 and removed when work began on the new stadium.

The museum is split into sections dealing with all aspects of the game. First there's a reconstruction of the 1930s changing rooms at Twickenham, complete with medical centre, followed by a history of the game. The origins date back centuries,

but in England the game developed in the 1820s in the Warwickshire town that gave rugby its name. Display cases are filled with early shirts, caps and memorabilia, as well as photographs, cartoons and video screens highlighting players and teams from around the world.

Striking trophies include the impressive Challenge Cup and the famed Calcutta Cup, made from 270 melted-down silver rupees. A section shows the history of Twickenham stadium from "Billy Williams' Cabbage Patch" in the early 1900s to the state-of-the-art ground that it is today. The final section is a small cinema, which runs a film of rugby's historic moments.

The stadium tour will appeal mostly to devotees. A well-informed guide whisks visitors to the top of the North stand for a breathtaking view, before taking them to the council and presidents' rooms, the changing rooms, hospitality suites, through the tunnel and out to the pitch side.

Food and drink: There are no bars or restaurants open on non-match days at the stadium. Head back into Twickenham, and about 50 metres past the station on the right is the Cabbage Patch (the original name for the stadium). A large popular pub, especially on match days, serving all kinds of food from hot meals to sandwiches.

Wimbledon Lawn Tennis Museum

How a genteel pastime has become an international sports industry

Map reference: page 22, D5
The All England Lawn Tennis & Croquet Club,
Church Road, Wimbledon, SW19.
Tel: 020-8946 6131. www.wimbledon.org
Tube: Southfields. Rail: Wimbledon. Bus: 93,
39, 200.
Daily 10.30am–5pm. During the championships,
the museum is open only to tournament visitors.
Closed the Friday, Saturday and Sunday imme-
diately before the championships, the middle
Sunday and the Monday immediately after they
finish. Also closed 24–26 December and 1
January. Admission charge. Wheelchair access.
The museum shop sells a wide range of tennis
merchandise and souvenirs.

The museum, located within the grounds of The All England Lawn Tennis and Croquet Club, illustrates the story of tennis from its medieval origins as Real, Royal or Court tennis to today's international multi-million dollar professional sport.

The rich collection of material on display includes paintings, photographs, ornaments and jewellery. All reflect the social history of the game, as do the various tableaux. The Victorian parlour and Home Counties garden party of 1895 show the quintessentially English nature of the game. The other scenes depicted are of a gentlemen's changing room in around 1900 and a racket-maker's workshop from the same period. It is worth comparing these wooden rackets with the latest titanium ones.

Apparently, the development of the sport into such a hi-tech activity would not have been possible without the invention of the lawn mower and the rubber ball. An exhibit shows how a tennis ball is made. Given that the ball can travel at speeds up to 140mph (225kph) when served, it's not surprising that there are so many production stages involved.

The later part of the museum profiles great players of the past and the famous players of today. Player memorabilia includes Pat Rafter's tennis shoes and Bjorn Borg's racket. There are also video clips of notable moments at the Championships and touch-screen interactives on which the visitor can select areas of interest and compete in a quiz. You can also see the original Championship trophies –

Ladies' Singles salver and the Men's Singles cup, the famous prizes of one of the world's most celebrated tennis tournaments.

The costume gallery shows how ladies tennis fashion has changed over the years. Full-length Edwardian dresses (special aprons were worn with pockets to hold the balls) gave way to slightly shorter "flapper" style dresses and then to skirts rising above the knee. A certain amount of outrage was caused by the first appearance of women in shorts. The latest development has been from polyester to lycra, as illustrated by a replica of Virginia Wade's dress when she won the Ladies Championship in 1977, to the backless outfit that Venus Williams wore in 2000.

Guided tours of the grounds are available, although it is advisable to book in advance; they are quite expensive – £12.50 at time of going to press). These do, however, provide an opportunity to see behind the scenes at the Club. Highlights include access to the

"It was Out!", Two Women Watching a Man Play Tennis, an 1898 drawing by John da Costa.

Centre Court via the International Box. The BBC studio can be seen within the Broadcast Centre, as well as the roof garden with its Players' Terrace. A landmark at Wimbledon is the statue of Fred Perry, erected in 1984, half a century after his first Championship win.

The Kenneth Ritchie Wimbledon Library, which contains an extensive collection of tennis publications, can be visited only by appointment.

Food and drink: Café Centre Court: refreshments are available in tennis-themed surroundings: snacks, lunch and afternoon tea.

Mainly for Enthusiasts

You name it and somebody collects it – from old toys to vintage sewing machines – and professionals, whether accountants or morticians, have a heritage to celebrate. Here are a few of London's more unusual museums

The original penicillin culture plate

The Alexander Fleming Laboratory Museum

A guided tour of the Alexander Fleming Laboratory Museum leads you in the footsteps of Fleming in the days when antibiotics were not being used to to fight often lethal bacteria. See the small laboratory in which he discovered penicillin, now restored to its cramped condition in 1928 when a petri dish of bacteria became contaminated with a mysterious mould, and experience the thrill of the story of the discovery of penicillin. Then retrace through displays and a video the remarkable story of Fleming, the man and scientist, and the discovery and development of penicillin destined to play a vital part in the ever continuing fight against bacteria and disease.

How to get to the Museum

By Underground: Circle, District, Bakerloo or Hammersmith & City lines to Paddington.
British Rail: Paddington, five minutes from the Museum. **Buses:** 7, 15, 27, 36.
We regret that there is no disabled access to the Museum.

The Museum is open
Monday-Thursday
10 am - 1 pm
Guided tours on the
hour, last tour
commences at 12 noon

Closed Public
Holidays

Open at other times
by appointment only
Monday-Thursday
2-5 pm and Friday
10 am - 5 pm

Individuals and
groups welcome

To arrange your visit,
please contact:
The Curator
Alexander Fleming
Laboratory Museum
St. Mary's Hospital
Praed Street,
London W2 1NY
Tel: 071-725 6528

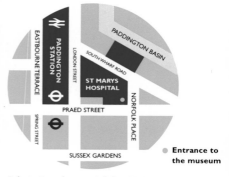

Entrance to the museum

Admission charge: Adults £2.00.
Children, students, senior citizens, UB40's £1.00
The Museum is staffed by volunteers, some of whom have personal experience of Fleming and the impact of penicillin, which they look forward to sharing with you.

The Alexander Fleming Laboratory Museum has been made possible by the generous support of SmithKline Beecham.

SmithKline Beecham

ALEXANDER FLEMING
LABORATORY MUSEUM

Discover
Penicillin
just as
Alexander
Fleming
did in 1928

St. Mary's Hospital
Paddington, London
The birthplace of penicillin

Alfred Dunhill Collection

The history of a classy brand

Map reference: page 20, B4
30 Duke Street, W1. Tel: 020-7838-8000.
Tube: Green Park or Piccadilly Circus.
Mon–Fri 9:30am–6pm; Sat 10am–6pm.
The museum allows smoking and may be
unsuitable for children. Admission free.

This corporate museum is filled with classy trinkets and intricate minutiae from the 20th century. The exhibited items are set in a plush downstairs room that feels more like a luxurious international hotel lounge than a museum. Guests are warmly invited to sit in the leather sofas and read the coffee table books while enjoying a cigar (Dunhill, of course). The items themselves trace the history of the company from its beginnings as a "motorities": a supplier of motor accessories such as windshield pipes, smart leather coats, and Bobby Finders (binoculars sold with the promise that they'll help you spot police half a mile away).

Along with the familiar Dunhill pipes and lighters, there are Japanese pens, vanity cases, watches and fragrances, all mixing details of social history and advertising that was innovative in its day. Some gain significance thanks to their famous owners. Lighters used at royal occasions are prized, along with ones owned by Elvis Presley, Yugoslavia's Marshal Tito, Noël Coward (complete with lipstick) and Harpo Marx. A key attraction is a lighter purchased in the 1930s by Pablo Picasso for his mistress Dora Maar, the Parisian photographer. Before giving it to her, he engraved her profile on the tiny lid of the lighter.

Food and drink: Green's
Restaurant (36 Duke Street,
020-7930 4566) is an expensive
and sophisticated restaurant.
Walker's of St James, 32
Duke Street. A cosy wine bar
with sandwiches and pub grub
at a moderate price.
Mokaris, 61 Jermyn Street. A
nicer than average café with
moderate prices and outdoor
seating in good weather.

Chartered Insurance Institute Museum

Covers the history of insurance companies

Map reference: page 21, G3
The Hall, 20 Aldermanbury, EC2.
Tel: 020-7417 4425. www.cii.co.uk
Tube: Moorgate, Bank, St Paul's.
Mon–Fri 9am–5pm. Free admission. It is essen-
tial to phone to arrange visit in advance and
non-specialist visitors are not encouraged.

This small museum, occupying a single room on the second floor of the handsome Chartered Insurance Building, explains the evolution and changing role of insurance and insurance companies. Much of the early history is linked with fire, and the exhibits reflect this – there are Victorian fire helmets, buckets and truncheons used by firefighters to ward off looters. Pride of place is given to a 19th-century horse-drawn fire cart.

Wall panels and displays deal with loss adjusters, life assurance (with stupendously complicated policy forms), and 17th-century maritime insurance for ships and their cargoes. One exhibit explains how the remarkable success of British insurance companies at meeting claims in the aftermath of the great San Francisco earthquake of 1906 underpinned London's status as the insurance capital of the world.

Fan Museum

A must for devotees of hand-held fans

Map reference: page 23, H4
12 Crooms Hill, Greenwich, SE10. Tel: 020-8305
1441 or 020-8858 7879. www.fan-museum.org.
Rail: Greenwich. Tourist cruise boat: from
Westminster, Charing Cross and Tower piers.
Tues–Sat 11am–5pm; Sun noon–5pm. Closed
Mon (except Bank Holiday Mondays).
Study, research and disabled facilities.
Admission charge. Senior and disabled visitors
admitted free on Tuesday afternoons.

Visiting this museum, housed in two early-Georgian townhouses across from the Greenwich Theatre, is an elegant experience. The rooms are airy and painted a pretty shade of green that mirrors the foliage from the garden in the back, which is planted in the Japanese style, with

OPPOSITE: vintage teddy bear at Pollock's Toy Museum.

LEFT: chic motoring attire, part of a 1904 Dunhill advertisement.

a pond, stream, and curving bridge.

For visitors who feel cool towards fans, it can also be a brief experience; the exhibits are displayed so meticulously that the entire museum can be seen in less than half an hour. Devotees will linger on the ground floor, where a permanent display chronicles the history and craft of fan making, while others will go directly to the first floor, where changing exhibitions include treasures from the museum's collection of 3,000 exhibits, which date from the 11th century. These include a Fabergé *point de gaze* lace fan surrounded by rose diamonds; fan leaves painted and signed by Gauguin (1887); and the unusual mask fan from 1740, in which the centrepiece is a face with cut-out eyes, through which the owner would coyly gaze.

The earliest fan remains were discovered in Egyptian tombs, the most famous being the Tutankamun fan, found complete with ostrich feathers. By the 18th century, fans were an important fashion accessory, so popular that Queen Elizabeth I authorised the formation of the Worshipful Company of Fanmakers in 1709. The organisation still exists.

Food and drink: Afternoon tea is served on Tuesdays and Sundays between 3pm and 5pm in The Orangery, a charming building overlooking the Japanese garden with glass chandeliers and hand-painted murals. Across the street from the museum is the Spread Eagle Restaurant, (1–2 Stockwell Street, 020-8853 2333), an elegant, expensive French restaurant housed in a 17th-century coaching inn known for its good food and wine.

An ivory painted fan from the 18th century.

the art gallery *(see page 204)* and turn right, away from Gresham Street. The whole collection is housed in one small room next to the library.

One of the greatest technological advances – the development of the marine chronometer for navigation – took place around Guildhall, where clockmakers worked from the earliest times of the guild (founded in 1631). Most of the timepieces date from between 1600 and 1850.

What is most interesting about clocks and watches is what they say about the preoccupations of their makers and owners, and the collection is built around this theme. A royal timepiece (with a ball rolling down a zig-zagging channel) is as ornamental as Edmund Hillary's watch for climbing Everest is plain and functional; a table clock indicates astrological details significant at the time but of lesser importance in the 21st century. Owners also include a 19th-century mail guard whose clock was locked so that it could

Guildhall Clock Museum

The world's oldest collection of timepieces

Map reference: page 21, G3
Guildhall Library, Aldermanbury, EC2.
Tel: 020-7332 1868 or 7332 1870.
www.clockmakers.org.
Tube: St Pauls, Moorgate, Bank.
Mon–Fri 9.30am–4.30pm (not bank holidays).
Free admission. Wheelchair accessible.

The Mary Queen of Scots Skull Watch, made in London in the 18th century by Victor Kullberg.

Around the back of the architecturally eclectic Guildhall Yard is the cosy little museum of the Worshipful Company of Clockmakers: go through the modern arches on the opposite side to

not be tampered with. His other equipment in those dangerous days would have included a pistol, cutlass and blunderbuss.

The intricate, painstaking detail of some of the timepieces reflects the analytical mind-set of 18th- and 19th-century society. They may also say something about our obsession with controlling time by dividing it into tidy – and quite arbitrary – slices. An alternative, and more organic, perspective can be seen in a Japanese piece, which divides time into several blocks of differing lengths: these are adjusted as the seasons change the hours of daylight. For aficionados, the best book on the collection is *The Clockmakers of London* by George White, available in the book and souvenir shop.

Food and drink: Mason's Avenue, an alley with Tudor-style houses leaning over it, contains Corney and Barrow's stylish modern wine bar, which offers pub fare at moderate prices.

London Funeral Museum

Coffins, curios and a bit of embalming

Map reference: page 23, J2
Victoria House, 10 Woolwich Manor Way,
Beckton. Tel: 020-7476 1855.
www.tcribb.co.uk
Tube: Canning Town.
Due to open in 2003.

The East London funeral firm of T. Cribb & Sons, a family enterprise founded in 1881 and known for its Victorian-style horse-drawn hearses, is adding this museum to its head office. It will house a collection of funeral and memorial arte-facts, as well as providing a library and reference facilities. The embalming process will be explained and there may be some exhibits on permanent loan from the Victoria and Albert Museum.

Traditional horse-drawn funerals have given the firm a high profile. "The combination of our award-winning Dutch Friesians and our range of carefully restored Victorian hearses and mourners' carriages is guaranteed to stop the traffic and provide a good send-off," its publicity claims.

Since Cribb provides specialist funeral services for many of East London's ethnic population (including Buddhists, Taoists and Muslims), the scope for cultural comparisons is wide. It could be just the place to go for those enthused by the British Museum's mummies.

London Sewing Machine Museum

Hundreds of antique sewing machines.

Map reference: page 22, E5
300 Balham High Road, Tooting Bec, SW17.
Tel: 020-8682 7916. www.sewantique.com
Tube: Tooting Bec.
Open 2–5pm on the first Saturday of every
month. Free admission. No children under 14.
40 steps make disabled access difficult.

This rare collection of nearly 600 domestic and industrial machines, housed in a retail store in a south London suburb, was assembled by Thomas Albert Rushton (1900–74). The two-room museum includes a replica of his first sewing machine shop and engineering workshop.

A funeral with style.

A Britannia "hood", made from 1868 to 1870 and thought to be one of only two surviving.

Pollock's Toy Museum

London's largest collection of toys

Map reference: page 20, C2
1 Scala Street, W1. Tel: 020-7636 3452.
www.pollocks.cwc.net or
www.tao2000.net/pollocks
Tube: Goodge Street. Buses: 10, 24, 29, 73.
Mon–Sat 10am–5pm. Closed holidays.
Admission charge.
Toy theatre performances during school
holidays (by appointment). Toy shop.

Named after Benjamin Pollock (1856–1937), the owner of a toy shop in Hoxton, East London, this museum, set up in 1956, will appeal to children as well as adults. Its small rooms are crammed full with a wonderful assortment of dolls, toy soldiers, teddy bears, puppets, cards, board games and other children's playthings from all over the world. Much of what is on display dates from the 19th and early 20th centuries.

The premises consist of two small houses joined together; small really is the key word – the exhibits are housed in a series of tiny rooms linked by steep, narrow staircases. The confined space, low ceilings and creaking floorboards adds to the nostalgic feel of the place, but as soon as there are more than about 10 people inside, things start to get crowded (it's best to try to avoid school holidays if possible).

You enter the museum directly into the narrow stairwell, with displays occupying every possible corner – it can be a little difficult to see some of them properly. Look out for the old-fashioned parlour games, with the illustration on the boxes invariably showing fresh-faced young men and women in dinner jackets and ball gowns enjoying a round or two of "Scramblejack" or "Spear's Comical Quoits… the jolliest of fun". There are also some more familiar games, such as Ludo and Snakes & Ladders, with informative captions explaining their sometimes exotic origins – both of these, for example, are based on games that developed in India thousands of years ago.

At the top of the first set of stairs is a room dedicated to boys' toys; an alcove represents a boy's den from around 1900, with a jack-in-the-box, a set of "boy's conjuring tricks" and other period items. The overall effect is rather poignant. Also in the room are some early train sets, a glittery collection of "space toys" dating from the 1940s through to the 1970s,

The centrepiece is a striking German machine made especially for Princess Victoria, eldest daughter of Queen Victoria, as a wedding gift. Also on display and in pristine condition is the original Singer No. 1, the first sewing machine developed in 1855 under the guidance of Isaac Merritt Singer (1811–75), who created the Singer Sewing Machine empire. While mass production introduced a certain homogeneity into the market, some designers kept originality alive: one curiosity from 1904 has a casing in the shape of a lion, which opens to reveal a sewing machine inside.

The industrial machines recall the era when the textile mills in the north of Britain flourished. Today, most of the mills and factories have gone but the machines have been saved by the museum and remain as an important piece of history.

and a decidedly primitive Swiss Action Man from 1921, complete with penknife.

On the next floor, beyond the room full of puppets and tin toys, you climb six steps into the adjoining house to reach the wax dolls' room. The intricate process of their manufacture is explained in detail. The next room houses the world's oldest known teddy bear: Eric, from 1905, looks a bit worn out, with one ear and an unusually small head. Teddy bears originated some time around 1903, after an American political cartoonist, Berryman, had sketched President Teddy Roosevelt on one of his hunting trips, unable to bring himself to shoot a cute little bear cub. The bear soon became a sort of motif for Berryman's illustrations.

Follow the stairs down past displays of folk toys from around the world. The next room is devoted to dolls of all shapes and sizes, made from wood, rags, celluloid and china. On this staircase is the remarkably short-lived Falklands War Game, on sale for just a few days in 1982 (it's hard to believe it ever went on sale). Other military-themed games include "Billeting Bullies", where the bullies have German names such as Von Tirpitz and Hindenberg.

The final room in the museum features the toy theatres that made Pollock's shop famous. These became extremely popular in the 19th century, but as interest waned in the early years of the 20th, the dimly-lit Pollock's became known as the last

remaining toy theatre shop in London. The cardboard and paper constructions were faithful reproductions of London theatres, and were sold with different backdrops, actors and scripts.

Before you leave, have a look in the toy shop, which sells well-made traditional toys and model theatres. There is a selection of books for sale in the main lobby. The booklet *Pollock's World of Toys* provides interesting background reading.

ABOVE AND BELOW: past playthings recalled at Pollock's Toy Museum.

Food and drink: The immediate area is full of cafés, pubs and restaurants. There are a number of lively Italian places on Goodge Street, and El Navarra tapas bar on Charlotte Street is also a good bet.

Vinopolis

Learn about wine with glass in hand

Map reference: page 21, G4
1 Bank End, SE1. Tel: 0870-4444 777.
www.vinopolis.co.uk
Tube: London Bridge (Borough High St exit).
Mon 11am–9pm, Tues–Fri 11am–6pm, Sat 11am–8pm, Sun 11am–6pm. Last tour starts two hours before closing.
Admission fee includes wine tasting.

Just across the street, in Bankside, from the venerable Anchor Inn is the main entrance to Vinopolis, City of Wine, which takes a very different approach to the pleasures of drinking. Occupying 2½ acres (1 hectare) of old warehouses and

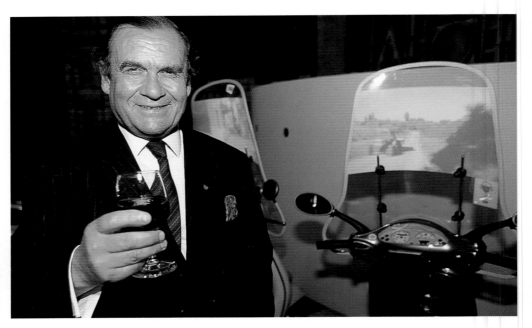

Duncan Vaughan-Arbuckle, founder of Vinopolis, in the museum's Italian cellar.

cathedral-like spaces under railway arches, this sprawling attraction is an innovative combination of entertainment and education. As well as a strikingly visual wine tour through exhibits of the world's major wine regions, there are shops, restaurants, conference facilities and an art gallery.

"I tried to give it a feeling of theatre," says Duncan Vaughan-Arbuckle, the former wine importer who founded Vinopolis. Set designers from West End musicals were hired to provide themes for the various vaults. The Italian vault, for example, has imposing Roman statuary and arches; it also has five Vespa scooters on which you can sit and, as film is projected onto their windshields, have the illusion that you are driving through Italian vineyards. The South African section has a frontage of an old Dutch colonial house, with a garden containing a variety of (artificial) local plants. The California section has old Hollywood movie cameras. Reproductions of Van Gogh, Renoir, Cézanne and Monet lend atmosphere to the France section, as does a battered Citroën delivery van and a statue of the wine-loving François Rabelais.

The education element is provided by individual audio units and earphones giving access to four hours of recorded commentary in six languages. As you walk into each country area, an introductory commentary – delivered by well-known wine journalists such as Hugh Johnson, Jancis Robinson and Oz Clarke – is triggered automatically. Many individual exhibits display a number which, when keyed into the audio unit, supplies a specialist commentary. The information ranges from details of wine production techniques to interesting titbits (for example, until as recently as 1990 it was illegal for supermarkets in New Zealand, one of the world's more respected wine producers, to sell the stuff).

The admission fee to the wine tour (£11.50 at time of writing) looks pricey at first but does include tickets for five wine tastings at tables along the route; these offer a choice of more than 200 wines plus the advice of knowledgeable staff. Any of these wines can be bought by the bottle from the Majestic Wine Warehouse store at the end of the tour. An adjacent gift shop claims to stock the world's widest selection of champagne and wine glasses plus accessories (e.g. 43 different corkscrews) and gourmet food (e.g. caviar, chocolates and a huge range of olive oils). Entrance to the shops and restaurants is free if you don't wish to take the tour.

But is the tour worth taking? Yes, if you like wine, want to know more about it, and have time to listen to a reasonable portion of the commentary. Wearing earphones can inhibit sharing the experience with companions, and children (who are denied the fun of the wine tastings) may get fidgety.

Food and drink: Cantina Vinopolis offers Modern British food and more than 200 wines by the glass. In the same complex, Wine Wharf has tapas-like snacks. Across the road is the Anchor Inn, an historic pub.

Wimbledon Windmill Museum

Models, machinery and milling tools

Map reference: page 22, C5
Windmill Road, Wimbledon Common, SW19.
Tel: 020-8947 2825. www.wpcc.org.uk
Tube: Wimbledon. Rail (from Waterloo):
Wimbledon or Putney. Bus: 93.
Apr–Oct, Sat 2–5pm, Sun and public holidays
11am–5pm, school parties at other times by
arrangement. Admission charge.

Appropriately, this museum devoted to the history of windmills and milling is itself housed in a windmill. Wimbledon Windmill, built by Charles March in 1817, is one of the few remaining examples in England of a hollow post mill. It ended its working life in 1864, when it was converted into six cottages. Each had a window and a fireplace (the 16 chimneys can still be seen). The Victorian tableau, on the first floor of the museum, shows how a room looked in this period, while a recorded commentary describes life in the mill at the time.

The windmill has been repaired and restored several times over the years and in 1976 the first floor was opened as a museum. Major renovation work was carried out with the aid of Heritage Lottery Funding in 1999 when the ground floor was incorporated into the museum and the sails were restored to working order.

Bert Follen, a millwright and carpenter who worked on the restoration of the windmill, donated the tools, which are on display in the museum. Follen's collection includes woodworking tools from the 16th century to the present.

On entering the museum, you see a diorama of the mill being built and the tools which would have been used in its construction. Moving into the centre of the ground floor, there is a display of agricultural tools, but the space is dominated by the cast-iron Great Spur Wheel rotating overhead, which would have driven the millstones on the floor above. In an adjoining room, the different types of windmill and their development are fully and clearly explained with the aid of working models.

The first floor illustrates the milling process and the machinery used in the process. Various types of windmill sails are displayed, and it is explained that the position of the windmill sails could be used to convey messages – for example, to explain that the miller would be back shortly. Visitors can also try their hand at milling by using a saddle stone, pestle and mortar or a hand quern. A remarkably detailed cut-away working scale model shows the windmill as it was in 1825. It includes some of the equipment and tools (in miniature) which are on display in the museum.

Wimbledon Windmill is also associated with the birth of the scout movement. In the adjoining Mill House in 1908, Robert Baden-Powell wrote *Scouting for Boys*, the handbook of the organisation.

From the windmill, visitors can follow the Windmill Nature Trail over part of Wimbledon and Putney Commons, which total more than 1,140 acres (460 hectares) of woods, scrub and heathland. Much of the area is protected as a Site of Special Scientific Interest (SSSI), including 10 ponds providing habitats for a wide variety of wildlife.

Food and drink*: A small café adjoins the windmill.*

Sectional model of Wimbledon Windmill.

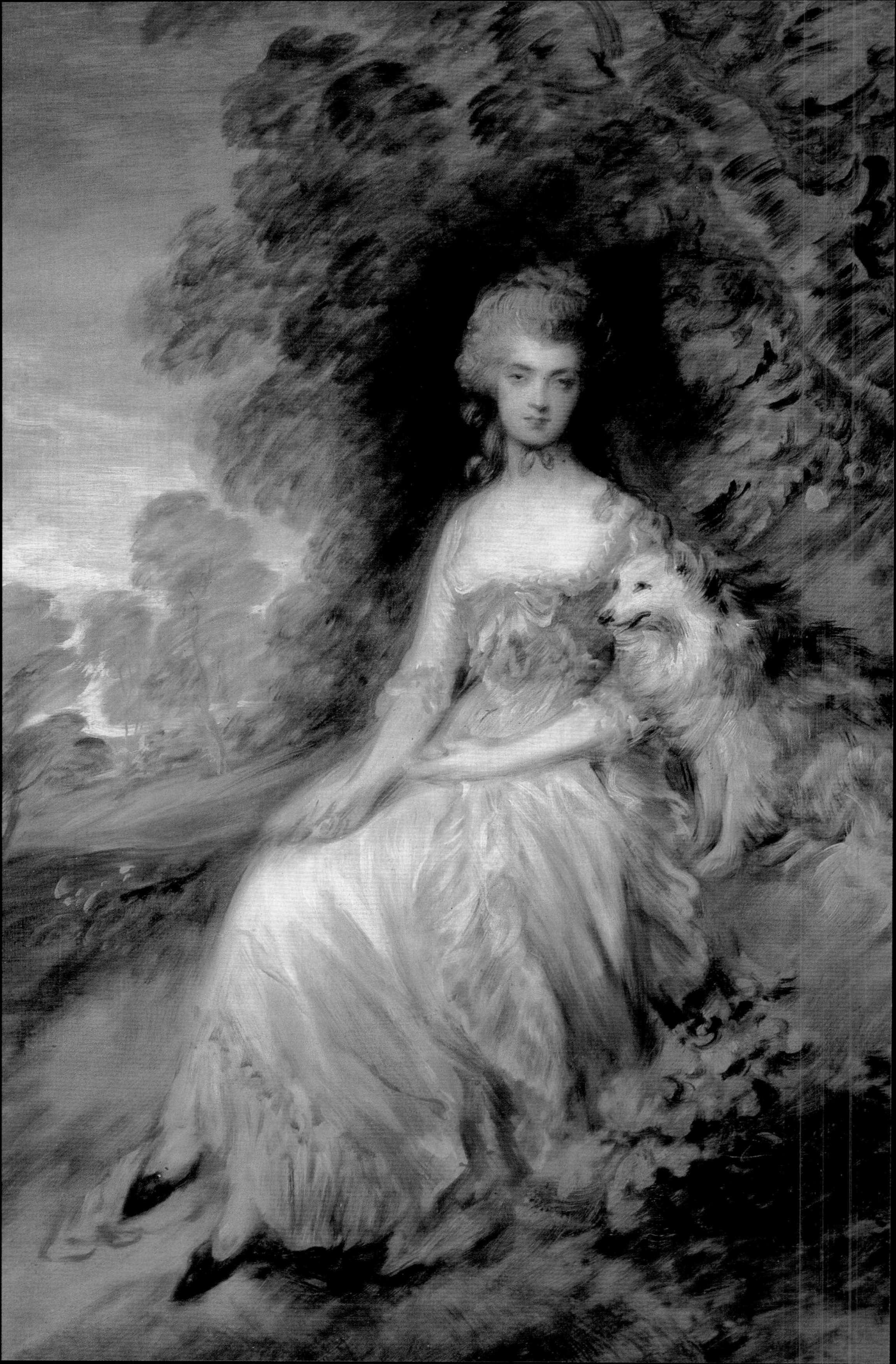

THE GROWTH OF THE GALLERIES

Art critic William Feaver traces the beginnings of London's major galleries and nominates the ones most worth a visit

Hubert le Sueur's Charles I on horseback, larger than life, moderately Baroque and shiny with self-esteem, gazes down Whitehall towards the spot where, in 1649, 15 years after the statue was cast in bronze, the king himself was executed. Traffic streams around the eroded heraldry of the plinth – designed by Sir Christopher Wren, architect of St Paul's Cathedral – on which Charles II had his father's effigy re-erected in 1675.

That the statue survived the Commonwealth regime was fortuitous. That it is now dwarfed by Nelson's column is unfortunate. To anyone standing beneath the portico of the National Gallery and looking out over Trafalgar Square it is barely noticeable, a distant figure beset by red buses. Yet in relation to the National Gallery and the national collections it is a highly significant object significantly placed: the vital chesspiece.

A dignified representation of the arrogance of Charles I, it is also a monument to his distinction as one of the few English monarchs with an informed passion for art. It stands midway between the inclusive world of a public gallery established by Act of Parliament and the exclusive realm of royal patronage – halfway, that is, between the National Gallery and the Banqueting House. The latter, designed by Inigo Jones in the early 1620s, is the only surviving building of the Palace of Whitehall, for the ceiling of which Charles I commissioned Rubens to produce paintings glorifying his father, James I, and asserting the "the Divine Right of Kings to Govern." Rubens's *Apotheosis of James*, culminating in the enthronement of the squat monarch in clouds of glory, was also the apotheosis of Charles I as connoisseur.

Francis Bacon's Head VI, 1949, from the Hayward Gallery.

On that cold January morning 20 years later, when Charles stepped from a first-floor window of the Banqueting House onto the scaffold, he did at least go to his death with the satisfaction of having employed Rubens and Van Dyck to splendid effect, and of having bought Raphaels and Titians and two or three of the latest Rembrandts.

PRECEDING PAGES: Thomas Miles Richardson's The City from Bankside (1820s), in the Museum of London; Claude Monet's The Thames below Westminster (1871), in the National Gallery.

Besides ordering Le Sueur's statue of "the man Charles Stuart" to be scrapped (it was buried instead for the duration somewhere in Covent Garden), the Commonwealth government sold off much of the Royal collection. Paintings went to the Louvre (Giorgione's *Concert Champêtre*, Titian's *Entombment*), to the Hermitage and other palaces. A few eventually came to the National Gallery, notably Rubens's *Peace and War* and Van Dyck's *Equestrian Portrait of Charles I*, a more idealised image than Hubert Le Sueur's.

The National Gallery

LEFT: Thomas Gainsborough's Mrs Mary Robinson ('Perdita'), 1781, from the Wallace Collection.

Britain possesses the only great national gallery which was not originally a royal collection or royal palace. Founded in 1824 and built on the site of the royal stables on the north side of the newly laid-out Trafalgar Square, London's National Gallery is a long narrow building, designed by William Wilkins. It does not stand comparison, its critics say, with Sir Robert Smirke's British Museum, let alone Karl Schinkel's formidable Berlin museums. The cupola, in particular, has been dismissed as substandard. "A sadly misconceived object which nobody has ever tried to defend," architectural historian John Summerson wrote. Actually, it is all the better for being too small to overawe anybody.

One wing of the building housed the gallery's starter pack, the Angerstein Collection; the other was home, for a while, to the Royal Academy, which transferred here from Somerset

House on the Strand, a mile away. As works were acquired, suites of rooms were built for Italian 15th Century, Italian 16th Century, Early Netherlandish and so on, extending northwards in increasingly ornate style. The limits of the site, and the limitation of the collection to painting only, prevented the National Gallery from becoming as encyclopaedically exhausting – as bulky indeed – as the Louvre. Behind the unimposing facade, coherence lies.

Before entering, pause at the top of the steps and look across the road, past the fountains and the bronze lions, to the equestrian statue. In July 1941, Charles I was removed to Buckinghamshire for safety, not to be returned until well after the end of the war. Two years before that, in the summer of 1939, the entire contents of the National Gallery were packed off for shelter to a Welsh slate quarry. Whereupon, in the absence of the collection, the gallery itself assumed a peculiarly symbolic status as a cultural landmark to rival St Paul's, which had been memorably photographed looming through smoke during the blitz. The portico became the country's number one rendezvous and the rooms of the gallery were given over to temporary exhibitions, photographs mostly, though after a while the director, Kenneth Clark, decided to bring one picture back to London each month to boost morale. Concerts were held daily.

For his emotive wartime documentary *Listen to Britain*, made in 1942, the poetic surrealist Humphrey Jennings filmed Dame Myra Hess playing a Mozart piano concerto to a touchingly rapt lunchtime audience which happened to include the then Queen, seen sitting next to Sir Kenneth Clark and smiling as the music swells and the people step out into the open air and go about their business, spiritually refreshed.

A common ownership

Early museums and galleries gave artists an opportunity to perfect their techniques.

The National Gallery's position, at the very heart of London, and its free admission, encourages all who happen to be passing to drop in and take in one or two pictures at a time. There is a sense of common ownership. Other national galleries have special strengths – the Prado has Titian and Velazquez, the Kunsthistorisches has the Bruegels, the Louvre has its French masterpieces – but there is no greater representative collection of European painting than here in Trafalgar Square, all the more extraordinary in that it did not begin as a nationalised royal collection. Its first director, Sir Charles Eastlake, bought a number of key works, among them Bellini's *Doge Loredan*,

Uccello's *Rout of San Romano* and, pre-eminently, Piero della Francesca's *Baptism of Christ*.

The main entrance to the National Gallery nowadays, for those who like to start with Duccio and Cimabue, is by way of the Sainsbury Wing's grand staircase, a Piranesian link between William Wilkins and the post-modern devised by the architect Robert Venturi and opened in 1991. The galleries are a well-lit, faintly corporate, setting for Renaissance works originally designed to grace altars and bedchambers. The sequences are dazzling: six Duccios, Cimabue and Giotto through to Uccello, the beady-eyed formality of van Eyck's *The Arnolfini Marriage*, three Piero della Francescas, Mantegna and Bellini, Botticelli's *Venus and Mars*, Raphael, Leonardo. Over in the main building, across a covered bridge, ripe neo-Edwardian decor takes over, enveloping the glories of Venetian painting (Tintoretto, Titian, Veronese) and Dutch pictures of places where nothing much ever happens.

The National Gallery is the best place in the world in which to explore the proliferation of European painting since the 15th century. Tiring of flighty Bolognese Mannerism, you can pass on and almost immediately light upon the privacy of Rembrandt's *Woman Bathing*, or the smoothness of Velazquez's *Rokeby Venus* or the discreet come-hither of Vermeer's *Young Woman standing at a Virginal*. Before you leave, pay your respects to Ingres's *Madame Moitessier*, magnificent in her corn-fed complacency and floral chintz. And spare a glance for the mosaic floor by Boris Anrep, inside the main entrance, in which Churchill in a boiler suit personifies Defiance and Greta Garbo is Melpomene the tragic Muse. The man looking at the Loch Ness Monster, representing Leisure, is T. S. Eliot.

(margin) Diego Velazquez's "Rokeby Venus", National Gallery.

National Portrait Gallery

Further images of Churchill and Eliot are to be found, of course, round the corner from the National Gallery in the National Portrait Gallery. Founded in 1856, half a century later than Madame Tussaud's, it is an institution as reliant as any waxworks on people's fascination with likeness, particularly famous likeness and celebrity likeness.

(margin) William Larkin's *Portrait of Frances Howard (c. 1615)* in the National Portrait Gallery.

A lengthy escalator elevates us (like James I in the Banqueting House ceiling) to Tudor England, where Henry VIII braces himself in a formidable Holbein drawing and Elizabeth I is truly iconic, decked out like a glorified butterfly. Old enmities are preserved here. Honthorst's Charles I is forever disdainful of Robert Walker's Oliver Cromwell. We see royalty gradually phased out, in importance if not in status, their portraits degenerating to the pop-up book idiom of Bryan Organ's pictures of the current Prince and late Princess of Wales. The National Portrait Gallery is the ideal place for studying British character. Stereotypes multiply: the fops, the bluff radicals, the interchangeable royal mistresses, the ruddy Empire builders.

Since the mid-19th century, photographers have gradually got the better of the portrait painters, to such an extent that photos of footballers and comedians now far outnumber the gallery's commissioned paintings, which are mostly bravura kitsch. There

remain some splendid historic portraits: the Brontë sisters painted by their dissolute brother, Sickert's incandescent Churchill and his full-length study (worked up from a photo) of Lord Beaverbrook, the newspaper owner, hands in pockets, about to dictate an editorial diatribe.

Tate Britain

Like kings, tycoons find patronage to be a pleasant exercise of power. Lord Beaverbrook founded an art gallery in his name in New Brunswick, Canada. In 1897, Sir Henry Tate, a sugar magnate, founded a National Gallery of British Art on Millbank, a former prison site by the Thames. It also became the national collection of modern foreign art, perfunctorily so until the 1960s when, coinciding with the rise of Internationalism, serious consideration began to be given to transforming it into a Museum of Modern Art proper. Consequently, in Millennium year, the Tate divided itself into Tate Britain, on Millbank, and Tate Modern, a mile and a half downstream at Bankside.

Tate Britain begins with paintings that would otherwise have ended up in the National Portrait Gallery and then gains zest and originality with Hogarth, the acerbic narrative genius, Stubbs the horse painter and Gainsborough, master of shimmery elegance. There are worthy sectors – the 18th-century formal portrait, the sort painted by Sir Joshua Reynolds, founder-president of the Royal Academy, whose ambition it was to raise the status of painters, through royal patronage and higher prices, and to achieve results as good as Michelangelo's.

Happily, the Tate collection is rich in works without pretensions, notably the Constables and Blakes and Pre-Raphaelites. The Turner Bequest, the contents of the artist's studio, which includes some 19,000 watercolours, is housed in the Clore gallery. And there are masterpieces:

Turner's *Hannibal Crossing the Alps*, Constable's *Hadleigh Castle*, intense Pre-Raphaelites, the inspired parochialism of Stanley Spencer's *Resurrection*. Sickert and Francis Bacon, Henry Moore and successive waves of sculptural fashion (stone and metal, painted metal, sticks and stones, Gilbert and George in person) and the so-called School of London (principally Bacon and Lucian Freud, Michael Andrews, Frank Auerbach and Leon Kossoff) and the recent Britart generation are shown in changing displays.

Tate Modern

This is a dramatically different gallery: a disused post-war power station

Maurizio Catalan's *Nove Cento*, one of Tate's temporary exhibitions.

across the river from St Paul's converted by the Swiss architects Herzog & de Meuron into a culture mall on seven floors. The most impressive approach to Tate Modern is across the river on the newly built (and rebuilt: it swayed too much) Millennium footbridge over the Thames. The best entrance way is the west door. You walk down a ramp, wide and long enough to make you feel antlike – and yet proprietorial because, as at Tate Britain and the other national galleries, admission is free as a matter of principle.

The galleries have been inserted along one side of the building; the other side still hums with electricity generators. The rooms are best suited to Minimalism (Donald Judds look dandy here), to installation art and video blackout. Paintings suffer. Since it opened in May 2000, Tate Modern has been phenomenally popular, so much so that there has been talk of turnarounds in mass perception of contempory art.

But the popularity is provoked more by the novelty of the building than by what's on show.

For the Modern collection is scanty by the standards of museums of modern art, seriously lacking in what may now be safely termed Twentieth Century Classics beyond Picasso's *Three Dancers* of 1925, Matisse's paper cut-out *The Snail* of 1953, and quite a bit of Surrealism. Oh, and the room of steak-tartare-tinged paintings commissioned from Mark Rothko for the Four Seasons Restaurant in the Seagram Building in New York, given instead in 1970 to the Tate, where they remain balefully on view.

The Tate has little prospect of making good its past failings and so, reasonably enough, the emphasis at Tate Modern is on the current century. Temporary exhibitions ("Matisse and Picasso", for example, in 2002) compensate for the lack of first-rate exhibits. On the other hand, the British collection (some of which qualifies for inclusion in Tate Modern) is unrivalled in scope and depth. The question arises: where does Britishness end and Internationality begin? It's a non-issue to most artists but, to the Tate, a burning question.

The Tate is a past master at generating controversy.

Scattered treasures

A number of London's public galleries have long histories of changing use. The Imperial War Museum in Lambeth was formerly Bethlem Hospital, the country's leading lunatic asylum. (Thanks to a remarkably enlightened Official War Artists scheme, thousands of works recording the impact of war, non-bombastically for the most part, are kept there; Stanley Spencer and Paul Nash worked memorably in both world wars.) Palaces have become Experiences and charity foundations have become time capsules.

Getting to them can be something of a pilgrimage. In London, as in Rome, everywhere dates back; you may become confused; but an awareness of telling resonances and extended perspectives is something that develops only when you stray from the signposted attractions and discover, for instance, in an outer suburb, Mantegna's greatest surviving work.

Fifteen miles (24 km) upstream from Tate Modern, Hampton Court Palace houses paintings from the Royal Collection, among them Titian's *Lucretia* and Bruegel's *Massacre of the Innocents*, in which a later hand altered slain babies turned into bundles. Andrea Mantegna's *Triumph of Caesar* is kept in the Orangery, a set of nine paintings commissioned by the Gonzagas of Mantua, bought from them by Charles I and subsequently retained by the Commonwealth Council of State instead of being sold off. Even the Roundheads were impressed by so solemn a celebration of the fruits and responsibilities attendant on victory. Processional, majestic but partly ruined by zealous restorers, the paintings are packed with spoils and captives, trumpeters and foot soldiers, trailing in procession.

It's a more impressive spectacle, by and large, than the selections from the post-Carolean Royal Collection (Michelangelo and Leonardo da Vinci drawings, from the Royal Library at Windsor Castle, George III's Canalettos) shown in past years at the Queen's Gallery, a snooty sideshow attached to Buckingham Palace. This has been replaced with a new gallery for the collection, commemorating the Queen's Jubilee in 2002.

Variety at the Victoria and Albert Museum

Prince Albert of Saxe-Coburg, Queen Victoria's consort and a distinguished campaigner for the elevation of public taste, was the leading figure promoting the idea of the Great Exhibition, a survey of manufactured goods from around the world, held in the Crystal Palace, a colossal glasshouse in Hyde Park in 1851. Profits from this, the first expo, went into the establishment of the Victoria and Albert Museum, dedicated to the improvement of design and manufactures. The V&A *(see pages 46–51)* grew and flourished, hiving off the Sciences, which went over the road to museums of their own, but absorbing immense quantities of fine and applied art, English, Indian, French, Japanese.

The Raphael cartoons (for tapestries) owned by Charles I were placed there: grandly dim, on permanent loan. Renaissance and Rodin bronzes were acquired, plaster casts of Trajan's Column and the portals of Amiens and other sculptural masterpieces were marshalled together in one court. Among the anomalous bequests was that of Isobel Constable, the artist's daughter: dozens of the oil sketches that transformed the idea of landscape in art.

The museum has an excess of treasures. It has not been able to accommodate and display them well enough in a leaky building laid out like some fabulous but hopelessly outdated department store. The opening in 2001 of the revamped British Galleries was meant to mark a fresh start.

Art in other museums

There's a similar excess at the British Museum, founded in 1753 as a "great treasury of learning." It has resisted change, remaining a temple of supreme achievement, a bank vault of knowledge, rather than a tourist-friendly destination. Wonders are not so much presented as left to be discovered. The Prints and Drawings department puts on displays in which rival collections are trumped, effortlessly it seems.

Detail from one of the 15th-century Devonshire hunting tapestries at the Victoria and Albert Museum.

Chairing the Member, one of William Hogarth's *Election* series at the Sir John Soane's Museum.

Other institutions, founded in the same period, developed differently, or did not develop at all. The Thomas Coram Foundation in Brunswick Square is the surviving offices of the Foundling Hospital. Captain Coram established it to save infant lives and enrolled Hogarth as a governor. Hogarth, in turn, painted Coram's portrait and persuaded fellow painters, Gainsborough among them, to donate pictures to form a gallery that could serve as a fundraising attraction. Handel chipped in with the score of his *Messiah*.

The Sir John Soane's Museum in Lincoln's Inn Fields *(see page 60)* is an amazing monument to the taste and obsessions of one man. Between the 1790s and the 1820s, Soane, an architect, knocked three houses into one and filled every corner with finds ranging from architectural fragments to the alabaster sarcophagus of Seti I, a British Museum reject for which

he built a "Sepulchral Chamber" in his cellars. Lacking wall space, he hung pictures on hinges, to be swung out for viewing. These include Hogarth's *Rake's Progress* and *Election* series, paintings busy with caustic topical detail.

Sumptuous surroundings

Soane was the architect of the Bank of England (demolished) and the designer in the early 1800s of the first purpose-built public art gallery in England: the Dulwich Picture Gallery. This stands in one of London's greener suburbs, housing a collection put together for a putative National Gallery in Warsaw. The King of Poland, who commissioned the dealer Joseph Desenfans to put together this collection, abdicated in 1795, leaving Desenfans holding the pictures. Warsaw's loss was South London's gain for, having failed to set up a National Gallery for London, he gave upwards of 400 pictures to the College of God's Gift, or Dulwich College, now a private school. Paintings by Rembrandt, Rubens, Murillo, Claude, Poussin,

Gainsborough and many Dutch landscapes and genre pictures make this elegant gallery a monument to enlightened dealerdom and, indeed, enlightened architectural design.

The Wallace Collection, in Hertford House, Manchester Square, is an opulent mix, put together in the 19th century by Lord Hertford and augmented by his illegitimate son, Sir Richard Wallace. Here, massed Sèvres china, Limoges enamels, suits of armour and ormolu-encrusted furniture, enlivened by the occasional Watteau, do their best to distract one from the masterpieces, among them Titian's *Perseus and Andromeda*, Rubens's *Rainbow Landscape* and Poussin's *Dance to the Music of Time*.

A brewing magnate, Lord Iveagh, left Kenwood House on Hampstead Heath to the nation together with Vermeer's *Guitar Player* and arguably the finest Rembrandt self-portrait. A textiles magnate, Samuel Courtauld, left a number of the paintings he bought (others include Van Gogh's *Chair* and Seurat's *Grande Baignade* in the National Gallery) to the Courtauld Institute Galleries, which he endowed. These now occupy Somerset House, formerly occupied by the Royal Academy. In the Great Room, where once Turner competed with his lesser contemporaries, the bored barmaid in Manet's *Bar at the Folies-Bergères* wearily presides in a realm of Impressionists and Post-Impressionists.

The Royal Academy moved to Burlington House, Piccadilly, in 1869. Artists belong to it, by election, and largely run it. Their Summer Exhibition remains almost as prominent on the social calendar as it was 200 years ago. It's best regarded as an annual celebration of the whole business of painting and sculpture, professional and amateur. The RA organises exhibitions, large ones (Impressionism, Van Dyck, Soane, Rembrandt's Women) in its main galleries, smaller ones in the Norman Foster Sachler Galleries on the top floor, accessible by elevator, a dramatic ride between brick walls. Michelangelo's *Tondo*, the Virgin and Child and Infant St John in white marble, is kept there.

Exhibition spaces

Changing programmes of museum-quality exhibitions are staged at the Hayward Gallery on the South Bank, a 1960s redoubt in grubby reinforced concrete; at the Serpentine Gallery in Kensington Gardens, a former tea room; at the Institute of Contemporary Arts in the Mall, an incongruously grand setting for programmatic radicalism; and at the Barbican Art Gallery, an unlovely exhibition space in a culture complex underwritten by the City of London. The Whitechapel Art Gallery, next door to Aldgate East Underground station, in a part of London's East End that has regularly served as first base for immigrants, is the oldest (founded in 1901) and most deeply rooted of these 20th-century creations. Picasso's *Guernica* was shown at the Whitechapel in 1938 at a time when Mosleyite Fascists did their utmost in the streets outside to intimidate the local Jews.

The Saatchi Collection, due to move to the South Bank, shows works owned by Charles Saatchi, an advertising tycoon and devourer of art. He has boosted many reputations (he bought the shark that gave Damien Hirst his big break) and has snapped up many recent works that Tate Modern would love to own. Dedicated, impulsive, arrogant it may be said, much criticised, and admired, Charles Saatchi could claim to be king in relation to the contemporary scene. That's an exaggeration, of course. For one thing, there's no statue to him as yet.

Anthony Lowe's *Blackfriars Bridge and St Paul's* (1995), at the Guildhall Art Gallery.

The Major Galleries

The work of the world's top painters and sculptors can be found among these overwhelming collections, from the greatest of the Old Masters in the National Gallery to the most controversial contemporary artists in Tate Modern

Courtauld Gallery

Old Master drawings and one of the world's finest collections of Impressionist paintings

Map reference: page 20, E4
Somerset House, The Strand, WC2.
Tel: 020-7848 2645; www.courtauld.ac.uk
Tube: Charing Cross, Holborn, Waterloo.
Bus: 13, 91, 68, 91, 168, 188.
Mon–Sat 10am–6pm, Sun 2–6pm;
last admission 5.15pm.
Wheelchair access. Lift. Bookshop. Art library and Witt Library photographic collection by appointment. Admission charge except Mon 10am–2pm (not including bank holidays) and after 5pm.

The Courtauld Institute Gallery opened to the public in 1958, housed in cramped conditions in Woburn Square. In 1990 it moved, along with the Courtauld Institute of Art, to larger premises in the north wing of Sir William Chamber's handsome Palladian Somerset House *(see pages 118–19)*. The gallery's Fine Rooms, once home to the Royal Academy and now containing the Institute's 16th- to 18th-century works, were refurbished in 1997–8.

The Institute takes its name from its main benefactor, the textile magnate Samuel Courtauld. In 1932, Courtauld funded the founding of an institute offering a university degree course in art history, the first of its kind in England; he also donated his Impressionist and Post-Impressionist pictures to the Institute, establishing the current art collection. He gave the lease of his home, a late-18th-century Robert Adam house in Portman Square, for the Institute's exclusive use.

Courtauld didn't start collecting until after World War I, and his first acquisition in 1921 was probably Gainsborough's portrait of his wife. By the following year, influenced by the English painter and critic Roger Fry, he was touched by the "magic" of Cézanne's work and bought a number of Cézannes and Seurats for himself and the Tate. In 1925, he bought his first important modern painting, Renoir's *La Loge*, and in 1926 acquired Manet's last main painting, *A Bar at the Folies-Bergère*.

A bequest from Fry contributed a major nucleus of works by the Bloomsbury artists and added to Courtauld's French paintings collection. In subsequent years a collection of Old Master paintings and drawings was amassed, along with a gift of English watercolours. The collection is still expanding and now includes examples of the 20th-century British School.

The collection

The earliest work, shown on the ground floor, includes an exquisite portable tabernacle by Bernardo Daddi, a fragment from an altarpiece by Lorenzo Monaco and a *predella* by Fra Angelico, all noted for their fine painting and gilding. A triptych of the *Entombment* by the Master of Flémalle, rich in colour and heartfelt emotions of pain and sorrow, is one of the great examples of Netherlandish realism. A later artist of the same School, Pieter Bruegel the Elder, painted the visionary panorama, *Landscape with the Flight into Egypt*, one of his most admired pictures and originally owned by Rubens.

The collection has several notable works by Rubens on the first floor, among them a landscape, romantically depicted by moonlight, and a superb oil sketch for *The Descent from the Cross*. Claude's idyllic little *Landscape with an Imaginary View of Tivoli* is painted on copper, enhancing what suggests itself to be the Eternal City, gloriously illuminated by the setting sun. Two studies by Tiepolo for a ceiling decoration and an altarpiece confirm the care and attention he brought to his compositions and their first spirited expression.

The core collection contains key works by Impressionist and Post-Impressionist artists, and includes masterpieces by Manet, Degas, Monet, Renoir, Cézanne, Seurat, Van Gogh and Gauguin. Manet's *Déjeuner sur l'herbe* (*c.*1863) is a smaller, simplified replica of the painting now in the Musée d'Orsay, in Paris, which shocked its contemporary audience for showing a naked woman in the presence of two men. It's thought that this version was commissioned because its owner was unable to hang the larger original. Equally unconventional and

Bruegel's *Landscape with the Flight into Egypt* (1563), Courtauld Gallery.

OPPOSITE: A sketch for Rubens' *The Descent from the Cross* (1611), is on show at the Courtauld. The image captures a moment of poignant drama.

LEFT: Manet's *A Bar at the Folies-Bergère* (1881–2).

BELOW: Renoir's *La Loge* (1874).

controversial was his *A Bar at the Folies-Bergère*, in which, as Professor John House has pointed out, the illogical reflections in the large glass mirror the uncertainty of human relationships.

As with Gainsbrough's portrait of his wife, Courtauld probably chose Renoir's *La Loge* for its lusciously painted, appealing femininity. Cézanne's *Montagne Sainte-Victoire* of *c*.1887 is the artist's most accomplished view of this stretch of Provençal landscape. Systematically structured and painted with short brush strokes, the artist brilliantly integrates the foreground tree and distant mountain peak on a flat, coherent surface. Admire, too, in the later, dusky *Lac d'Annecy*, the way a similar surface coordination is achieved by sweeping the diagonal movement of overhanging branches and mountain slope down into the vertical reflections on the lake.

In *Young Woman Powdering Herself*, a famous example of Seurat's scientific explorations with light, colour and form, the artist creates a vibrating surface of dots of colour. Though oddly artificial in effect, it makes an extraordinarily strong visual impact. Van Gogh's famous self-portrait "with bandaged ear" is probably the most tantalisingly unexplained picture – why did the artist mutilate himself? It has recently been suggested that it was Gauguin who lashed out at Van Gogh when the pair failed to get on in Arles. The expressive brush-strokes, creating a textured finish, and Van Gogh's self-absorbed appearance suggest a very different artistic personality to the one who painted the exotic pleasures of *Nevermore*, with its smooth, sensual surface.

Food and drink*: The Courtauld has a café in the basement, serving snacks and coffees. There are also two other inexpensive cafés in the south wing of Somerset House, one with riverside seating in the summer. For a treat, lunch or dine at the chic but expensive Admiralty Restaurant.*

Hayward Gallery

One of the largest, purpose-built exhibition spaces in Britain

Map reference: page 20, E4
South Bank Centre, Belvedere Road, SE1
Tel: 020-7960 5226 and 020-7261 0127 (recorded information); www.hayward-gallery.org.uk
Tube and rail: Waterloo. Buses 4, 68, 168, 188.
Open: daily 10am–6pm (Tues, Wed until 8pm).
The main entrance is on an overhead walkway; access from Waterloo Bridge or via spiral steps from ground level. Wheelchair access via a lift from ground level. Lift. Bookshop. Audioguides. Gallery talks. Admission charge.

The idea for the South Bank Centre, situated, as its name implies, on the south bank of the Thames, was born with the Festival of Britain in 1951. The Festival was intended to celebrate better times after years of austerity following World War II and to rejuvenate an under-used area of London. At its heart was the Royal Festival Hall, a state-of-the-art concert hall. Since 1951, two more concert halls, the Hayward (named after Sir Isaac Hayward, one-time leader of the London County Council), the

National Film Theatre and the National Theatre have been added to the site.

The Hayward was designed by the Greater London Council (GLC) Department of Architecture and Civic Design, led by Geoffrey Horsefall. Built as a cluster of abstract blocks in reinforced concrete, its cold and oppressive 1960s brutalist style is little loved by the public but is now considered an architectural classic of its time. Inside, the exhibition space is designed as five separate galleries over three levels, joined by a massive ramp and staircase.

The organisation is, in theory, versatile, but is difficult to unify. Attempts to demolish or disguise the 1960s additions have been resisted, although most of the monumental pedestrian walkway has been removed as part of the recent renovation and humanisation of the area. On the Hayward's roof is the "Neon Tower", composed of alternating coloured strip-lights; designed in 1970 by Philip Vaughan and Roger Dainton, it has become the gallery's distinguishing sign on the South Bank.

The Hayward, until 1987 funded by the Arts Council of Great Britain, is now managed by the South Bank Centre. The Gallery shows a varied exhibition programme covering art, architecture and design in its permanent home, and a range of National Touring Exhibitions to regional centres throughout the country. Every five years it selects and organises The British Art Show, a large-scale exhibition designed to demonstrate the strength and vitality of British art. Its main programme includes monographic shows by international contemporary artists, such as Bridget Riley, Jasper Johns, Lucio Fontana, Antony Gormley,

Malcolm Morley and Pierre Bonnard; thematic exhibitions offering fresh and exciting insights into subjects and movements; the art of other cultures; and contemporary group shows. Recent exhibitions of note include "Spellbound: Art and Film", "The Art of Ancient Mexico" and "Art and Power: Europe under the Dictators 1930–1945".

Food and drink: The Hayward has a café, with a small terrace with views onto the Thames. Light refreshments only are served. For more substantial fare, try the Royal Festival Hall's People's Palace (moderate). East along the river you'll find the Oxo Tower (expensive) and a few trendy pubs at Gabriel's Wharf.

National Gallery

An outstanding collection of Old Masters from the early Renaissance to 1900

Map reference: page 20, C4
Trafalgar Square, WC2.
Tel: 020-7747 2885. www.national gallery.org.uk
Tube: Charing Cross, Leicester Square.
Buses: 24, 29, 91, 139, 159 (Mon–Sat).
Open: daily 10am–6pm (Wed until 9pm).
There are two main entrances: one into the old building and one into the Sainsbury Wing, on the northwest corner of Trafalgar Square. Wheelchair access is via the Sainsbury Wing. The two buildings are linked by a bridge on the main floor. Bookshops. Archive and library (by appointment), micro gallery (computer points), audioguides, lecture theatre, gallery talks, lifts. Admission free except for some exhibitions.

ABOVE: a late 20th-century addition to the National Gallery: the Sainsbury Wing.

LEFT: Vaughan and Dainton's iconic tower stands proud on the roof of the Hayward Gallery.

The National Gallery was founded in 1824, when a private collection of 38 paintings was acquired by the British Government for

The Wilton
Diptych
(1395–99).

the sum of £60,000 and exhibited in the owner's house at 100 Pall Mall. *(For a detailed history, see pages 171–73).* Included in the initial collection were several outstanding works that set the standard for today's gallery of masterpieces: *Bacchanal* by Poussin, *St Ursula* and *The Queen of Sheba* by landscape master Claude, paintings by Van Dyck, two admirable Rembrandts and a superb Aelbert Cuyp. The British contribution was represented by William Hogarth's famous narrative, *Six Pictures called Marriage à la Mode.*

An early addition was Correggio's exquisite little *Madonna of the Basket.* This was followed by unique acquisitions such as Titian's *Bacchus and Ariadne* and Poussin's *Bacchanalian Revel.* Sir George Beaumont's gift included Rembrandt's portrait of *A Jew Merchant and Deposition*, Rubens' landscape, the *Château de Steen,* and Canaletto's *View of Venice.* The first modern landscape to enter the collection was Constable's *The Cornfield*, which remains today one of the most popular English national icons.

Building improvements

As the collection grew in size and stature, a new building in which to accommodate it was planned. William Wilkins' long, low construction, with its classical façade in white Portland stone and crowned with a dome, opened to the public in 1834 in the then-recently created Trafalgar Square. The building has been remodelled in various ways over the years, notably with the imposing three-way staircase leading to the main floor.

However, the most prominent addition to the

building is the Sainsbury Wing, situated on the west corner of the square. It was designed in 1991 by the American architect Robert Venturi in witty post-modern style to add a stylish coda to what is regarded as Wilkins' rather bland classicism. The two buildings are bridged by a circular link, and the pleasant paved area between the two buildings offers a neat short-cut to Leicester Square. It's well worth taking a peek round the corner at the west wall – Venturi's colourful touches are taken up in the interior details.

In fact, the general public probably feels more affection for Wilkins' maligned façade than they do

John
Constable's
The Cornfield
(1826),
National
Gallery.

National Gallery

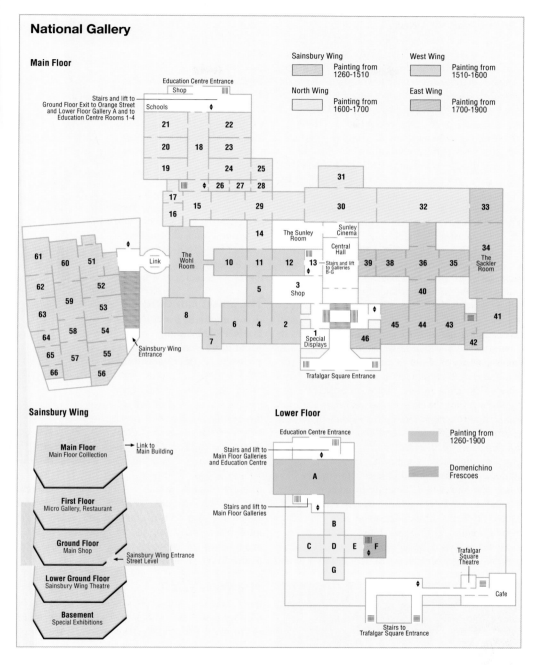

Main Floor

Education Centre Entrance
Shop

Stairs and lift to
Ground Floor Exit to Orange Street
and Lower Floor Gallery A and to
Education Centre Rooms 1-4

Schools

Sainsbury Wing — Painting from 1260-1510

West Wing — Painting from 1510-1600

North Wing — Painting from 1600-1700

East Wing — Painting from 1700-1900

Link

The Wohl Room

The Sunley Room

Sunley Cinema

Central Hall

Stairs and lift to Galleries B-G

Shop

Special Displays

Sainsbury Wing Entrance

Trafalgar Square Entrance

The Sackler Room

Sainsbury Wing

Main Floor
Main Floor Collection

→ Link to Main Building

First Floor
Micro Gallery, Restaurant

Ground Floor
Main Shop

Sainsbury Wing Entrance
Street Level ←

Lower Ground Floor
Sainsbury Wing Theatre

Basement
Special Exhibitions

Lower Floor

Education Centre Entrance

Stairs and lift to
Main Floor Galleries
and Education Centre

Stairs and lift to
Main Floor Galleries

Painting from 1260-1900

Domenichino Frescoes

Trafalgar Square Theatre

Cafe

Stairs to
Trafalgar Square Entrance

---

for its 20th-century variation. For, although the Sainsbury Wing has been visited by more than 25 million people since its opening, the most popular entrance to the National Gallery is still via the old building. With its double flight of steps up to a covered portico overlooking Trafalgar Square, this is still a favourite spot to meet, socialise and photograph the admired vista towards Nelson's Column and down Whitehall. Giant Corinthian columns frame the elegantly spired church of St Martin in the Fields, to the east, and, to the west, the jutting curve of the Sainsbury Wing.

The Sainsbury Wing

The collection is arranged chronologically, from the 13th century to the end of the 19th century, through four wings starting in the Sainsbury Wing. Here, Venturi's grand staircase takes you up to the main floor. At the top, turn left into a suite of 16 recently refurbished galleries evocative of a great basilica, with a central nave and monumental windows on the eastern side giving onto the staircase. Remarkably, this early collection is still being added to.

Turn immediately left into room 52 to see the *Virgin and Child enthroned with two Angels* (*c.*1280–5), by Cimabue, and paintings by Giotto and Duccio, leaders in the break from Byzantine formality towards more naturally human representation. One of the Gallery's treasures is the Wilton Diptych, a beautiful, French or English, portable altarpiece, which is painted and gilded with jewel-like delicacy. The startling clarity of the blue makes an indelible impression. It shows Richard II kneeling with his patron saints before the Virgin and Christ Child, who makes to present him with a standard. Exciting new research revealed that the tiny painting on the orb depicts an island with a castle, an image of England, which Richard is about to receive as a divine gift.

In the last of this sequence of rooms is *The Marriage of Arnolfini*, an intriguingly realistic and ever-popular work by the early Netherlandish master, Jan van Eyck. From here, turn right and immediately on your left hangs Antonio and Piero del Pollaiuolo's famous painting, *The Martyrdom of St Sebastian*. This accomplished, if somewhat contrived, figural composition was painted in late 15th-century Florence at a time when the study of anatomy – and particularly, as here, the muscular structure of the body – fascinated artists. The panoramic landscape behind is a *tour de force* and repays a long look.

Move ahead into the far rooms. Rooms 61 and 62 contain works by Mantegna and Bellini. As you com-plete the circuit, don't forget to look back again at the St Sebastian, which forms the apex of the central enfilade. In the final room, Michelangelo's early *Manchester Madonna* now joins work by his teacher, Domenico Ghirlandaio, and Leonardo da Vinci's celebrated *Virgin and Child with St Anne and St John the Baptist* (known as *The Virgin of the Rocks*), *c.*1508.

From this point, you can walk across the bridge into the West Wing of the old Gallery and continue your chronological journey with 16th-century Italian and German masterworks of the High Renaissance period.

The main building

If you approach the collection from the old building, a magnificent flight of stairs offers you a choice of three directions. Take the left flight to the West Wing and the Renaissance galleries. Go straight ahead, through the Central Hall, for the North Wing and the great masterpieces of the 17th century, including Velazquez's *Rokeby Venus* (1647–51). Turn right into the East Wing for Monet and the Impressionists, Van Gogh and Cézanne. As you go round admire the 19th-century grandeur and variety of the rooms in this part of the gallery. Now richly restored and refurbished, they present a contrast to the relative restraint of the Sainsbury Wing.

The West Wing

Not to be missed in the West Wing are paintings of the German School in room 4. Here you can see Holbein's magnificent double portrait of *The Ambassadors,* with its sober *momento mori,* a hidden skull, in the midst of worldly success. Stand to the right, parallel to the painting. From here, the puzzlingly distorted image, or anamorphosis, in the centre will reform as a human skull. Holbein's virtuoso realism in the painting of the two men, the complexity of the instruments on the buffet and the intricate mosaic, based on a pavement in Westminster Abbey,

Hans Holbein's *The Ambassadors* (1533).

(1815), which he considered his masterpiece, and *Sun Rising through Vapour* (exhib. 1807), on the understanding that were hung alongside two paintings by Claude, *Seaport with the Embarkation of the Queen of Sheba* (1648) and *Landscape with the Marriage of Isaac and Rebekah* (1648), as if to demonstrate that his blazing evocation of sunlight and atmospheric colour rivalled, and even surpassed, those of Claude. Two of Turner's best-known masterpieces are hung with British work in the East Wing, room 34: *Rain, Steam and Speed* and his romantically heroic picture of the *Fighting Téméraire*, as he imagined the battleship tugged down the Thames at sunset to be broken up.

In room 16 hang one of Vermeer's rare and exquisite pictures, *A Young Woman Standing at a Virginal*, as fascinating in its handling of paint as in the suggestiveness of its subject matter. Beyond, room 17 houses Samuel van Hoogstraten's peep-box, showing realistic interiors of a Dutch house.

Turn back into room 15 and from here turn left into the extension and, not to be missed, a suite of galleries redecorated to theatrical effect. The long gallery (room 18), hung with portraits of the French School against crimson damask, draws the eye to a bravura full-length portrait on the end wall, Philippe de Champaigne's *Cardinal Richelieu*, showing France's chief minister under Louis XIV. Notice how the arched doorways leading on either side to the National Gallery's Education Centre wittily echo the architecture in this painting, as though the sitter had stepped out of the Gallery. Appropriately, this room of rich dress and fabrics was donated by fashion designer Yves Saint Laurent.

Johannes Vermeer's *A Young Woman Standing at a Virginal* (17th century).

must have helped promote his appointment as Court Painter to Henry VIII.

The following rooms, 7–12, are richly hung with work by El Greco, Tintoretto, Michelangelo, Bronzino, Veronese and Raphael. The large Wohl Room (room 9) displays paintings by Titian, including his brilliant and spirited *Bacchus and Ariadne* (1523). As you complete the circuit of the West Wing, you move into the Central Hall, a useful resting point. From here you can continue, either left into the Sunley Room, a space for special exhibitions, and the North Wing, or straight ahead into the East Wing.

The North Wing

Straight ahead at the end of the Wohl Room is the North Wing's octagonal room 15. Here, you can see two paintings from the Turner Bequest, now mostly hung in the Clore Gallery at Tate Britain (*see page 193*). He gave these, *Dido Building Carthage*

The rooms leading out of this long gallery are hung against dramatically contrasting cool grey walls. Here, if you follow the rooms in numerical order, you can see a group of fine paintings by Claude (19), Poussin (20) and Aelbert Cuyp (21), a favourite with English patrons. Crossing room 18, Netherlandish masters continue in the parallel suite. There's a representative range of paintings by Rembrandt in room 23 that are splendid in their human sympathy and understanding. As you move through a warren of small rooms, out into

The Marriage of Arnolfini (c.1434) by Jan van Eyck.

Da Vinci's
*Madonna of
the Rocks*
(*c.*1508),
National
Gallery.

the hexagonal room 29, a group of pictures exemplifies Rubens' versatility as a mythogical painter, portraitist and, in *The Château de Steen*, a landscape painter *par excellence*.

The two largest rooms in the North Wing contain, in room 30, paintings by the Spanish artists, Murillo, Zurbarán and Velazquez. The last's powers of observation are expressively realised in paint, and, most daring for its time, in the sensuous nude, *The Toilet of Venus (The Rokeby Venus)* of *c.*1655–60 (*see page 173*). In room 32, Caravaggio's dramatic use of chiaroscuro, exploiting the contrasting effects of bright light and deep shadow, is still effective in conveying the story of Christ's startling appearance at *The Supper at Emmaus* (1601). The rooms opening out of 32 take you to the East Wing, to English, continental and Scandinavian painting of the 18th and 19th centuries.

The East Wing

In the East Wing, the long gallery 34 provides the architectural balance to the West Wing's Wohl Room. Here, a magnificent collection of portraits and landscapes by Gainsborough, Constable, Turner and Stubbs is on display. In the smaller, square room 35, there are paintings by Hogarth – the vitality of his *Shrimp Girl* (*c.*1740s) gives as accurate a picture of his times as does his satirical narrative *Marriage à la Mode*.

The final rooms in this wing display an outstanding selection of French late 19th-century paintings by Courbet, Manet, Degas, Cézanne, Monet, Renoir, Gauguin, and Dutch-born Van Gogh.

Although the National Gallery's and Tate Britain's historic collection of British and European art officially divide at 1900, the two galleries pursue a fruitful policy of exchange and overlap. If there is a particular work you want to see, it's worth checking on its whereabouts in advance of your visit.

Food and drink: For snacks and coffees, try the inexpensive Gallery Café, entered through the main building, or direct from Trafalgar Square. For more substantial, Italian-influenced fare (drinks only also available), there's Criveli's Garden Restaurant and Italian Bar in the Sainsbury Wing, named after the mural by Paula Rego that decorates its walls.

National Portrait Gallery

The home of one of the strongest traditions of national portraiture in the world

Map reference: page 20, C4
St Martin's Place, WC2.
Tel: 020-7312 2463; www.npg.org.uk
Tube: Charing Cross, Leicester Square.
Buses: 24, 29, 91, 139, 159.
Open: Mon–Wed, Sat and Sun 10am–6pm,
Thurs and Fri 10am–9pm.
Wheelchair access on Orange Street. Lift for
the disabled. Bookshop, archive and library
(by appointment). Audioguides, lecture theatre,
IT Gallery. Admission free except for some
special exhibitions.

A British Historical Portrait Gallery was established in 1856 on the initiative of the 5th Earl of Stanhope. It had no collection as such, relying on gifts and bequests, the first of which was the famous "Chandos" picture of Shakespeare, attributed to John Taylor, *c*.1610, and arguably the only portrait of Britain's most famous playwright done from life. From the start, additions to the collection (initially comprising traditional paintings, drawings and sculpture, with photography a later addition) were determined by the status of the sitter and historical importance of the portrait, not by their quality as works of art; these criteria still pertain today. Portraits of living people were not admitted until 1968, when the policy was changed to encourage younger artists and a fresh exploration of the genre.

In the late 20th century the definition of portraiture widened hugely, and gallery acquisitions included the collection's first conceptual, genomic portrait. By Marc Quinn, it remarkably employs the DNA of the sitter, Sir John Sulston, one of the UK's leading figures in the development of DNA analysis.

Location

In its early days, the gallery had no fixed home. Eventually, the collection was hung in a Georgian terraced house, only to be moved on again and again as it outgrew its venues. The collection and visitor numbers increased so rapidly that the Government assigned it a permanent home on its present site, northeast of the National Gallery on the corner of St Martin's Place. Financed, at the time anonymously, by the philanthropist William Henry Alexander, the gallery was purpose-built to designs by his favourite architect, Ewan Christian, in his favoured style – Florentine Renaissance – and faced with Portland stone to complement its neighbour, the National Gallery. It opened in 1896.

In the course of the 20th century the gallery has expanded. In 1933, the Duveen Wing opened on Orange Street, and, in the early 1980s, this space was remodelled to create a gallery for special shows. In 1993 an attractive suite of galleries was opened on the ground floor. Designed by John Miller and Sue Rogers to display contemporary portraits, this is one of the most popular attractions in the gallery. A recent, spectacular development is the Ondaatje Wing, designed by Jeremy Dixon and Edward Jones with a vast entrance hall and one of the longest escalators in London, sweeping the visitor to the top floor, where the displays begin with 16th-century portraiture.

Medieval times to the 17th century

Surveying the history of British portraiture over five centuries, the collection is arranged on five floors. Its displays are broadly chronological, with thematic sub-divisions in each period: the Medieval and Tudor Period, the 17th century, the Georgian age, the Victorian period and, on the first-floor Balcony Gallery and the ground floor, work of the 20th and 21st centuries.

The early part of the collection, on the top floor, contains many notable royal portraits. The very large drawing of Henry VII and his son Henry VIII (*c*.1536–7) is by Hans Holbein, probably the most memorable image of Henry VIII. With this majestic figure, legs astride and bulked out by his court dress,

Queen Elizabeth I (c.1600), anonymous, National Portrait Gallery.

Holbein created an unforgettable icon of royal power. The curiously distended image of Prince Edward amazed its 16th-century audience and still continues to intrigue visitors. It was painted when Edward was nine, a year before he succeeded Henry VIII as King. If you look through the peephole at the side, the portrait of a boy wearing a feathered cap and contained in a roundel, springs into correct perspective.

One of the most important portraits of Queen Elizabeth I is the very life-like, three-quarter length view of the Virgin Queen, sumptuous in brocade and pearls *(see page 187)*. It was almost certainly painted from direct observation, when she was about 40. A later image, known as "The Ditchley Portrait", shows the Queen in her more familiar stiff and stylised guise. It commemorates the Queen's visit to one of her subjects, Sir Henry Lee, and shows her

standing on a symbolic globe, her feet planted, significantly, in Oxfordshire where Lee lived.

In the 17th century there was a remarkable flowering of naturalistic portraiture, stimulated by foreign example. Rubens, while on a diplomatic visit to England, made a sympathetic likeness of the great art patron and connoisseur, Thomas Howard, Earl of Arundel, whose collection of classical sculpture, known as the Arundel Marbles, is now in the Ashmolean Mueum in Oxford. The finished portrait is in the Isabella Stewart Gardner Museum, Boston.

The most reputed foreign artist to satisfy the English taste for portraiture, however, was Rubens' pupil, Van Dyck. The portrait of Venetia Stanley, Lady Digby, is an allegory of a virtuous wife – a former concubine – commissioned by her distraught widower, and shows her stamping on profane love, while angels crown her with laurels.

Van Dyck's successor in the field was German-born, British-based Peter Lely, who made his name in the Restoration court of King Charles II. One of his masterpieces is a beautiful double portrait of the future James II and Anne Hyde (*c*.1660–90), married in secret after she became pregnant. Although her father disapproved of the match, Charles II admired her and supported his brother's choice. Lely has captured the warmth and intimacy of the couple in a socially elegant picture, complemented by a fine contemporary frame.

A German artist, Godfrey Kneller, painted a noble portrait of one of England's greatest architects, Christopher Wren, whose rebuilding of London after the Great Fire included St Paul's Cathedral. The plan for the cathedral's west end hangs over the table beside him. He was 79, and could look back confidently on the trials involved in the project.

Georgian and Victorian portraiture

The superb terracotta bust of George I dressed as a Roman emperor in togas and laurel crown is yet another example of a continental artist, this time the Flemish artist Ruysbrack, receiving notable commissions. The sensitive portrait of the Great Augustan poet, Alexander Pope, is also by him.

By the 18th century, British portraitists such as Thomas Hudson and Allan Ramsay were responding to foreign challenge. Hudson's portrait of Handel is magnificently framed, its gilded carving topped appropriately with a trophy of musical instruments. The self-portraits of Hogarth, Gainsborough and Reynolds, which, respectively, are almost comic in honest informality, intelligently composed, and melodramatic, are telling indications of their personalities. The official portraits of the Victorian and Edwardian periods are some of the last examples of stylish formality. Sargent's bravura treatment of Sir Frank Swettenham shows a successful portrait painter working in the lush Van Dyck tradition.

The 20th century and beyond

The later works are housed on the first-floor Balcony Gallery and the ground floor. The Balcony Gallery parades a splendid array of well-known per-

Musician David Bowie (1994) by Stephen Finer.

Royal Academy of Arts

Major temporary exhibitions and a small permanent collection at the home of the English Royal Society of Art

Map reference: page 20, B4
Burlington House, Piccadilly, W1.
Tel: 020-7300 8000, 020-7439 4996 (recorded information); www.royalacademy.org.uk
Tube: Piccadilly Circus, Green Park.
Buses: 8, 9, 14, 19, 22, 38.
Open: daily 10am–6pm, Fri until 10pm.
Lunchtime tours of the Fine Rooms and selection from the Academy Collections, free. Shop. Lift to upper floor. Archive and library, the oldest collections of fine arts books in the country (by appointment). Audioguides. Lectures. Admission charge to exhibitions; combined tickets available.

sonalities, such as Rodrigo Moynihan's controversial portrait of the former Conservative Prime Minister, Margaret Thatcher, sent back by its sitter for some cosmetic surgery to one eye. Some of the most successful 20th-century portraits are characterised by their informality and their attempt to catch the sitter unawares, and vie with casual photographic poses. Note the Labour Prime Minister, Harold Wilson, seen through a cloud of pipe smoke, and the Conservative Prime Minister, Alec Douglas-Home, off-duty, fishing. The matinée idol Dirk Bogarde and the former Beatle Paul McCartney are depicted in private, dreamy moments, out of the limelight.

Also on the first floor are modern-day royal portraits including Annigoni's sweetly lyrical handling of the young Queen Elizabeth II; this piece achieved a popularity that was not repeated with his later, still controversial, attempt at a regal image.

On the ground floor, contemporary portraits delight the gallery's visitors. Look out for images of artists Frank Auerbach, Sarah Lucas and Tracy Emin, writer Martin Amis, actor Ewan McGregor, architects Norman Foster and Richard Rogers, sports star David Beckham and politicians William Hague and Tony Blair. Note that excellent temporary exhibitions are also mounted at the gallery.

Food and drink: There are two good options at the NPG. In the basement, there's the Portrait Café, serving drinks and snacks. On the top floor, there's the more expensive Portrait Restaurant, a minimalist eating place with splendid views over London's skyline (open late Thurs and Fri).

The entrance to the Royal Academy (RA) is through a grand arch in the centre of a long classical façade and across a large courtyard. The society was founded in 1768 under George III, with Joshua Reynolds as its first President. Originally based in Pall Mall, it moved in 1780 into purpose-built premises in William Chambers' new Somerset House on the Strand *(see pages 118–19)*, where its annual exhibition was hung in an overcrowded display in the Great Room on the top floor.

In 1868, the Academy moved to its present headquarters in Burlington House, so called because the core of its building, on the north side of the courtyard, was the home of Richard Boyle, 3rd Earl of Burlington. In the 1720s the building had been remodelled in Palladian style and in 1815 it was faced with Portland stone. The site was extensively remodelled from 1868 by Sydney Smirke RA, who added 12 exhibition galleries, a lecture room and studios on the gardens behind the house.

In 1983, an ambitious redevelopment programme, which included restoring Smirke's suite of galleries, began. In 1991, the Sackler Wing, by architect Norman Foster, opened, with three top-lit galleries,

Taddei Tondo (1502) by Michaelangelo, Royal Academy of Arts.

whose work is judged to be good enough) have been positive. Recent temporary exhibitions include, in the main galleries, the controversial "Apocalyse" and "Sensation" shows, and monographs such as "Giacometti" and "Frank Auerbach", and, in the Sackler Galleries, "Botticelli's Dante: The Drawings for the Divine Comedy". The most popular exhibitions have timed tickets, which must be bought in advance.

The permanent collection

The Academy's little-known permanent collection includes masterpieces such as Michelangelo's *Taddei Tondo* (displayed outside the Sackler Galleries), Constable's *The Leaping Horse*, Gainsborough's *A Romantic Landscape* and Sargent's *Venetian Interior*. Diploma work, submitted by each Academician on election to membership, includes Walter Sickert's *Santa Maria Maggiore*, Stanley Spencer's *A Farm Gate* and David Hockney's *Grand Canyon*.

Food and drink: The café in the Sackler Wing serves snacks and drinks, while the restaurant on the ground floor does more substantial fare. In summer, you can eat outside in the attractive main courtyard.

reached by a sleek glass lift and staircase. The courtyard, often used to display sculpture, is now repaved and car-free, and will eventually sprout jets of water.

In 2001, the Academy bought 6 Burlington Gardens, once the garden to Burlington House and, more recently, home to the Museum of Mankind. Architect Michael Hopkins was commissioned to link the two historic sites with a building containing galleries for the show of work by academy members and students, for architecture exhibitions and for extra premises for the Royal Society of Art. A second front door, in Burlington Gardens, and many new facilities are planned as part of this grand project due for completion in 2007.

Promoting the fine arts

The RA's founding mission is the promotion of the Fine Arts through its membership (the Academicians), schools, major (temporary) exhibitions and education programme. Its hesitant attempts to modernise its traditional, increasingly old-fashioned, image in the late 20th century and to acknowledge the new aesthetic concerns of younger artists, particularly in its summer exhibition (held annually for the display of members' work but open to anyone

Tate Britain

The country's main gallery of British art

Map reference: page 23, E3
Millbank, London SW1.
Tel: 020-7887 8000; 020-7887 8008 (recorded information); www.tate.org.uk
Tube: Pimlico, Westminster. Rail: Vauxhall.
Bus: 2, 3, C10, 36, 77A, 88, 159, 185, 507.
Open: daily 10am–5.50pm.
Wheelchair access on Atterbury Street and via the Clore Gallery. Wheelchairs available. Reserve a parking space for disabled visitors on tel: 020-7887 8888 or via tate.ticketing@tate.org.uk.
Bookshop. Art library and Tate Archives, Turner library (Clore Gallery), all by appointment only. Audioguides, lecture theatre, gallery talks, lift in the Clore Gallery. Admission free except for special exhibitions.

The Tate Gallery was relaunched and rebranded as Tate Britain and Tate Modern in 2000, as part of an ambitious programme of expansion and redevelopment, which includes the gallery's regional branches, Tate Liverpool and Tate St Ives.

At Tate Britain on Millbank, the original Tate Gallery, British art from the 16th century to the present day is collected and displayed. Tate Modern *(see page 194)* is a show-case for international modern and contemporary art, including some British art.

The Tate has been continually criticised for showing only a fraction of its holdings of some 5,000 works. Its policy since 1990 of turning the collection over by hanging new annual displays provided one solution, which was exciting to some, but dismayed those expecting to find old favourites in familiar places. With increased space for the exclusive display of British art, visitors can expect to find some of the following masterpieces described here, but do check that 20th-century works are not displayed in Tate Modern. If you are visiting to see a particular work, you are advised to telephone the Information Department in advance to find if the piece is at Millbank.

The building

The original Tate Gallery was designed in classical style by Sydney Smith with a grand flight of steps leading to a large entrance portico. It was financed by a public benefactor, Henry Tate, who made his fortune from sugar refining and the invention of the sugar lump. The Tate opened in 1897 as a department of the National Gallery in Trafalgar Square; its original purpose was to celebrate British art, and the gallery was inaugurated with Tate's own collection of 67 Victorian paintings, including Millais' *Ophelia* and works from the National Gallery.

The original gallery has been enlarged several times, first by Sir Henry Tate, and then by Joseph Duveen, who paid for a gallery to house the Turner Bequest of well over 20,000 of J.M.W. Turner's oils, watercolours and drawings. In 1917, in the nationalistic atmosphere generated by World War I, and in a desire to compete with the example set by the Musée du Luxembourg, in Paris, the Tate began to build up a collection of modern foreign art with the Hugh Lane Bequest of Impressionist paintings and later funding from Samuel Courtauld *(see page 179)*.

Through the 1920s there was a focus on enlarging the Tate's collection of contemporary British art, and important acquisitions include Stanley Spencer's painting *The Resurrection, Cookham,* purchased in 1927, the year in which it was completed. It was Duveen's son who financed new galleries for foreign art in 1926 and the grand Duveen Sculpture Galleries in 1937. New show spaces, designed by John Weeks in 1979, were controversial at the time, but have proved to be versatile and attractive as a setting for art of all kinds. In 1987 the Clore Gallery, built in pavilion-style to designs by the internationally renowned British architect James Stirling, provided a permanent home for the Turner Bequest.

A major centenary development at Millbank, which had been underway since 1998, was completed in 2001. This exciting project mainly involved the redevelopment of the northwest corner of Tate Britain by architects John Miller and Partners. It also included external improvements, notably the landscaping of the front gardens with new seating by Allies and Morrison. Miller's design for new galleries of early English painting has substantially increased the display area and created a new entrance on Atterbury Street, with full wheelchair access, educational and other public facilities.

The Cholmondeley Ladies, British School, 17th century, Tate Britain.

The early collection

The detailed *Queen Elizabeth I* (*c*.1575), showing the Queen resplendent in a jewel-encrusted dress, is one of only two large paintings known to be by Nicholas Hilliard (he is best known as a miniaturist). Here, he has given Elizabeth an air of luxury and flawless beauty, similar to a religious icon, which was much to her taste. Hogarth, working over a hundred years later, painted his anti-French satire *O The Roast Beef of Old England* in equally patriotic mood. He was furious at being arrested at Calais as a suspected spy because he was sketching and took revenge by comparing the fat side of beef, the English national dish and symbol of a nourished people, with the emaciated French brought up on gruel.

Hogarth dominated British painting in the early 18th century, and you can see some fine examples of his portraits and narratives at Tate Britain. Later in the century, Joshua Reynolds and Thomas Gainsborough adopted a grander manner. Gainsborough's dashing brushwork brings the vivacity of *Giovanna Baccelli* (1782) alive brilliantly in a portrait which is generally regarded as one of his masterpieces.

John Constable is associated with pictures of a new kind of naturalistic landscape painted from observation rather than from classical models, and is credited with the creation of a national landscape tradition. Some of Constable's best-known paintings are in Tate Britain, including *Flatford Mill* (1817), the first of his large-scale paintings of the River Stour in Suffolk, where he grew up and acquired his love of nature. His range of greens flecked with white brings the lush English countryside to life for the first time in painting. Although mostly remembered for his rural scenes, Constable also painted superb coastal subjects, such as *Chain Pier, Brighton* (1826–7), with its dramatic expanse of sky. For him, the sky set the mood for a scene, and he excelled at its rendering. His *The Opening of Waterloo Bridge* (1832) is one the most impressive works in English art, not least for its sparkling effects of light and colour over the water and in the clouds. Although only a preparatory work, the full-scale *Sketch for Hadleigh Castle* (*c*.1828–9) is a dark masterpiece in its own right; here, Constable poured his emotions into the sombre landscape, reflecting his unhappiness after his wife's death.

Among the most popular 19th-century painters represented are the Pre-Raphaelites. The group's leading members were Millais, Holman Hunt, Rossetti and, later, Burne-Jones, who rebelled against dark, "sloshy" painting and trivial subject matter, creating instead sharply realistic paintings in pure, brilliant colours. Millais' *Ophelia* (1841–2), derived from Shakespeare's *Hamlet*, is a perennial favourite. Another influential artist was the American-born artist Whistler, whose ideas shifted the course of English painting towards modernism.

The 20th century and later

In the 20th century, Stanley Spencer's personal and imaginative pictures, such as *The Resurrection, Cookham* (1927), are acclaimed as a high point in a figurative tradition that constitutes a strong strand of originality in English painting. Today, Lucian Freud is celebrated as Britain's greatest living painter of the figure, particularly the erotic nude. The work in Tate Britain allows us to compare the psychological intensity and immaculate finish of the early *Girl with a White Dog* (1950–1) with the later *Standing by the Rags* (1988–9), in which the palpitating presence of flesh, closely scrutinised, is revealed in the physical texture of the pigment.

Of the post-World War II painters, Francis Bacon is pre-eminent. *Three studies for Figures at the Base of a Crucifixion* (1944) is where, he said, "I began", and it shows his fine handling of paint coupled with

Rossetti's *Beata Beatrix* (*c*.1864–70), Tate Britain.

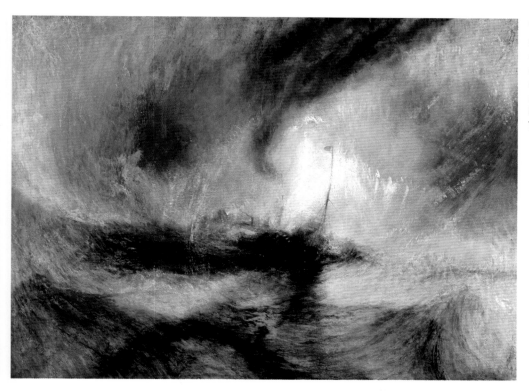

Turner's evocative *Snow Storm: Steam-Boat off a Harbour's Mouth*, exhibited in 1842, Tate Britain.

his violent treatment of the figure in the creation of contemporary images. A later, powerfully expressive development of his theme is called *Triptych – August 1972*, painted in memory of his partner.

David Hockney belongs equally to this parade of prestigious British artists preferring figurative to abstract art, and whose work is strongly autobiographical. *Mr and Mrs Clark and Percy* (1970–1) is a major contribution to British painting and one of the most popular Tate paintings. Traditional in its composition, and modern in its treatment of a contemporary relationship, it could be called a "celeb" portrait of "swinging" London society.

Among the British 20th-century sculptors represented, Jacob Epstein (*Doves, c.*1914–15), Barbara Hepworth (*Three Forms,* 1935) and Henry Moore are towering figures. Moore is the most celebrated for his works with a human subject and modern vision that resonate with audiences all over the world. His *Four-Piece Composition: Reclining Figure* (1934) and *Reclining Figure* (1951) deal with a theme central to his work. For Moore, the reclining figure, usually female, is related to the landscape and alludes to motherhood, childbirth, and to the primal image of mother earth.

The Clore Gallery

Leave time to visit the Clore Gallery, home to a magnificent collection of oil paintings and works on paper by Turner. This incredible artist carried the handling of light and weather to heights never matched by any other artist. Two paintings, *Snow Storm: Hannibal and his Army Crossing the Alps* and *Snow Storm: Steam-Boat off a Harbour's Mouth* show the artist's fascination with elemental forces, particularly storms in the mountains and at sea. In the former, the army is about to be engulfed by the sweeping curve of thunder clouds. In order to paint the sensational effect achieved in the latter, Turner tells us in his subtitle that "The Author was in this Storm on the Night the Ariel left Harwich", lashed, at his own request, to the ship's mast. By contrast, note the serene *Norham Castle, Sunrise* (*c.*1845–50), one of his most brilliant evocations of light.

Food and drink: Dine in style in Tate's Rex Whistler-designed Restaurant (to reserve, tel: 020-7887 8877), complete with mural by Howard Hodgkin. There are also drinks and light meals available in the inexpensive self-service café in the basement. On a fine day, picnic in the gallery's front gardens or in the attractive, quiet public gardens behind. Excellent sandwiches are available in the nearby John Islip Street.

Tate Modern

Britain's spectacular museum of modern and contemporary international art

Map reference: page 21, G4
Bankside, London SE1.
Tel: 020-7887 8000; 020-7887 8008 (recorded information); www.tate.org.uk
Tube: Southwark, Blackfriars, London Bridge.
Bus: 45, 63, 100 (to Blackfriars Bridge Road); 381 (Southwark Street); 344 (Southwark Bridge Road).
Open: daily Sun–Thurs 10am–6pm (last entry 5pm), Fri–Sat 10am–10pm (last entry 9pm).
Main entrance is the West Entrance on Holland Street. Access for wheelchair, prams and buggies: via North Entrance on river walkway. Bookshop. Admission free except for special exhibitions.

In 2000, the Tate Gallery's collection was divided between two sites in response to a growing need to expand display space. It now dedicates its building on Millbank (Tate Britain, *see page 190*) to its original purpose of displaying British art, having moved its modern works to Tate Modern, located on the south bank of the Thames. At Tate Modern, modern and contemporary international art from *c*.1900 to the present, including some British art, is shown.

A new powerhouse

Tate Modern has captured the public's imagination in a quite unprecedented way, both for its displays and its building, which establishes a magnificent presence on the South Bank. The bold decision not to build a new gallery, but to purchase and transform the redundant Bankside Power Station was taken in 1998. The post-war industrial building was designed Sir Giles Gilbert Scott, also architect of Battersea Power Station and designer of the red telephone kiosk. The Swiss architects Herzog & de Meuron won an open international competition to redevelop the former electricity station.

The existing brick structure, a massive horizontal block with huge central tower, has been smartened up and the monumental windows re-opened, but in other respects the industrial character of the building still asserts itself. What now identifies it as a museum of art is "The Swiss Light", created by the artist Michael Craig-Martin in collaboration with the architects. The light is a two-storey beam that runs along the top of the building and functions as a beacon on the London skyline.

The new development involved removing the machinery from within the old power station to create a vast cathedral-like entrance the whole height of the building, and piling three gallery floors, shops, cafés and restaurant into a compact bank on one side. Hundreds of visitors can pour into the museum down a huge ramp and quickly disperse.

On your way round you can enjoy views down into the Turbine Hall from the mezzanine bridge on level 2 and various gallery levels. Between the two suites on each of the gallery floors there is seating where you can rest, read, watch the Thames traffic and enjoy the superb vistas across London.

The collection

Do not expect to find the art arranged chronologically, or displayed in a modernist progression of stylistic "-isms" that leads to abstraction and ignores traditional forms. In order to make the collection both more accessible to, and more popular with, the general public, Tate has ordered the work by theme. The displays replace a single historical account with many different stories of artistic activity and suggest their relationship to the wider social and cultural history of the 20th and early 21st century. Note that the displays change from time to time, so the examples picked out here may not all be on show when you visit.

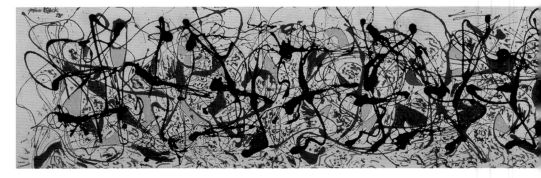

Tate Modern's imposing Turbine Hall.

Four classic themes have been chosen: landscape, still life, history painting and the nude. The genre of landscape painting has been reconceived as "Landscape/Matter/Environment", still life as "Still Life/Object/Real Life", history painting as "History/Memory/Society" and the nude as "Nude/Action/Body". Hung in four separate suites, on two floors, the selections show how artists continue to use these traditionally familiar subjects, renewing and transforming them in ways that transcend movements.

Landscape

In landscape, highlights include Monet's atmospheric painting of *Water-Lilies* (after 1916), Emil Nolde's emotional outpouring in *The Sea B* (1930), Dalí's surreal vision *Autumnal Cannibalism* (1936), Naum Gabo's representation of space in his beautiful plastic-and-glass *Construction in Space with Crystalline Centre* (1938–40) and Fontana's *Spatial Concept "Waiting"* (1960). Note Jackson Pollock's entirely abstract response to the landscape outside his studio in his drip painting *Summertime* (1948) and the

abstract expression of the magnificent and numinous in nature in Clyfford Still's visualisation of a metaphysical landscape in *1953* (1953) and in Mark Rothko's sombre *Seagram Murals* (1958–9) for the Four Seasons Restaurant in New York. Joseph Beuys' *Untitled (Vitrine)* of 1983 contains objects made of, or containing, wax and fats – healing, energy-giving symbols of the natural world. Richard Long's *A line Made by Walking* (1967) is an example of work by an artist working directly in the landscape.

Still life

This genre has opened up enormous possibilities for modern artists, whose experiments with actual objects have become increasingly sculptural and, increasingly, an aspect of, and comment on, real life. The traditional means used by Cézanne to paint his immediate surroundings in *Still Life with Water Jug* (*c*.1892–3) are discarded in Braque's exploration of forms in the Cubist *Clarinet and Bottle of Rum on a Mantelpiece* (1911). The approach of many later artists, such as Morandi in *Still Life* (1946), a painting

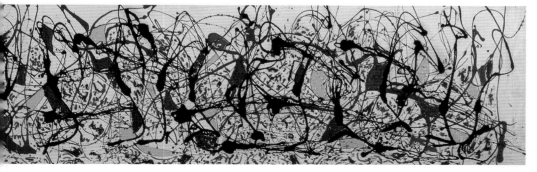

Jackson Pollock's *Summertime: Number 9A* (1948), Tate Modern.

of utter simplicity, and Caulfield in his complex investigation, *Interior with a Picture* (1985–6), are basically traditional.

Other artists chose a different path. Picasso's collage *Bottle of Vieux Marc, Glass, Guitar and Newspaper* (1913) is made more real by the inclusion of elements from the everyday world, in this case pieces of *Le Figaro*, while Spoerri "trapped" the remains of a whole meal on the wall in his *Prose Poems* (1959–60). Duchamp's *Why not Sneeze Rose Sélavy?* (1921) is composed entirely of ready-made objects – sugar lumps, a thermometer and a cuttlefish in a bird cage – but in a curious combination rendered all the more enigmatic by its title. The Surrealists reinvented the still life as the even more elusive Surrealist Object, of which Dalí's famous *Lobster Telephone* (1936) is an intriguing example of an innocent item in daily use charged with sexual meaning. Rachel Whiteread's mystifyingly prosaic *Untitled (Air Bed II)* of 1992 is resonant with personal and symbolic meaning.

History painting

This genre expands from depictions of war and its consequences, such as Grosz's lurid *Suicide* (1916) and Picasso's *Weeping Women* (1937), representing

the agonised despair of women in Republican Spain in the aftermath of the Guernica bombing, to expressions of personal revolt, as in Baselitiz's anti-heroic *Rebel* (1965). Some works focus on individual heroism, such as Hamilton's powerful triptych *The citizen, The subject, The state* (1981–3, 1988–90, 1993), which depicts different sides of the sectarian struggle in Northern Ireland. Anselm Kiefer, a child of conscience-stricken, post-World War II Germany investigated and celebrated more distant heroes of his country's past in *Parsifal I* and *Parsifal II* (1973). Christian Boltanski's *The Reserve of the Dead Swiss* (1990) is a sad reflection on the anonymity of death in war and peace, while Andy Warhol's detached and unemotional attitude to the *Electric Chair* (1964) makes a similar comment on our time.

The nude

Man and the human condition has long been a theme that preoccupies artists. The subject of the naked body has been treated romantically in Rodin's famous sculpture *The Kiss* (1901–4), or darkly, as in Sickert's grossly realistic painting *La Hollandaise* (c.1906), almost certainly a Camden Town prostitute. It has been portrayed with unlicensed joy in Kirchner's nudist *Bathers at Moritzburg* (1909–26), and with delight in Bonnard's sun-dappled painting of his wife in *The Bath* (1925) and Matisse's exploration of a naked bather in four progressively simplified sculptures, *The Backs* (1956–6).

Later in the 20th century, American artists, such as Bruce Nauman, used film and video to explore human behaviour, particularly its violent extremes in *Violent Incident* (1986), while Bill Viola in *Nantes Triptych* (1992) reflects on birth, procreation and the inevitability of decline and death. *Post-Partum Document* (1975) by Mary Kelly treats a central theme in art – motherhood – not in images, but in a series of pseudo-scientific notes and diagrams recording her relationship with her small son.

Temporary exhibitions

Level 3 is used for temporary exhibitions, recent examples of which include "Arte Povera" and a retrospective on Andy Warhol. Large-scale installations of commissioned art in the Turbine Hall have included Louise Bourgeois's steel towers: *I do, I Undo, I Redo* (2000) and Juan Muñoz's *Double Bind* (2001).

Food and drink: There are cafés on levels 2 and 7, as well as an Express Bar on level 4. Don't miss the fabulous panoramic views of the river, St Paul's Cathedral and other London landmarks from the café on level 7.

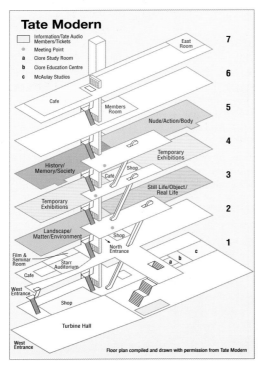

Tate Modern

☐ Information/Tate Audio
    Members/Tickets
• Meeting Point
a Clore Study Room
b Clore Education Centre
c McAulay Studios

East Room — 7

6

Cafe

Members Room — 5

Nude/Action/Body

4

History/Memory/Society

Temporary Exhibitions

Shop

Café — 3

Still Life/Object/Real Life

Temporary Exhibitions — 2

Landscape/Matter/Environment

Shop

North Entrance — 1

Film & Seminar Room

Starr Auditorium

Cafe

West Entrance

Shop

Turbine Hall

West Entrance

Floor plan compiled and drawn with permission from Tate Modern

FAR LEFT:
François
Boucher's *Mme
de Pompadour*
(1759), Wallace
Collection.

LEFT: Sir Joshua
Reynolds' *Miss
Jane Bowles*
(1775), Wallace
Collection.

Wallace Collection

A fine private collection of 18th-century French paintings, porcelain and furniture

*Map reference: page 20, A3
Hertford House, Manchester Square, W1.
Tel: 020 7563 9500.
www.the-wallace-collection.org.uk
Tube: Bond Street, Baker Street. Buses: 2, 10,
12, 13, 30, 74, 82, 94, 113, 137, 274.
Open: daily Mon–Sat 10am–5pm, Sun noon–5pm.
Bookshop. Lecture theatre. Gallery lectures.
Library and archives by appointment.
Wheelchair access. Admission free.*

The Wallace Collection was bequeathed to the nation by Lady Wallace, wife of Sir Richard Wallace, in 1897. It was opened in 1900 in Hertford House, the main London residence of the Marquesses of Hertford, and still retains the air of an aristocratic residence. Hertford House was badly bombed in World War II, but has since been repaired. Improvements to the museum and its facilities for its centenary were designed by architect Rick Mather, notably the addition of an elegantly glazed roof to the central courtyard and the inventive opening up of the basement to provide new spaces.

The closed collection ranks among the most superb assembly of French art outside Paris. In addition to pictures by Watteau, Boucher and Fragonard, it also contains Rembrandt's portrait of his son and favourite model, Titus, and his self-portrait *The Artist in a Cap*, Velazquez's *Lady with a Fan*, Rubens' *Rainbow Landscape*, Franz Hals's *Laugh-*

ing Cavalier, Poussin's *Dance to the Music of Time*, and Gainsborough's *Lady Robinson as "Perdita"*.

The nucleus of the collection was formed by generations of the Hertford family in the 18th century and included pictures by Reynolds and Romney's *Mrs Robinson*. It was the 3rd Marquess, a connoisseur and adviser to the Prince Regent, who laid the foundations by acquiring 17th-century Dutch paintings, French furniture and Sèvres porcelain, and such notable pictures as Titian's *Perseus and Andromeda*, painted for Philip II of Spain.

The 4th Marquess of Hertford, one of the richest men of his day, built on these collections with paintings, sculpture, furniture and porcelain of the highest quality. He lived mostly in France, where, as a bachelor recluse, his world centred on collecting. In this, he was assisted by his protégé (some say his son), Richard Wallace, whom he made his sole heir.

In the 1840s and 1850s, the 4th Marquis purchased Watteau's *The Music Party*, a characteristically idyllic scene of aristocratic leisure, and *The Music Lesson*, by the same painter. He also acquired *The Italian Comedians* by Lancret, *The Swing* and *The School Mistress* by Fragonard, and Boucher's *Madame de Pompadour*. Paintings from the English School include the ever-popular *Miss Jane Bowles* and *The Strawberry Girl*, both by Reynolds.

In addition to this impressive collection of paintings, the house also holds an array of priceless furniture and European and Far Eastern armour acquired by Sir Richard Wallace. Changing exhibitions, highlighting aspects of the collection, are also held.

Food and drink*: Highly recommended is Café Bagatelle in the glazed central courtyard of the Wallace Collection.*

While the major collections may be overwhelming,
London's smaller galleries often display more specialist
works and are sometimes housed in buildings whose
architectural interest alone makes them worth a visit

Bankside Gallery

Watercolours and prints on the South Bank

Map reference: page 21, F4
48 Hopton Street, SE1.
Tel: 020-7928 7521; www.royalwatersociety.com
Tube and rail: Blackfriars, Southwark.
Bus: 45, 63, 172 (to Blackfriars Bridge).
Open (during exhibitions only): Tues 10am–8pm,
Wed–Fri 10am–5pm, Sat, Sun 11am–5pm.
Special collections by appointment only. Shop.
Events, courses, workshops. Wheelchair access.
Admission charge to most exhibitions.

The Bankside Gallery, home to the Royal Society of Painters in Watercolour (RWS) and the Royal Society of Painter-Printmakers (RE) occupies a space originally intended as a supermarket for a nearby council block on the now-fashionable south bank of the Thames. The RE had long been a guest-exhibitor in the premises of the RWS, in Conduit Street, W1, and the two societies joined forces on a move into what was then an undeveloped area of London.

Both societies attract leading members of their profession, supporting traditional and experimental work. Some of the treasures from the permanent collections include, from the RWS, work by John Sell Cotman, David Cox, Russell Flint, David Jones, Arthur Melville, Samuel Prout, John Singer Sargent, John Varley and Leslie Worth. From the RE, the permanent works on show include pieces by Alphonse Legros, Laura Knight, Auguste Rodin, Walter Sickert and Graham Sutherland. The gallery also holds temporary exhibitions.

Food and drink*: The gallery does not have its own café, but the Founder's Arms pub, which has splendid views of the river and St Paul's Cathedral, is opposite the gallery front entrance. See also Tate Modern, pages 194–6.*

The Barbican

Two lively exhibition venues in a unique entertainments complex

Map reference: page 21, G2
Barbican Centre, Silk Street, EC2
Tel: 020-7638 8891; www.barbican.org.uk
Tube: Barbican, Moorgate (follow yellow lines on ground). Buses: 4, 153

Open: Mon, Tues, Thurs–Sat 10am–6pm, Wed 10am–8pm, Sun and bank hols noon–6pm. Wheelchair access in Silk Street. Admission charge to Art Gallery. The Curve is usually free.

The Barbican is an ambitious housing scheme built in reinforced concrete faced with dark grey granite. It takes its name – and some would say its forbidding appearance – from an early fortification on the site. The complex was conceived with the intention of attracting people back to the ruined City of London in the wake of World War II, and its bleak geometry is somewhat softened by the picturesque lake and water garden at its centre.

The arts centre, comprising a splendid concert hall, two theatres – a main auditorium and a studio space (The Pit) – a cinema, art gallery and public lending library is the lifeblood of the site, which also incorporates parts of the medieval London Wall and the Museum of London *(see page 33)*.

The Barbican Art Gallery has two spaces: an open-plan area on the first floor, and, above, a series of cell-like spaces opening off a continuous corridor. The Gallery mounts six or seven exhibitions a year, and often has two separate, but thematically sympathetic shows, in its two spaces. Both shows are included in the price of a ticket. Past exhibitions include "Bacon's Eye", on Francis Bacon, documentary photography in "Reporting the World", retrospectives of the work of the designers Robin and Lucienne Day, fashion photographer Helmut Newton and landscape photographer Fay Lucas, and "The Americans", showing new art from the USA.

The Curve space, near the Silk Street entrance, shows five contemporary fine art exhibitions a year. Recent exhibitions include "The Barbican as a

Watercolour and pencil work from the Bankside Gallery by Charlotte Halliday, RWS.

OPPOSITE: Portrait of Doctor François Brabander (1918) by Amedeo Modigliani, Estorick Collection.

Concept", in celebration of the centre's 20th anniversary, and "Contemporary Nordic Painting".

Note that it's a good idea to pick up, or request in advance, a Barbican Centre monthly guide containing details of all events and useful practical information.

Food and drink: There are various eating options within the complex. On level 0, there's the Waterside Café (inexpensive), a self-service spot with open-air lakeside seating. On level 1 is the Balcony Café (tel: 020-7628 3331; moderate), where you can drink, order snacks or have a full meal. On level 2 is Searcy's Restaurant (tel: 020-7588 3008; expensive), where modern British food is served with style and a French twist. There are also bars and coffee points across the site.

Brunei Gallery

African and Asian art and culture

Map reference: page 20, C2
School of Oriental and African Studies (SOAS), Thornhaugh Street, Russell Square, WC1.
Tel: 020-7898 4046; www.soas.ac.uk/gallery
Tube: Russell Square.
Buses: 68, 91, 168, 188 (alight Russell Square).
Open: Mon–Fri 10.30am–5pm during exhibitions (times sometimes change, so it's advisable to check before you visit). Group booking must be made in advance. Bookshop. Wheelchair access. Admission free.

The Brunei Gallery, funded by the Sultan of Brunei Darussalem, was designed by Nicholas Hare Architects and opened in 1995. The building comprises a beautiful, light-filled reception area crowned by a circular drum, which acts as a hinge between two wings. The left-hand door leads into the busy teaching, conference and office block, while the other door leads to what was originally intended as a three-storey Islamic Arts Centre, housing a permanent collection of Islamic art, and the Brunei Gallery showing loan exhibitions.

The upper and lower galleries are cool, finely proportioned, windowless spaces, with massive barrel vaults that create a sense of gravity and calm. These open onto a brilliantly conceived glass staircase, awash with natural light, which rises to what was once a top-floor, open-air water garden, but was redesigned in 2001 as a Japanese garden.

The building is no longer a designated Islamic Arts Centre and lacks a permanent collection. Instead, it now presents and promotes independently funded exhibitions, past examples of which have covered

Islamic antiquities, Chinese textiles, 18th-century Iranian painting, contemporary Nigerian art, Tibetan jewellery, and the art of contemporary Arab women.

Food and drink: The centre has an inexpensive and pleasant university-style café on the ground floor.

Dalí Universe

A popular introduction to Salvador Dalí

Map reference: page 20, D5
County Hall, South Bank, SE1.
Tel: 020-7620 2720; www.daliuniverse.com
Tube: Waterloo, Westminster.
Buses: 11, 12, 24 (alight Parliament Square), 53, X53, 76, 77, 159, 211, 341, 381.
Open: daily 10am–5.30pm (last entry). Late-night opening in summer (check in advance). Shops. Wheelchair access. Admission charge.

Dalí Universe is situated near the start of Jubilee Walk (also known as the Millennium Mile), the pedestrian way along the south bank of the River Thames, which offers splendid views of Big Ben and the Houses of Parliament. It is the latest newcomer to be given house-room in County Hall, the former headquarters of the London County Council, later the Greater London Council (GLC). This monumental symbol of local government was designed prior to World War I by the architect Ralph Knott; it opened in 1922 but was not fully completed until 1933. Since the GLC was abolished in 1986, the building was bought by a Japanese Corporation and let out to various enterprises.

The gallery, curated by the President of the Stratton Foundation, Benjamin Levi, is devoted to the late work of the Catalan Surrealist artist, Salvador

The eccentric Salvador Dalí, Dalí Universe.

Dalí (1904–89). It is arranged in a sequence of spaces painted in black, with the exhibits theatrically spot-lit. Useful biographical information is presented in the entrance lobby, from where you plunge down a long corridor decorated with random quotations and images, into the main display area.

The exhibits are arranged according to three themes – "Dreams and Fantasy", "Sensuality and Femininity" and "Religion and Mythology" – and date from the 1960s to the 1980s. The works on show include reproductions of classic Surrealist sculpture of the early 1930s, when Dalí was at the height of his fame, such as *Nue Féminine Hystérique et Aérodynamique*, *Buste de Femme Rétrospectif*, and the sensational crimson-satin sofa in the shape of the actress Mae West's lips. A series of multiple-edition bronzes, commissioned from Dalí by Levi, is also on display.

The exhibition is augmented with Dalí's book illustrations, such as *Caprices de Goya reintepreted by Dalí*, erotic drawings for Boccaccio's *Decameron* and illustrations for the Bible and various works by Dante. There is also some gawdy Daum Frères *pâte-de-verre* glass sculpture and the large oil painting that Dalí painted for Alfred Hitchcock's iconic 1945 movie, *Spellbound*.

Food and drink*: The gallery does not have its own café but within County Hall there is a Chinese restaurant, Four Regions (tel: 020-7928 0988; expensive) and the County Hall restaurant, which has great views over the Thames. For snacks, try York Road, where you exit the Dalí Universe.*

The Madonna of the Rosary by Bartolomé Esteban Murillo (1617–82), Dulwich Picture Gallery.

Dulwich Picture Gallery

European Old Masters of the 1600s and 1700s

Map reference: page 23, F5
Gallery Road, Dulwich Village, SE21.
Tel: 020-8693 5254, 020-8693 8000 (recorded information); www.dulwichpicturegallery.org.uk
Rail: West Dulwich (from Victoria). Turn right out of station, left along College Rd (10-min walk).
Open: Tues–Fri 10am–5pm, Sat, Sun 11am–5pm.
Gallery tours: Sat, Sun 3pm, except Easter.
Bookshop. Lectures. Wheelchair access.
Admission charge except Fri (free daily for students, children and the disabled).

The nucleus of the Dulwich College collection was formed by Edward Alleyn, the school's 17th-century founder. It was transformed around 200 years later with an outstanding collection of 17th- and 18th-century masters assembled in the late 18th century by Noël Desenfans, a French picture

Panel showing *Ceres and Two Nymphs with a Cornucopia* (early 17th century) by Rubens, Dulwich Picture Gallery.

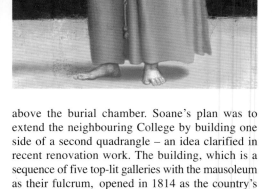

The early Italian pictures in the collection at Dulwich include two small panels of saints Francis of Assisi and Anthony of Padua by Raphael.

dealer. Commissioned to buy work for a planned National Gallery of Poland, Desenfans was left with this collection when King Stanislas of Poland was forced to abdicate. When Desenfans offered the redundant body of work to the British Government, as a core for a British National Gallery, the government wavered, and the collection passed on Desenfans' death to his English wife, then to his friend, Sir Peter Francis Bourgeois, RA, who continued to add to it. It was Mrs Desenfans as sole survivor who gave the Desenfans-Bourgeois collection to Dulwich for the foundation of a Picture Gallery, according to the terms of Bourgeois's will.

The gallery

In 1811, Sir John Soane, Bourgeois's friend and fellow-Academician, designed a gallery for the collection, incorporating a mausoleum for its three benefactors. The Neo-Classical exterior with its distinctive dome is austere, while the interior is undecorated and beautifully proportioned. Lanterns pitched high above deeply coved vaults bathe each gallery with natural light. By contrast, the central mausoleum, entered down some steps, is a shadowy space, lit dramatically from a vault immediately

above the burial chamber. Soane's plan was to extend the neighbouring College by building one side of a second quadrangle – an idea clarified in recent renovation work. The building, which is a sequence of five top-lit galleries with the mausoleum as their fulcrum, opened in 1814 as the country's first major public picture gallery.

Additions and extensions were undertaken in the 19th and early 20th centuries, including a new entrance hall and five new galleries along the east side. The building suffered extensive bomb damage in 1944, towards the end of World War II, but was rebuilt from Soane's drawings; the gallery re-opened in 1953. The most extensive renovation, finished in 2000, was architect Rick Mather's restoration of Soane's original design, particularly the front elevation; a glass-sided extension with a café, a lecture theatre and visitor facilities was also added.

The collection

Some 300 pictures are shown in the gallery, which is especially rich in 17th-century European painting and includes work by Claude, Poussin, Cuyp, Hobbema, Rembrandt, Rubens, Van Dyck, Reni and Murillo. Apart from Joshua Reynolds's *Mrs Siddons* and Wilson's *Tivoli*, the English School was poorly represented in the Desenfans-Bourgeois collection, as modern British work was deemed inappropriate for a public gallery in the 17th century. Major pictures by Peter Lely, William Hogarth and Thomas Gainsborough were donated in the 20th century.

In room 1 you can see Gainsborough's small portrait, *An Unknown Couple in a Landscape*, one of the finest of its kind. Most of these appealing portraits in a natural setting were painted in the 1750s in Ipswich, before Gainsborough moved to fashionable Bath. The strong realist influence of the Dutch 17th-century landscapists is evident from Meindert Hobbema's *Wooded Landscape with Water-Mill*. Notice, too, his dreamy portrait of the visionary De Loutherbourg, Bourgeois's teacher.

One of the great highlights of the gallery is a group of seven paintings by Poussin, one of the finest assembled in Britain. Admire the rigorous logic of *The Roman Road* and the colour of *Rainaldo and Armida*. *Sta Rita of Cascia,* which is unique as a piece of topography, is Poussin's earliest landscape.

Also on show in this genre is *Jacob with Laban and his Daughters*, by Poussin's contemporary, Claude. With Claude, the figures and sheep are absorbed into a vast natural expanse based on the landscape of the Roman Campagna. By contrast, the effervescence of the French Rococo is typified by Watteau's *tour de force*, *Le Bal Champêtre*.

A group of sketches and paintings by Rubens is also worth seeing, notably a gently sympathetic portrait of a sitter thought to be Catherine Manners, Duchess of Buckingham, and an outstanding example of his late style in full flourish, *Venus, Mars and Cupid*. The Dutch pictures are among the most outstanding strengths of the Dulwich collection, which includes three portraits by Rembrandt. His likeness of the engraver *Jacob III de Gheyn* shows his skills as a successful portrait painter, while *Girl Leaning on a Window-Sill* and *A Young Man, Perhaps the Artist's Son Titus* show his sympathetic yet unsentimental treatment of children. Among the outstanding group of Dutch landscape artists Cuyp is pre-eminent; the much-admired *A Road near a River* is one of the most beautiful of his late Italianate pastoral scenes, glowing in pale golden light.

In addition to the permanent collection, the gallery puts on temporary shows. Recent exhibitions have focussed on Murillo, Howard Hodgkin, William Beckford and Dutch landscape painters, 1600–1700.

Food and drink: The gallery has a licensed café in its attractive minimalist extension. Food is served until 5.30pm (tel: 020-8299 8717) and there is outdoor seating in summer. Other places to eat nearby include Le Piaf (020-8693 9331).

Gainsborough's *Unknown Couple in a Landscape* (18th century), Dulwich Picture Gallery.

Estorick Collection

Permanent collection of Italian Futurist and other 20th-century masterpieces

Map reference: page 23, F2
39a Canonbury Square, Islington, N1.
Tel: 020-7704 9522; www.estorickcollection.com
Tube: Highbury & Islington. Rail: Essex Road.
Bus: 271 (to Canonbury Square); 4, 19, 30, 43 (to Upper Street, Canonbury Lane); 38, 56, 171 (to Essex Road and Canonbury Road).
Open: Mon–Sat 11am–6pm, Sun 2–5pm.
Bookshop. Research library (by appointment only). Gallery talks. Wheelchair access to Galleries 1 and 2, shop and toilets.
Limited parking for disabled visitors (telephone in advance). Admission charge.

The Estorick Collection, put on public view early in 1998, is hung in Northampton Lodge, a smart Grade II-listed Georgian town house. The building was converted for the display of the collection by Nathaniel Gee Architect, who has retained the fine 18th-century proportions of its original domestic interior.

Eric Estorick (1913–93) discovered a passion for art as a graduate student of sociology in New York. After World War II, he went to Europe and began buying drawings by Pablo Picasso, Georges Braque and other modern French masters – a move that set the course of his own collecting. During his honeymoon in Italy, Estorick and his wife, Salome, laid the foundation of their Italian collection by acquiring Mario Sironi's drawings direct from the artist's studio. At the time he also met, and bought work from Massimo Campigli, who became a close friend. From that time the collection grew impressively, particularly in the 1950s, so much so that in 1956 the Italian Cultural Institute and the Tate Gallery collaborated on the exhibition "Italian Art from the Estorick Collection". The show stimulated great public interest, in Britain and internationally, when it went on tour to Italy and elsewhere.

By 1960, Estorick was dealing alongside collecting and, as Director of London's Grosvenor Gallery, exercised considerable influence on the gallery-going public. He showed Asian and African art, besides exhibitions of Magritte, Mucha, Erté and others. From 1975, he lived in Barbados, but before he died he set up the Eric and Salome Estorick Foundation, endowed with his Italian collection, which his family decided should remain in his adoptive country.

The collection

The core of this collection comprises Futurist art by Balla, Boccioni, Carrà, Severini and Russolo, as well as figurative art of the period from 1890 to the 1950s by Modigliani, Sironi, Campigli, de Chirico, Morandi and Marino Marini. Although the Estorick Collection changes its displays every six months, its highlights are advertised as on permanent exhibition. Don't miss these early modern masterpieces: Boccioni's *Modern Idol* (1911), Severini's *The Boulevard* (1910–11), Balla's *Hand of the Violinist* (1912), Carrà's *Leaving the Theatre* (1910–11), Russolo's *Music* (1911), Marini's *Quadriga* (1942), de Chirico's *Melancholy* (1912), Campigli's *Il Belvedere* 1930, Modigliani's *Dr François Brabandder* (1918) and Medardo Rosso's sculpture *Impressions of the Boulevard: Woman with a Veil* (1893).

Food and drink: The gallery has a pleasant café (inexpensive) with French windows giving onto the garden, where outdoor seating is provided in fine weather. Not surprisingly, Italian dishes (pasta, sandwiches, etc) are the speciality.

Guildhall Art Gallery

The Corporation of London's art collection

Map reference: page 23, G3
Guildhall Yard, EC2.
Tel: 020-7606 3030, 020-7332 3700 (recorded information); www.guildhall-artgallery.org.uk
Tube: Bank, St Paul's, Moorgate, Mansion House (Bow Lane exit). Buses: 242, 258, 501 (to Cheapside); 11, 15, 23, 26 (to Queen Victoria Street); 43, 76, 138, 141, 214, 271 (to Moorgate); 172 (to London Wall). Approach via Gresham Street; the Guildhall Art Gallery is on the east side of Guildhall Yard.
Open: Mon–Sat 10am–5pm, Sun noon–4pm (last admisssion 30 minutes before closing). Shop. Library and archives by appointment. Wheelchair access. Admission charge.

The Guildhall, which is medieval in appearance but is, in fact, a spectacular late 18th-century building, is the meeting place for the Corporation of the City of London and is used for special civic occasions. The new Guildhall Art Gallery, maintained by the Corporation, was opened in 1999, long after the original gallery was gutted by air raids on London in 1940 and 1941, destroying many valuable

Rossetti's *La Ghirlandata* (1873), Guildhall Art Gallery.

Everett Millais's *The Woodman's Daughter* (1851), Frederic Leighton's *The Music Lesson* (1877) and the gallery's ever-popular Pre-Raphaelite paintings.

My Second Sermon (1864) by John Everett Millais, Guildhall Art Gallery.

Food and drink: *For basic but wholesome vegetarian food, head for The Place Below (Cheapside; tel: 020-7329 0789; inexpensive), in the crypt of St Mary-le-Bow.*

Institute of Contemporary Arts

Cutting-edge art and cultural events

Map reference: page 20, C5
The Mall, London SW1.
Tel: 020-7930 3647; www.ica.org.uk
Tube: Charing Cross, Piccadilly Circus.
Buses: 3, 6, 9, 11, 12, 13, 14, 15, 19, 22, 23, 24, 29, 38, 77a, 88, 91, 139, 176.
Open: Mon noon–11pm, Tues–Sat noon–1am, Sun noon–10.30pm (galleries close at 7.30pm)
Bookshop (noon–9pm). Workshops, talks, films. Limited wheelchair access. Admission charge.

works. Although a temporary interior was built in the shell to house the collection, the arrangement was unsatisfactory, and in 1985 the Corporation of London decided to erect a new gallery. The demolition of the old building in 1987 revealed an exciting find: the archaeological remains of London's lost amphitheatre, which have now been incorporated into the basement of the new design. The architects Gilbert Scott and D.Y. Davies have produced a handsome building using traditional materials in keeping with the Guildhall.

The Corporation began collecting works of art in the 17th century, commissioning portraits of the judges who assessed property claims after the Great Fire of London in 1666. Its collection now numbers over 4,000 works, including royal portraits, historic and contemporary views of London, and important naval battles. The Guildhall now focuses on buying London subjects and work with significance for the capital. Around 250 pieces are displayed in the gallery at a time, with a programme of themed temporary exhibitions showing lesser-known works from its store. A selection of its best-known works are always on display, including Constable's *Salisbury Cathedral from the Meadows* (1829–30), Edwin Landseer's *The First Leap* (1829), John

First conceived in 1946 in emulation of New York's Museum of Modern Art, the Institute of Contemporary Arts (ICA), was founded under its new name in 1947. Unlike a museum, it was designed to be a hub for like-minded people, funded by and run for its members. Among its prime movers were the poet and modernist critic Herbert Read and the Surrealist artist Roland Penrose, whose friends included Picasso, Braque, Derain, Ernst, Breton, Man Ray and the photographer Lee Miller.

One of the founders' main intentions was to introduce the public to the history and development of modernism, which had been neglected by most British institutions, most glaringly the Tate. The ICA has also long been closely connected with the role of design and architecture in shaping society.

In the 1950s, although the institute had its detractors, its reputation as a crucible for ground-breaking ideas, initiatives, critical theory and debate grew. Seen as a showcase for new ideas and their experimental presentation, it was one of the first galleries to show photography and photo-generated imagery. Exhibitions crossing the boundaries between art and science and art and technology followed. In the forefront in recognising new trends, the ICA was the first gallery in the early 1960s to launch young Pop artists such as Peter Blake and David Hockney.

In 1968, it moved to its present premises in the Mall, where it is housed in part of Carlton House

Terrace, originally a huge building of stuccoed and painted mansions designed by John Nash just before his death in 1835. In the 1970s, the institute became increasing political, controversial and even scandalous, with exhibitions featuring conscience-riven work by German artists examining their homeland's recent history, the politics of gender and sexuality, including unsettling shows on the female body. In the 1980s and 1990s, the ICA's show policy reflected the impact of social and political events, such as the fall of the Berlin Wall. Aesthetically, it kept in touch with photographic trends, particularly developments in video and other media coming out of New York.

It is hard to separate the ICA's exhibitions from its programme of cultural debate. The 1991 conference "Towards the Aesthetics of the Future" and other debates examined digital technology, the use of the Web and interactive CD-roms. In 1997, a New Media Centre was opened. In 1999, the now-annual "Beck's Futures" art prize, open to artists working in any medium, was staged here for the first time. This, the biggest arts prize in Britain, encapsulates the institute's aims of spotting, celebrating and nurturing new ideas and talent.

Food and drink: The ICA has an inexpensive café serving hip modern food, plus a bar, where special events such as comedy and music are often held in the evenings. A small membership fee must be paid to gain access to both.

Jerwood Gallery

Contemporary art by young British artists

Map reference: page 21, G5
171 Union Street, SE1. Tel: 020-7654 0171.
www.jerwoodspace.co.uk
Tube and rail: Borough, London Bridge, Southwark. Buses: 45, 63, 172 (to Blackfriars Bridge); 40, 133, P11 (alight Southwark Street). Open: Tues–Sat 10am–6pm, Sun noon–6pm (Note: times and days may change, so it is advisable to check before your visit.) Wheelchair access. Admission free.

The Jerwood Space, designed by the architectural practice Paxton Locher, is housed in the converted buildings of what was a Victorian school, later an education centre. It retains the original purpose of the site by providing subsidised rehearsal rooms for young dance and theatre companies. The rooms are also available to the rest of the art profession at market rates – this largely funds the more glamorous front-of-house activities, including the art gallery.

The gallery, in which six exhibitions are mounted each year, has three areas for exhibitions of painting and other events, and an arena for sculpture, all of

Jerwood Gallery offers a versatile space to artists and performers.

which open onto a courtyard and garden with a pool. This is a significant exhibition venue, particularly for its Charitable Foundation awards, the Jerwood Painting Prize, launched in 1994, and the Jerwood Sculpture Prize, awarded for the first time in 2001.

Food and drink: Jerwood has a minimalist licensed restaurant, Café 171 (tel: 020-7654 0100; moderate; open 10am–6pm Tues–Fri, noon–2pm weekends), serving great-value meals and snacks (good vegetarian options), in a calm, chic ambience. There's some outdoor seating and a fountain.

Leighton House

An 1860s studio-house in the exotic taste of the Victorian artist Frederic Leighton

Map reference: page 40, A2
12 Holland Park Road, W14. Tel: 020-7602 3316.
www.rbkc.gov.uk/leightonhousemuseum
Tube: Kensington High Street. Buses: 9, 10, 27, 28, 33, 49, 328 to Odeon Cinema/Commonwealth Institute stop.
Open: daily except Tues 11am–5.30pm.
Garden (restored to original layout and planting scheme) open Apr–Sept, depending on weather. Drawings collection by prior appointment only. Guided tours. Shop. No wheelchair access. Admission free.

L eighton House *(see also page 114)* was built as a studio-house by its namesake, the Victorian artist, Frederic Leighton (1830–96). After an early life spent travelling, Leighton settled in England in 1860. A fine draughtsman and classical academic painter, he became a Royal Academician in 1868, the Academy's President 10 years later, and a peer in 1896. His decision to build a house was unusual; he chose an area of London that was becoming fashionable and was in residence by 1866, two years after planning the project with his architect, George Aitchison. This is one of the most extraordinary houses of the late 19th century, its interiors decorated with Far Eastern tiles and hung with paintings by Leighton's contemporaries. It gives remarkable insight into Leighton's private and professional world, and is also a unique place in which to study Victorian aesthetic values.

The core of the building consisted of the hall and drawing and dining rooms (for entertaining such distinguished guests as the Prince of Wales), all on the ground floor, and a large imposing studio and a simply

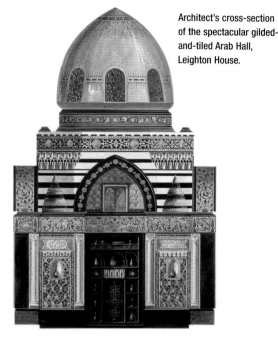

Architect's cross-section of the spectacular gilded-and-tiled Arab Hall, Leighton House.

furnished bedroom (in which Leighton died) on the first. Corot's *Times of the Day*, now in London's National Gallery, once hung in the drawing room. The most spectacular area of the house, the Arab Hall, rising through two floors, was added in 1879, as was the library.

The design of the Arab Hall, an exotic space, richly decorated in blues, greens and purples, with a small pool at its centre, was based on the banqueting room in the Arabian palace of Lazisa in Palermo, Sicily. It was conceived as a place in which to display Leighton's extraordinary collection of 16th- and 17th-century Damascus ceramic tiles.

In Leighton's last years, the studio was extended into a winter studio for his painting materials, leaving the large area free as a kind of show studio, for visitors and entertaining. The Silk Room, added on the first floor in 1895 to provide room to hang the collection of paintings given to Leighton over the years, was finished after his death. The grand staircase in the hall was intended to make an impact and is indeed one of the most impressive features of the house. Leighton's visitors would be shown upstairs to his studio, while models took the back stairs.

Notable artworks

Around 80 of Leighton's oil paintings, many of them oil sketches produced as part of the meticulous

Francis Leighton's
*A Noble Lady
of Venice*
(19th century),
Leighton House.

process of creating a major painting, are displayed in the house. Among these paintings are the lovely portrait sketch, *The Countess of Brownlow* (*c*.1878–9), and the oil sketch, *When the Sea gave up the Dead* (*c*.1891). The most important early finished work is *The Death of Brunelleschi* (1852), depicting one of the most notable architects from Florence, where Leighton first studied. The artist was just 22 years old when he painted the picture, and it already demonstrates his mastery of the academic method.

Clytemnestra* (*c*.1874) shows the tragic heroine standing on the battlements of Argos watching for the beacon to be fired that will announce the return of her husband, Agamemnon, from the Trojan Wars. Agamemnon had sacrificed their first-born daughter to the gods in exchange for a fair wind for his fleet. Clytemnestra plots his murder, and Leighton's picture shows her at this critical moment, keyed up with inner anger and emotion. There are also around 700 drawings in the collection, mostly acquired after Leighton's death; some are on show in the studio.

Food and drink: There are no refreshments at the house, but there are eating places on nearby Kensington High Street.

Percival David Foundation

One of the world's finest collections of Chinese ceramics

Map reference: page 20, C1
School of Oriental and African Studies (SOAS), 53 Gordon Square, WC1. Tel: 020-7387 3909. www.pdfmuseum.org.uk
Tube: Russell Square.
Buses: 10, 24, 29, 73, 134, 68, 91, 168, 188.
Open: Mon–Fri 10.30am–5pm. Tours for large groups by arrangement only. Children are allowed if accompanied by an adult. Reference library by advance application only (charge for use). Shop. No wheelchair access to entrance but lift to gallery floors inside. Admission free.

In 1950 by Sir Percival David (1892–1964) offered his collection of 1,700 rare items of Chinese ceramics and his remarkable library of books in Chinese and European languages to London University. Following the collection's acceptance, a Foundation, administered by the School of Oriental and African Studies (SOAS) on behalf of the university, was established. The Foundation is, as its benefactor intended, a public museum and a unique learning resource for SOAS students, collectors and dealers.

The collection is housed in a 19th-century town house and arranged by dynasty on two floors, starting on the first floor. Temporary exhibitions are shown on the ground floor, and the *Scroll of Antiquities* is also usually exhibited here – don't miss this piece of 18th-century court painting laid out in fine detail with art objects from the Imperial Collection. First-time visitors may find it helpful to buy a leaflet giving a tour of the highlights. For international scholars the collection is of incomparable value, being the largest and most representative outside the Imperial Collection in the Palace Museum, Taiwan.

The strength of the collection covers work from the Song (960–1279) to Qing (1644–1911) dynasties, but on the first floor you'll find earlier examples, including one of the first images of a Buddha moulded into the band around a jar (3rd or 4th century) and a beautiful stoneware vase in the shape of two carp, covered in a semi-opaque, grey-green celadon glaze (Tang dynasty, 9th century). As ceramic art in China goes back 9,000 years, it was already highly developed by the time the earliest work here was made.

The first floor

Work on the first floor is mostly monochrome, either white, some with subtle incised decoration, or black (some perfectly potted tea bowls with a metallic glaze), and celadon. In the centre case in the East Gallery there are also some very fine pieces of Jun ware, on which 12th-century potters added copper splashes to the unfired pale-blue glaze. The experiments produced beautiful effects, which vary from a soft mauve to bright purple. Sir Percival David's own favourite, a small 13th-century bottle vase in Guan, or official, ware (catalogue number: PDF 4), is in Case 6. This is one of the most exquisite pieces in the collection, finely potted, with a delicate brown crackle and bound in metal; it came originally from the Imperial Collection.

The second floor

By contrast with the first floor, the second, with its spectacular range of blue-and-white porcelain and polychrome enamelled ware, is ablaze with colour. It offers a fine intro-

Chun ware bottle from the Sung dynasty, Percival David Foundation.

duction to the development of Chinese porcelain from the 13th to early 20th centuries. Sir Percival David's knowledge of classical Chinese and his fascination with inscriptions enabled him to acquire two exceptional "David" vases (PDF B613 and B614). These fine temple vases carry inscriptions on their necks giving the date on which they were commissioned, so giving a firm reference for the dating of other 14th-century blue-and-white pieces.

Food and drink: In summer, you can picnic on Russell Square. Otherwise, try the brightly coloured Coffee Gallery (23 Museum Street; inexpensive), where imaginative Italian-style meals and great coffees are served.

Photographers' Gallery

Changing exhibitions in Britain's first independent space devoted to photography

Map reference: page 20, C4
5 and 8 Great Newport Street, WC2.
Tel: 020-7831 1772; www.photonet.org.uk
Tube: Leicester Square. Buses: 24, 29.
Open: daily Mon–Sat 11am–6pm, Sun noon–6pm.
Talks, tours and events. Library by appointment.
Bookshop. Wheelchair access. Admission charge.

The British art world was fairly late in taking photography seriously in the 20th century, and in establishing it on an equal footing with fine art. The medium still lacks the encouragement given to photography in other European countries and the US, but the Photographers' Gallery has done sterling work in attempting to remedy the situation and give photography the credibility it deserved.

Galley background

Founded in 1971 at 8 Great Newport Street, this was the first independent gallery in Britain devoted exclusively to photography. This building now houses the main exhibition space and bookshop. In 1980, the Gallery expanded to 5 Great Newport Street. One of its great achievements was to establish photography within the gallery tradition, to popularise it and to make it more accessible. It was the first place in the country to show, in changing exhibitions, such key names in photography as André Kertezsz, Jacques-Henri Lartigue and Irving Penn, and it has given historic status to Robert Capa, Gordon Parks and Gary Winogrand.

Portrait of Marilyn Monroe (1954) by Milton H. Greene, The Photographers' Gallery.

The gallery now leads the way in presenting innovative developments in photography and new talent, and names of now-established British photographers encouraged here include Fay Godwin and Martin Parr. It has also introduced notable international artists working with photography, among them Rineka Dijestra, Catherine Opie and Boris Mikhailov.

Although the gallery was refurbished by Nick England in 1993, there are now plans to move it to a new building. Gallery staff are working closely with the Dutch architect Erick van Egeraat to think of ways of enhancing its image as a leading European venue for photography and of building on its success in helping to increase the interest in and commitment to the medium. The Citibank Private Bank Photography Prize, for the most significant contribution to photography over the previous year, for example, was established in 1996 and is now an annual event here; it is open to a wide range of work, including photojournalism, documentary, fashion and fine art photography.

Food and drink: *The funky café at 5 Great Newport Street is open Mon–Sat 11am–5.30pm and Sun noon–5.30pm.*

Queen's Gallery

Treasures from the Royal Collection

Map reference: page 20, B6
Buckingham Palace, Buckingham Palace Road, SW1. Tel: 020-7839 1377. www.royal.gov.uk
Tube: Green Park, Victoria, St James's Park.
Buses: 2, 11, 24, 73, 82, 211, C1, C10.
Open: daily 10am–5.30pm (last entry 4.30pm).
Admission charge. Bookshop.

The Queen's Gallery opened in July 1962 on the southwest corner of Buckingham Palace, at the suggestion of Queen Elizabeth II and the Duke of Edinburgh, who wanted to establish a public gallery displaying works of art from the Royal Collection. The collection is held in trust by the Queen for her successor and the nation and is entirely self-funded. While offering a welcome chance for the public to see some of the 9,000 works of art usually displayed in the Royal palaces or kept in store, the gallery barely publicised its presence on Buckingham Palace Road, had only limited space and sat

Portrait of Agatha Bas (1641) by Rembrandt, Queen's Gallery.

awkwardly on the site. The Golden Jubilee of Queen Elizabeth seemed an ideal moment to give the gallery a stronger identity, and it reopened in May 2002 to new designs by architects John Simpson and Partners.

The collection is a remarkable tribute to the discriminating taste of Kings and Queens from the 16th to the 21st centuries and their enlightened patronage. It is rich in royal portraits, notably by Holbein and Van Dyck. However, it is in the portraits of one or two sitters outside the court circle, such as Derick Born, that Holbein demonstrated his profoundest insight into character. Equally revealing is a triple portrait of Charles I, which Bernini asked Van Dyck to paint for him as a reference for the marble bust he was sculpting of the King. Among three early Rembrandts is a painting of the artist's mother, acquired by Charles I when the artist was hardly known abroad. Charles I also commissioned the virtuoso self-portrait by Rubens, perhaps the most spectacular example of his work in the collection.

George III was another important royal collector. He commissioned around 50 landscape paintings and 100 drawings by Canaletto, including some memorable views of 18th-century London and romantic scenes of Venice's Grand Canal. The collection of drawings – an unrivalled selection of work by Da Vinci and Holbein, drawings by Raphael, Michelangelo, Poussin and Claude, sketches by Hogarth and a superb series of watercolour views of Windsor by Paul Sandby – is especially fine.

Food and drink: *For a range of restaurants and good old-fashioned British pubs, head across Green Park behind Piccadilly to the area known as Shepherd's Market.*

Saatchi Collection

One of Britain's largest and most exciting private collections of contemporary art

Map reference: page 23, F2
30 Underwood Street, EC1.
Tel: 020-7336 7362; www.saatchigallery.org.uk
Tube: Old Street. Bus: 394.
Open: Thurs–Sun noon–6pm. Admission fee.

The Saatchi Gallery opened in 1985 in architect-designed premises in St John's Wood to display the collection of contemporary art built up by Charles and Doris Saatchi (now separated) since the 1970s. Charles and his brother Maurice made a fortune with their advertising company, Saatchi & Saatchi. The St John's Wood gallery closed in late 2001, and shows are currently held in temporary premises in London's Old Street. Saatchi's plan is to open a massive "art museum" on a scale to rival Tate Modern, probably in London's former County Hall, provocatively close to Tate Modern.

The collection, which is still growing, comprises over 2,000 paintings, sculptures and installations, with emphasis on Saatchi's predilection for figurative work. A strength of Saatchi's patronage is that he acquires the work of an artist or a period in depth, rather than buying one of everything. The gallery's aim is "to introduce new art, or art largely unseen in the UK, to a wider audience".

With controversial touring exhibitions such as "Sensation", seen in 1997 at London's Royal Academy (and later on tour in Berlin and New York), Saatchi's patronage has helped win recognition for a group in which he has particular interest: a generation of young British artists, among them Damien Hirst, Gary Hume, Sarah Lucas, Chris Offili, Marc Quinn, Jenny Saville and Rachel Whiteread. Tate Modern would love to have more of these artists' work and, if Saatchi becomes Tate's neighbour, it will further emphasise the much discussed rivalry.

Food and drink: Try The Wenlock Arms (26 Wenlock Road, tel: 020-7608 3406), a traditional pub serving great real ales. On the corner of Shepherdess Walk and City Road is The Shepherdess Café (221 City Road, tel: 020-7253 2463), for cooked breakfasts, coffees and sandwiches.

Serpentine Gallery

Modern and contemporary art on show in a 1908 tea pavilion in Kensington Gardens

Map reference: page 40, B2
Kensington Gardens, London W2.
Tel: 020-7298 1515; www.serpentinegallery.org.uk
Tube: South Kensington, Knightsbridge.
Bus: from Knightsbridge, 9, 10, 52 (alight Exhibition Road).
Open: Mon–Sun 10am–6pm.
Bookshop. Wheelchair access. Admission free.

Taking over what had been a classical tea house, built by Henry Tanner in 1934, the Arts Council of Great Britain founded the Serpentine Gallery in 1971 as a temporary exhibition space for modern and contemporary art. It is set in one of London's loveliest locations, near the Serpentine lake, amid extensive lawns, trees, wooded dells and shrubberies, dotted here and there with sculptures, including Jacob Epstein's *Rima* – a memorial to the naturalist and writer W.H. Hudson (1841–1921).

For many Londoners a visit here forms a regular attraction on an afternoon out in Hyde Park. Since the early 1990s, the Serpentine has been one of London's leading venues for important exhibitions of recent work by established artists such as Damien Hirst and Rachel Whiteread, and for major retrospectives of artists including Bridget Riley, Man Ray, Henry Moore and Andy Warhol.

In the late 1990s, the gallery underwent extensive redevelopment and renovation by architects John Miller and Partners. It reopened in 1998 as a hip white space, thus balancing its image as a picturesque garden pavilion (a Grade II-listed building), with a state-of-the-art environment for international art, a flexible space, and a specially designed education area. In 2001, a separate, temporary pavilion, an ingenious structure called *Eighteen Turns*, was designed by Daniel Libeskind with Ove Arup for the lawn in front of the gallery.

In addition to exhibitions, regular events are held here, including talks and (in July and August) the Poetry Proms – poetry readings held prior to the Prom Concerts in the Albert Hall.

Food and drink: There is no café in the museum itself, but there are several kiosks dotted throughout the park where cans, hot drinks, ice creams and snacks are available.

Angel (c.1997) by Ron Mueck, Saatchi Collection.

South London Gallery

Historic and modern artworks and changing exhibitions of contemporary art

Map reference: page 23, G4
65 Peckham Road, Camberwell, SE5.
Tel: 020-7703 6120, 020-7703 9799 (recorded information); www.southlondongallery.org
Tube: Elephant & Castle, then buses 171, 12, P3; Victoria, Oval, then bus 36.
Bus: 12. Rail: Peckham Rye.
Open: Tues, Wed, Fri 11am–6pm; Thurs 11am–7pm; Sat, Sun 2–6pm; closed Mon. Disabled visitors welcome but access is very difficult (ring in advance). Admission free.

The South London Gallery (SLG) was a cultural off-shoot of the South London Working Men's College, opened in 1868 at 91 Blackfriars Road. Its Principal was Professor T.H. Huxley, grandfather of the novelist Aldous Huxley; its manager was the philanthropist William Rossiter. When the gallery expanded 10 years later into larger premises, a free library was added, the first in South London. In 1878, an exhibition of pictures lent by private supporters was another pioneering development. The exhibition became, to all intents and purposes, a permanent institution, with the Prime Minster, William Gladstone, appointed President of the College and Art Gallery. In 1887, the library and gallery moved to 207 Camberwell Road.

Rossiter enlisted the support of leading artists, Watts, Burne-Jones and Sir Frederic Leighton (then President of the Royal Academy) and, two years later, bought the site of the present gallery in Peckham Road. Walter Crane, a contemporary of William Morris, donated the design for the magnificent marquetry floor in the gallery, which opened in 1891.

The aim of these social activists in establishing the SLG in a poor part of London was to bring art and beauty to what was considered the dreary wasteland south of the Thames. Following the examples of John Ruskin and William Morris, they believed in the power of art to heal the ills of an increasingly commercial and materialistic society.

Leighton initially gave 41 works of art to the gallery's collection and many more in subsequent years. Such was his contribution in terms of time and finance that, on his death in 1896, the gallery became known as the Lord Leighton Memorial. In 1892, a lecture hall and library were opened.

Another philanthropist funded a Technical Institute, later to become Camberwell College of Art, which was built on the site in 1896–8 by Maurice B. Adames, giving the gallery a new entrance.

The collection

From its inauguration to its temporary closure during World War II, the gallery showed changing exhibitions of fine and applied art, as well as displays of museum objects, such as coins and medals. The foundation of the gallery's permanent collection was formed during this period, when many pieces were

donated or bought by subscription. In 1949, the gallery re-opened and its exhibition programme of British artists reinstated, although its permanent collection remained mostly in store. Since 1992, exhibitions in the small gallery have focused on displaying international contemporary trends, enhancing SLG's profile with shows of work by Gilbert and George, Anselm Kiefer and Tracey Emin.

A budget has also been reinstated for buying new work for the permanent collection, which is open to view by appointment on the first floor. Highlights include work by Ruskin, Leighton, Millais, Sickert (*The Sick Doctor*) and Stanley Spencer (*Sarajevo*).

Vanishing Point, an installation by Charlotte Cullinan and Jeanine Richards at the South London Gallery.

Food and drink*: It's a 10-minute walk from the gallery to the centre of Camberwell, where there is a proliferation of bars, cafés and restaurants. Tadim's (41 Camberwell Church Street; inexpensive) is good for Turkish food, while bistro-style Seymours (2–4 Grove Lane; inexpensive) does good sandwiches and has an attractive terrace out the back. On Friday and Saturday evenings, note that jazz is performed in the crypt of St Giles' on Camberwell Church Street.*

LEFT: The grand arched entrance to the Whitechapel Gallery.

RIGHT: Installation by Carl Andre, Whitechapel, August 2000.

Whitechapel Art Gallery

Contemporary international art in one of London's most spectacular modern spaces

Map reference: page 23, G2
Whitechapel High Street, London E1.
Tel: 020-7522 7861; 020-7522 7878 (recorded information); www.whitechapel.org
Tube: Aldgate East. Rail: Liverpool Street.
Bus: 5,15, 15A, 25, 40, 67, 78, 253.
Open: Tues–Sun 11am–5pm, Wed 11am–8pm.
One parking space in front of gallery for disabled driver (tel. in advance). Wheelchair access. Bookshop. Talks. Archives by appointment. Admission free except to some exhibitions.

The Whitechapel Art Gallery (originally the East End Art Gallery) was founded in the late 19th century. Its establishment was a response to the spiritual and economic poverty of London's East End by Canon Samuel Barnett, the local vicar of St Jude's, and his wife, Henrietta, a noted philanthropist and educator. They were also prime movers behind Whitechapel's Toynbee Hall (est. 1884), the first "University Settlement".

The gallery itself was built in 1897–9, designed by the Arts and Crafts architect Charles Harrison Townsend. The building opened to the public in March 1901 and was an immediate success. In 1985,

the gallery underwent major rebuilding and refurbishment to designs by Colquhoun and Miller, with the aim of re-opening the upper gallery and providing an enhanced and flexible space for all forms of art. The result was a light, clean and very elegant venue, with a café, bookshop and an additional connecting staircase to the upper gallery.

The gallery never acquired a permanent collection, but focused on mounting an ever-changing programme of exhibitions. In its early years, displays included works from China, Japan and India, Jewish art, modern British art and the Pre-Raphaelites, as well as work by students and local schoolchildren. More recently, the Whitechapel Open Exhibition and the East End Academy have encouraged local artists and displayed their work. This exhibition takes place every summer and early autumn both in the gallery and in studios all over the East End. Visitors can use a link bus to transport them from venue to venue.

A notable highlight in the history of the Whitechapel was the display in 1939 of Picasso's *Guernica* as part of Stepney Trades Council's exhibition "Aid Spain". Other landmarks include "This is Tomorrow" (1959), a collaborative project between painters, sculptors and architects; a series of shows in the 1950s and 1960s of work by Mondrian, Turner, Stubbs, Henry Moore and Barbara Hepworth; and the first solo exhibitions in Britain of painting by contemporary American artists, among them Jackson Pollock, Mark Rothko and Robert Rauschenberg. More recently, the Whitechapel has mounted major exhibitions devoted to David Hockney (1970), Frida Kahlo (1982), Lucian Freud (1993), Nan Goldin and Liam Gillick (both 2002).

Food and drink: The gallery has a lovely café, which is open Tues–Sun 11am–4.30pm and Wed 11am–6.30pm during exhibitions and, between exhibitions, Tues–Fri noon–3pm.

William Morris Gallery

The only public space dedicated to the work of this great Arts and Crafts exponent

Map reference: page 23, H1
Lloyd Park, Forest Road, Walthamstow, E17.
Tel: 020-8527 3782.
www.lbwf.gov/wmg/home.htm
Tube/rail: Walthamstow Central. From the station turn left into Hoe Street, then left again into Forest Road. Bus: N73 stops nearby.
Open: Tues–Sat and the first Sun of each month, 10am–1pm, 2–5pm. Shop. Wheelchair access. Admission free.

William Morris, poet, painter, designer, craftsman, socialist and leading exponent of the Arts and Crafts Movement, which rallied to revive quality craftsmanship in the face of industrial mass production, was born in Walthamstow in 1834. In 1848, his family moved to Water House and it was here that Morris spent his later childhood. This smart Georgian brick house, with double bow front and Corinthian portico, dates from the early 1740s, and is set in pleasing grounds with a moat (now a lake), the source of its name. In 1898, a later owner, the publisher Edward Lloyd, gave the property to the local council, which opened the house to the public as the William Morris Gallery in 1950. The grounds were laid out as small park, and named Lloyd Park.

The collection

The gallery contains an outstanding collection of fabrics, rugs, wallpapers, furniture, stained glass and painted tiles. Most of the items here were designed by Morris and members of his circle who, in 1861, founded a firm of decorators and manufacturers under the name Morris, Marshall, Faulkner & Co. Among the designers were Burne-Jones, Philip Webb, Rossetti and Ford Maddox Ford. Outstanding exhibits include Morris's medieval-style helmet and sword, which he made as props for the murals he

and other Pre-Raphaelites painted in the 1850s in the Oxford Union.

The designs, particularly for wallpapers and furnishing fabrics, which Morris manufactured, were to have an enormous influence on public taste. Their principal inspiration was nature. Characterised by unaffected motifs including plants and flowers of the garden and countryside (daisies, roses, honeysuckles and willow leaves), they were – and still are – popular among those able to afford them. There are many beautiful patterns on display, including the design for "Trellis", the earliest of Morris's wallpapers. Look out for the later "Bird", a favourite design of 1878 in a woven-wool fabric, and another attractive design inspired by bird life, "The Woodpecker" tapestry, produced at his Merton works.

Morris's major role in improving standards of design extended to the decoration and printing of books. His most famous printed book, *The Works of Geoffrey Chaucer,* was produced at his private printing-press, the Kelmscott Press, which he founded in 1891 and named after a village in Hammersmith, his home from 1871. Morris was himself responsible for designing the splendidly ornamental title-pages, letters and borders.

His socialist doctrines were founded on the belief that art, work and life were interrelated. He disliked the machine and encouraged hand-craftsmanship along medieval guild principles. He thought that, by removing the tedium of mechanical labour and giving each worker the pleasure of crafting beautiful objects, society could be reformed for the better. One of the more personal items on display is the satchel that Morris used to carry around his Socialist pamphlets.

The work of other influential exponents of the Arts and Crafts Movement, which continued until the 1920s, is also on display, including designs by A.H.J. Mackmurdo and the Century Guild, William de Morgan, Ernest Gimson, Sidney Barnsley and C.F.A. Voysey.

Food and drink: *A good place to try in Walthamstow for coffees, sandwiches and other café fare is the Ecology Centre (Hoe Street; inexpensive).*

Pencil and watercolour design for "Dove and Rose" wool and silk fabric by William Morris.

THE ECONOMICS OF ART

William Feaver selects the best places to go window shopping

Commercial galleries are subject to the dictates of rent and market prospects, and their geographic centres shift accordingly. Bond Street and Cork Street in London's West End are as up-market as E.57th Street in New York and have been the high streets of the art trade since the late 19th century. Leases expire, though, and, one by one, the galleries there are being replaced by fashion outlets; the presence, nearby, of the Sotheby's and Christie's auction houses is reason enough for some to remain, however. They include Agnews and Colnaghi's, specialising in the traditional, which includes the Old Masters.

Gallery-going technique is a matter of nonchalance and confidence. You are not expected to buy: galleries are shop windows and the selling takes place behind the scenes, usually before an exhibition opens. So nothing is expected of you beyond your willingness to take a look.

A stroll from Oxford Circus to Green Park should be by way of Dering Street (Annely Juda, Anthony d'Offay and Anthony Reynolds), Bond Street (the Fine Art Society), Clifford Street (Bernard Jacobson), Cork Street (Waddington, Mayor, Browse and Darby) and, in adjacent streets, Sadie Coles HQ, Stephen Friedman and Marlborough Fine Art. The Frith Street Gallery is an elegant converted 18th-century townhouse in narrowest Soho. White Cube, in Duke Street, St James's, is small enough to be literally exclusive.

Art dealer Kay Saatchi with sculpture by Ron Mueck and painting by Alex Katz.

Away from the West End, and with the exception of the Lisson Gallery in Bell Street, NW1 (best visited on a Saturday morning when the street market outside offers a striking contrast to the smartness within), the concentration of commercial galleries now lies eastwards, around Hoxton Square off Old Street. Initially, dealers and galleries moved to the East End because the young artists were there, often squatting in empty porperties and making studios for themselves in redundant warehouses and factories. Art as fertiliser: the consequence invariably was that demand grew, artist-colonised areas became fashionable, maps altered and within a season or two urban desolation became urban chic.

The carousel of fashion

The art world operates on five-year cycles, approximately. Artists come in generations – "new generations" – and dealers, too. It is rare for a contemporary dealer to remain the latest and best for long. Soon, startlingly soon, the innovation becomes the done thing. This means that gallery guides too rapidly lose authority. One thing is certain, however: the pursuit of the new in art is not to be undertaken without some knowledge of the state of play. Otherwise, you are likely to be left sore-footed and chronically irritated.

In the East End, the more established galleries include Flowers East (Richmond Road), a large operation with a wide range of painters. In Hoxton Square, the dealer Jay Jopling has White Cube2, a larger and therefore more conventional version of his original premises in Duke Street. Others to note include lux in Hoxton Square, Maureen Paley/Interim Art in Herald Street, E2, Matt's Gallery (for large installations) in Copperfield Road, E2, Modern Art in Redchurch Streeet, E2, Victoria Miro in Wharf Road, N1, Artspace in St Peter's Street, N1, The Agency in Charlotte Road, EC2, and The Approach in Approach Road, E2.

Entertainment entrepreneur Bob Geldof (centre) at the opening of White Cube2 in Hoxton.

The rapid turnover in galleries, names and reputations is beneficial. Art in this age of cossetted sensation becomes increasingly competitive. Visiting the commercial, or would-be commercial galleries combines window shopping and talent-spotting. Competitiveness breeds collectors, but it also sustains the passionate interest of students of form. What matters is to keep up with the new – and that is what the latest galleries, however ephemeral, tend to show.

Commercial Galleries

This selection gives a range of notable galleries in the capital, from the most traditional establishments to small galleries nurturing up-and-coming young artists. Also included are a couple of the main online art sites, which are revolutionising the way art is sold and may appeal to those intimidated by art galleries. Note that many galleries close from mid-July to mid-September.

The Agency

35–40 Charlotte Road, EC2
Tel: 020-7613 2080
www.agency-gallery.
demon.co.uk
Sells works by contemporary artists including Ross Sinclair, Ken Lum and Kazuo Katase.

Agnew's

43 Old Bond Street, W1
Tel: 020-7290 9250
www.agnewsgallery.co.uk
Founded 1817, this established Old Bond Street gallery specialises in old master paintings, European drawings from 1200 to 1850, 17th–20th century British oils and watercolours, and works by some contemporary artists (including John Wonnacott). Holds up to eight solo shows a year in the space at the front of the gallery.

Annely Juda Fine Art

23 Dering Street, W1
Tel: 020-7629 7578
www.annelyjudafineart.co.uk
Has contemporary British artists, including Anthony Caro and David Hockney, plus European and Japanese artists on its books. Also shows themed exhibitions of contemporary art.

Anthony d'Offay

Tel: 020-7499 4100
www.doffay.com
Anthony d'Offay's Dering Street gallery is now open by appointment only. This dealer has an incredible number of major international names from the 20th and 21st centuries on his books including Joseph Beuys, Gilbert & George, Howard Hodgkin, Jasper Johns, Anselm Kiefer, Willem de Kooning, Jeff Koons, Roy Lichtenstein, Richard Long, Ron Mueck, Bruce Nauman, Gerhard Richter, Cy Twombly, Andy Warhol and Rachel Whiteread.

Anthony Reynolds Gallery

5 Dering Street, W1
Tel: 020-7499 4100
Shows work by contemporary artists such as John Wilkins, Keith Tyson and Richard Billingham.

The Approach

47 Approach Road, E2
Tel: 020-8983 3878
A small gallery, situated above an East End pub. Exhibited the work of Turner Prize nominee Michael Raedecker.

Bernard Jacobson

14A Clifford Street, W1
Tel: 020-7495 8575
www.jacobsongallery.com
A West-End gallery with an impressive list of artists, including Stanley Spencer, Graham Sutherland, Frank Stella, Phillip King, Ed Ruscha and William Tillyer, on its books.

britart.com

60–62 Commercial Street, E1
Tel: 020-7392 7200
www.britart.com
Here, the gallery-shy can surf through almost 4,000 works by around 400 artists (mainly emerging British artists). Photography is on sale in conjunction with Proud Galleries of 5 Buckingham Street, WC2 (tel: 020-7839 4942). Britart also have a showroom near Aldgate East.

Browse & Darby Ltd

19 Cork Street, W1
Tel: 020-7734 7984
www.browseanddarby.co.uk
Housed in elegant premises in London's main street of art dealers, Browse & Darby specialise in figurative and contemporary English painting. They cover late 19th- and early 20th-century European art.

Colnaghi's

15 Old Bond Street, W1
Tel: 020-7491 7408
www.colnaghi.co.uk
A grand old London gallery, founded in 1760, specialising in old masters and drawings from the 14th–19th centuries. Also covers English paintings and European sculpture.

Delfina Project Space

51 Southwark Street, SE1
Tel: 020-7357 6600
www.delfina.org.uk
This well-reputed art trust provides studios for the production and presentation of new work by contemporary artists. Delfina also has studios and a snazzy restaurant (in which artworks from resident artists are shown) in an old chocolate factory at 50 Bermondsey Street, SE1.

eyestorm.com

18 Maddox Street, W1
Tel: 020-7629 5678
A fabulously slick site, offering visitors the chance to "explore, discover and buy contemporary art and photography". Eyestorm is easy to navigate and offers an

extensive array of limited-editions from artists including Damien Hirst, Sebastião Salgado, Antony Gormley, Andy Goldsworthy and David Hockney, to name a few. The London gallery is in Maddox Street.

Flowers East
199–205 Richmond Road, E8
Tel: 020-8985 3333
www.flowerseast.com
Show work by artists including sculptor Eduardo Paolozzi and abstract painter John McLean. Another branch, Flowers Central, is at 21 Cork Street, W1.

Frith Street Gallery
59–60 Frith Street, W1
Tel: 020-7494 1550
www.frithstreetgallery.co.uk
An elegant West End gallery, representing contemporary artists such as Tacita Dean, Juan Muñoz, Cornelia Parker and Giuseppe Penone (all of whom have had work exhibited recently in shows at the Tate).

Lisson Gallery
52–4 Bell Street, NW1
Tel: 020-7724 2739
www.lissongallery.com
A well-respected gallery that opened in 1967 and now has a list of heavyweight international clients, including Robert Mangold, Sol Lewitt, Giulio Paolini, Anish Kapoor, Julian Opie, Tony Oursler and Tony Cragg.

Marlborough Fine Art
Scandia House,
6 Albermarle Street, W1
Tel: 020-7629 5161
www.marlboroughfineart.com
Claims to show the best in modern art in London, in six to eight exhibitions a year. Strong on figurative artists (Paula Rego, Celia Paul and Frank Auerbach).

Matt's Gallery
42–4 Copperfield Road, E2
Tel: 020-8983 1771
Trendy East-End gallery, promoting up-and-coming young artists. Good for large-scale installation art.

Maureen Paley Interim Art
21 Herald Street, E2
Tel: 020-7729 4112
An East-End gallery that, among others, represents photographer and Turner Prize-winner Wolfgang Tillmans.

Modern Art Inc
73 Redchurch Street, E2
Tel: 020-7739 2081
www.modernartinc.com
Past exhibitions have shown the work of contemporary artists Juergen Teller, Jake and Dinos Chapman, Mat Collinshaw and Clare Woods.

Sadie Coles HQ
35 Heddon Street, W1
Tel: 020-7434 2227
www.sadiecoles.com
One of London's most fashionable galleries focusing on contemporary art. Recent exhibitions have shown work by Sarah Lucas, Danny Oates, Elizabeth Peyton and Carl Andre.

Stephen Friedman Gallery
25–82 Old Burlington Street, W1
Tel: 020-7494 1434
www.stephenfriedman.com
Contemporary painters, photographers and installation artists including Thomas Hirschhorn, Tom Friedman, Catherine Opie and Kerry Stewart are shown in Friedman's stylish, modern space.

Victoria Miro Gallery
16 Wharf Road, N1
Tel: 020-7336 8109
www.victoria-miro.com
Dubbed "the most beautiful commercial gallery in London" by *Time Out*'s art critic Sarah Kent, Miro's gallery is a spectacular, light, lofty space. Established 1985, this firm was one of the big names on Cork Street until it moved to larger premises in 2000. The stress is on young artists emerging from the UK and abroad, and it's particularly good for photography. Names on the books include Jake and Dinos Chapman, Tracey Moffatt, Chris Ofili, Cecily Brown and Andreas Gursky.

Waddington Galleries Ltd
11 Cork Street, W1
Tel: 020-7851 2200
www.waddington-galleries.com
Shows paintings, works on paper and sculpture by 20th-century masters from Britain, Europe and the US, plus contemporary art and modern British art. Has Bridget Riley, Patrick Caulfield, David Hockney, Donald Judd, Picasso, Henry Moore, Patrick Heron, Frank Stella and Jean Dubuffet on the books.

White Cube/White Cube2
White Cube: 44 Duke Street,
SW1. White Cube2: 48 Hoxton Square, N1
Tel: 020-7930 5373
www.whitecube.com
Celebrity dealer Jay Jopling owns two of the slickest, most exclusive galleries in London, with a long list of headline-making "Young British Artists" on his books. Shows Darren Almond, Gary Hume, Mona Hatoum, Sam Taylor-Wood (Jopling's photographer wife), Tracey Emin, Antony Gormley, Damien Hirst and Gavin Turk. The original Duke Street branch is tiny, while there's more room to move at White Cube2.

Special passes

Although national museums and galleries are free, most others have entrance charges. Energetic visitors will benefit from the **London Pass**, which allows free entry to several dozen attractions, including many reviewed in this book. Free travel on the Tube and buses is also included. At press time, prices ranged from £18/US$26 for a one-day pass to £74/$106 for a three-day pass (children £11/$16–£38/$54). Details: tel: 01664 500 107 or check the website www.londonpass.com

Joining the **Art Fund**, the UK's leading art charity, costs £31 a year and provides free admission to more than 200 museums, galleries and historic houses around the country, plus discounts on some special exhibitions. Details on 0870-848 2003 or www.artfund.org

Disabled Access

The Museums Guide – London: an Access Guide for Disabled People is published by Artsline, covering London attractions from the Victoria and Albert Museum to Lord's Cricket Ground. Information includes the number of steps at entrances, steps inside the museum and ease of access around displays, plus touch tours and audio description for the visually impaired. It is available (in printed A4 booklet or on audio cassett at £3 plus p&p for disabled people) by calling 020-7388 2227.

Tourist information

The Britain Visitor Centre, 1 Regent Street, Piccadilly Circus, is the central source of tourist information on London and Britain. It has an accommodation and theatre booking service, a bookshop and bureau de change. There are 19 other smaller centres in Greater London, including one on Victoria Station forecourt and another in the arrivals hall at Waterloo International Terminal.

Events listings

Supreme in this field is the long-established weekly *Time Out*, but the *Evening Standard* newspaper includes a good (free) listings magazine, *Hot Tickets*, on Thursdays.

Getting Around

London Underground
The Underground ("Tube"), although ageing and creaking, is the quickest way to get around. Trains run from 5.30am (Sunday 7.30am) to just before midnight. Prices vary by distance according to a zoning system and tickets may be bought from a booking office or machine. A single ticket in Zone 1, where most museums and galleries are located, is £1.60. A carnet of 10 tickets is worth buying at £11.50. *See map on inside back cover.*

Buses
There are 129 red bus routes, numbered up to 300. They run between 6.30am and 11pm. The quicker Red Arrow buses are usually single-deckers, numbered from 500. They call only at stops serving main shopping centres and stations. An all-night (but less frequent) service runs between the centre and the outer suburbs. A book of six bus tickets costs £3.90.

Travel passes
A one-day Travelcard offers more or less unlimited use of the red buses and the Underground in the central zones for £4. A 7-day card costs £18.90 and requires a passport-style photograph.

Taxis
A taxi may be hailed if the yellow "For Hire" sign is lit. The black cabs (other colours are possible) are licensed and are recommended, but fares are high. A tip of at least 10 percent is usual. You can also telephone for a black cab: 020-7272 0272 or 7253 5000.

Tours

Bus tours
A good introduction to the sights of London are the tours on double-decker buses with English-speaking guides or taped commentaries in various languages. You don't usually need to book in advance, just turn up at a departure point such as Marble Arch or Trafalgar Square. Most tickets allow you to hop on and off at various points.

Operators include The Big Bus Company (tel: 020-7233 9533) and The Original London Sightseeing Tour (tel: 020-8877 1722).

Walking tours
These are an ideal way of getting to get to know the real London in the company of a qualified guide. Original London Walks (tel: 020-7624 3978) has almost 100 walks, many with literary and historical themes. Other operators include Historical Tours (020-8668 4019), Stepping Out (020-8881 2933) and Streets of London (07812-501418).

Black Taxi Tours of London
These offer a full commentary from knowledgeable cabbies. Tours are two hours long. Drivers will pick up from and deliver back to hotels. Cost £70 (approx US$100 or 112 euros) per cab – up to five passengers. 24-hour booking: 020-7289 4371.

River travel
Much of London's history was centred on the Thames and seeing the city from the river provides a fascinating perspective. City Cruises (tel: 020-7237 5134) serves the main piers down to Tower Pier and Greenwich; Westminster and Greenwich Cruises (tel: 020-7930 4097) runs tours from Westminster Pier to Greenwich; and Catamaran Cruises (tel: 020-7839 3572) operates from Embankment and Tower piers to Greenwich.

Public Holidays

1 January (New Year's Day), Good Friday, Easter Monday, the first Monday in May (May Day), the last Monday in May (Spring Bank Holiday), the last Monday in August, Christmas Day, Boxing Day.

Telephones

London's UK dialling code is 020. To call from abroad, dial the 44 international access code for Britain, then 20, then the eight-digit number. To call abroad from London, dial 00, then the country code (e.g. 1 for North America, 353 for Ireland). For police, fire, ambulance, dial 999.

Internet Cafés

London has many internet cafés. The most widespread is the EasyEverything chain which has mega cafés in Victoria, Oxford Street, Trafalgar Square, Tottenham Court Road and Kensington, all open 24 hours a day. www.easyeverything.com

Other smaller cyber cafés include Webshak in Soho , Cyberia in Whit-field Street,W1, Offshore Café behind Piccadilly Circus in Sackville Street. You can also surf at Waterstone's bookshop in Piccadilly.

Useful Websites

www.insightguides.com has updates to this book and details of notable exhibitions in London.
www.londontouristboard.co.uk Run by the London Tourist Board and Convention Bureau, the site is well designed and has information on maps, hotels, accommodation, restaurants, pubs and attractions.
www.thisislondon.com This site, maintained by the *Evening Standard* newspaper, has detailed listings of events in the city.
www.netlondon.com Internet directory. Includes links to hotels, museums, theatres and (if you are so inclined) Prince William.
www.londonnet.co.uk An online magazine style guide to London. Features cover certain aspects of travel but its more a resource for news and entertainment information.
london.hotelguide.net A comprehensive guide to London's accommodation.
www.londononline.co.uk Up-to-date going-out information for the city. More trendy than traditional.
ww.travelbritain.com/london/tourism A basic site for basic travel information for tourists.

Further Reading

Loot! Russell Chamberlin (Thames & Hudson, 1983).
Museums in Motion Edward P. Alexander (AltaMire Press, 1996).
Museums and Popular Culture Kevin Moore (Cassell, 1997).
The New Museology ed. Peter Vergo (Reaktion Books, 1989).
The Poetic Museum: Reviving Historic Collections Julian Spalding (Prestel, 2002).
The Rape of the Nile Brian M. Fagan (Macdonald & Jane's, 1977).
The Representation of the Past Kevin Walsh (Routledge, 1992).
The Story of Art E. M. Gombrich (Phaidon, 1995).
The Story of the British Museum Marjorie Caygill (British Museum Press, 2000).
The Turner Prize Victoria Button (Tate Gallery Publishing, 1999).

Art & Photo Credits

Permissions

Every effort has been made to trace the copyright holders, and we apologise in advance for any unintentional omissions.

Works of art have been reproduced with the permission of the following copyright holders:

Head IV, 1949 Francis Bacon © Estate of Francis Bacon 2002. All rights reserved, DACS: 171

Summertime, No 9A, 1948 © Jackson Pollock ARS, NY and DACS, London 2002: 194–95

Armadillo, 1998 © Carl Andre/Vaga, New York/DACS, London 2002: 214r

Portrait of David Bowie, 1994 © Stephen Finer, National Portrait Gallery, London, UK/Bridgeman Art Library: 189t

Big Cigar: Portrait of Lew Grade © Ruskin Spear, National Portrait Gallery,London, UK/Courtesy of Artist's Estate: 188

The Arrival of the Jarrow Marches, 1936 © Thomas Cantrell Dugdale, Courtesy of the Geffrye Museum, London: 75l

Blackfriars Bridge and St Paul's, 1995 © Antony Lowe, Courtesy of the Guildhall Art Gallery: 177

Novocento © Maurizio Catalan, Courtesy of the Marian Goodman Gallery, New York: 174

The Angel, 1997 © Ron Mueck Courtesy of The Saatchi Gallery, London: 212

The Royal Collection © Her Majesty Queen Elizabeth II: 211

South London Gallery © Charlotte Cullinan & Jeanine Richards Vanishing Point, 2000 Installation: 213

Credits

AKG London: 146, 154t
AKG/British Library: 155
AKG London/Paul Almasy: 140
AKG London/Eric Lessing: 145tl
Apsley House/Wellington Museum: 85
Atlantic Syndication: 119
Alexander Fleming Laboratory Museum: 147
Alfred Dunhill Collection: 159
Arcaid/Richard Bryant/Jerwood : 206
ASAP/Bridgeman Art Library/British Library: 25
Natasha Babaian/Apa: 18, 26t, 78b, 134t

Natasha Babaian: 116, 133, 144, 181b
Bank of England Museum: 53
Bankside Gallery: 199
Bettmann/Corbis:143, 145b
Bramah Tea & Coffee Museum: 69
Bridgeman Art Library: 24, 93,
Bridgeman Art Library/Arts Council Collection, Hayward Gallery, London: 171
Bridgeman Art Library/ Chelsea Physic Garden, London: 70l, 70r
Bridgeman Art Library/Courtauld Gallery, London: 178, 179, 180r
Bridgeman Art Library/Courtauld Institute Gallery, Somerset House, London: 180l
Bridgeman Art Library/Dickens House Museum, London: 86l, 86r
Bridgeman Art Library/Dulwich Picture Gallery, London: 201t, 201b, 202l, 202r, 203
Bridgeman Art Library/Estorick Foundation, London: 198
Bridgeman Art Library/Geffrye Museum, London: 68, 75l, 76
Bridgeman Art Library/Guildhall Library, Corporation of London: 64, 177, 204, 205
Bridgeman Art Library/Ham House 108b
Bridgeman Art Library/Horniman Museum: 3, 55b
Bridgeman Art Library/Jewish Museum, London: 56b
Bridgeman Art Library/Leighton House Museum and Art Gallery, London: 207, 208
Bridgeman Art Library/ Library and Museum of Freemasonry, London: 74
Bridgeman Art Library/Museum of London: 34
Bridgeman Art Library/National Maritime Museum, London: 36,
Bridgeman Art Library/National Gallery: 168–169, 173t, 182t, 182b, 185b, 186
Bridgeman Art Library/National Portrait Gallery: 173b, 187, 188, 189t
Bridgeman Art Library/Osterley Park, Middlesex: 117t, 117b
Bridgeman Art Library/Percival David Foundation, London 209
Bridgeman Art Library/Royal Academy of Arts London: 189b, 190
Bridgeman Art Library/Royal College of Physicians: 152b
Bridgeman Art Library/RIBA, London: 207
Bridgeman Art Library/Stapleton Collection: 83t
Bridgeman Art Library/Courtesy of the Trustees of Sir John Soane's Museum, London: 61
Bridgeman Art Library/Towneley Hall Art Gallery and Museum, Burnley, Lancashire: 12
Bridgeman Art Library/Victoria and Albert Museum: 16t, 48, 49
Bridgeman Art Library/Wallace Collection, London: 170, 197l, 197r
Bridgeman Art Library/Westminster Abbey: 67

Bridgeman Art Library/Whitehall: 103
Bridgeman Art Library/Wimbledon Lawn Tennis Museum: 157
Bridgeman Art Library/Worshipful Company of Clockmakers' Collection: 160b
Britain at War Experience: 131b
Courtesy of The British Museum: inside front cover, 4bl, 5bl, 13, 14b, 15t, 15b, 26b, 28t, 29, 30t, 30b, 31, 32t, 32b
Mike Bruce: 212
Brunel Engine House Tunnel Exhibition: 141
Cuming Museum: 72t
Deidi von Schwaenen/Dennis Severs' House: 74
Design Museum: 95b
English Heritage: 106, 107, 113
The Fan Museum: 160t
Fashion & Textile Museum: 73
Firepower: 123t, 123b
Florence Nightingale Museum Collection: 148
Freud Museum, London: 88
Geffrye Museum, London: 75r
Gilbert Collection: 118t, 118b
Glyn Genin/Apa: 62, 71, 77t, 95t, 97t, 120, 124, 126, 134b, 152t, 164, 200
Greenwich Observatory:146
Guildhall Library, Corporation of London: 177
The Guardian/Frank Baron: 10-11
Tony Halliday/Apa: 125
Handel House Trust: 89t
Historic Royal Palaces, Crown copyright: 63, 65t, 65b, 66t, 66b, 102, 109, 110t, 110b, 111, 112t, 112b
Horniman Museum: 54, 55t
Kit Houghton Photography/Corbis: 139b
Anna Hull/Leighton House: 115
Hulton-Deutsch Collection/Corbis: 161
Imperial War Museum: 122, 127
Britta Jaschinski: 195t
The Jewish Museum, London: 56t
Richard Kalina/Shakespeare's Globe: 99
Keats House: 91t
Kew Bridge Steam Museum: 142
LCP/Apa: 28, 77b, 79b, 81, 87, 114t, 181t
Pavel Libera: 98r
Sam Lloyd: 59
London Canal Museum: 135, 136
London Fire Brigade Museum: 78t
London Sewing Machine Museum: 162
London Transport Museum: 132, 137, 138
Lords Collection: 154
Madame Tussaud's: 19b, 79t
Marx Memorial Library: 91b
Francis G. Mayer/Corbis: 156
Museum of St Bartholomew's Hospital: 150, 151
Museum of Domestic Design & Architecture/Middlesex University/ McCrea 1955: 80
Museum of London: 5r, 33, 166-167
Museum of the Order of St John: 149t
Museum of the Royal College of Surgeons: 149b
National Army Museum: 127b, 128b
National Gallery: 90, 184l, 184–185

National Maritime Museum, Greenwich: 35, 37, 38b, 145tr
National Portrait Gallery: 89b
National Trust Photographic Library/ Matthew Antrobus: 96l
National Trust Photographic Library/ Nadia MacKenzie: 96r
National Trust Photographic Library/Nick Meers: 108t
Natural History Museum, London: 41, 42,
Richard Nowitz: 17
Old Operating Theatre and Herb Garret: 151
PA Photos: 6–7, 8–9, 174, 175
Petrie Museum: 57
Photographers Gallery/© 2001 Milton H. Greene Archives Inc: 210
Pollock's Toy Museum: 4br, 158, 163t, 163b
Polish Institute and Sikorski Museum: 128t
Ragged School Museum: 82b
Rex Features: 216, 217
RIBA: 14t
J. Miller/Robert Harding Picture Library: 38t
Royal Air Force Museum: 129, 130t
The Royal Collection © Her Majesty Queen Elizabeth II: 104, 105l (Derry Moore), 105r (Andrew Holt), 114b, 139t (David Cripps), 211
Royal College of Music, Museum of Instruments: 97t, 97b
Royal College of Surgeons: 151
The Royal Fusiliers Museum/HM Tower of London: 130b, 131t
Sherlock Holmes Museum: 92l, 92r
Sir John Soane's Musem/Martin Charles: 60l, 60r
Sir John Soane's Musem: 176b
Science & Society Picture Library: 16b, 19t, 43, 44, 45
Somerset House Trust: 172
South London Gallery: 213
Tate, London 2002: 191, 192, 193, 194-195
The Theatre Museum: 94, 98l, 100, 101
Topham Picturepoint: 121
Bill Varie/Corbis: 39
Victoria and Albert Museum: 2, 4bc, 47, 50, 51, 82t, 84, 87, 176t
Victoria and Albert Museum/Derry Moore: 46
Wellcome Trust: 153
Whitechapel Gallery: 214l, 214r
The William Morris Gallery: 215
Wimbledon Windmill Museum/Norman Plastow: 165
The Women's Library: 83b

Map and Plan Production:
Stephen Ramsay
© 2002 Apa Publications GmbH & Co Verlag KG (Singapore branch)

Cartographic Editor: Zoë Goodwin

Cover concept and design:
Klaus Geisler
Cover illustration created from works of art inside this book.

Index

● **Museums and galleries reviewed are in bold**